RS-0368

Public Participation in Development Planning and Management

Westview Replica Editions

The concept of Westview Replica Editions is a response to the continuing crisis in academic and informational publishing. Library budgets for books have been severely curtailed. Ever larger portions of general library budgets are being diverted from the purchase of books and used for data banks, computers, micromedia, and other methods of information retrieval. Interlibrary loan structures further reduce the edition sizes required to satisfy the needs of the scholarly community. Economic pressures on the university presses and the few private scholarly publishing companies have severely limited the capacity of the industry to properly serve the academic and research communities. As a result, many manuscripts dealing with important subjects, often representing the highest level of scholarship, are no longer economically viable publishing projects--or, if accepted for publication, are typically subject to lead times ranging from one to three years.

Westview Replica Editions are our practical solution to the problem. We accept a manuscript in camera-ready form, typed according to our specifications, and move it immediately into the production process. As always, the selection criteria include the importance of the subject, the work's contribution to scholarship, and its insight, originality of thought, and excellence of exposition. The responsibility for editing and proofreading lies with the author or sponsoring institution. We prepare chapter headings and display pages, file for copyright, and obtain Library of Congress Cataloging in Publication Data. A detailed manual contains simple instructions for preparing the final typescript, and our editorial staff is always available to answer questions.

The end result is a book printed on acid-free paper and bound in sturdy library-quality soft covers. We manufacture these books ourselves using equipment that does not require a lengthy make-ready process and that allows us to publish first editions of 300 to 600 copies and to reprint even smaller quantities as needed. Thus, we can produce Replica Editions quickly and can keep even very specialized books in print as long as there is a demand for them.

About the Book and Editor

This book examines the position held by most development administrators that citizen participation in the planning and management of development projects is crucial to their lasting success. The contributors view inadequate participation as part of the larger problem of ineffective management, policies, and planning. They show that development objectives have been hampered by failures in program implementation: Assistance agencies often falter in delivering projects, while their clients often fail to sustain them. Case studies from African and Asian countries are used to analyze successes and failures in efforts to create a participatory process of project planning and management.

Jean-Claude Garcia-Zamor is professor of public policy and administration at Howard University. Previously, he taught at the Brazilian School of Public Administration (EBAP) of the Getulio Vargas Foundation in Rio de Janeiro, and at the University of Texas at Austin. Among Dr. Garcia-Zamor's most recent publications is The Ecology of Development Administration in Trinidad and Tobago, Jamaica, and Barbados (1977). He also coedited The Financing of Development in Latin America (1980).

Public Participation
in Development
Planning and Management
Cases from Africa and Asia

edited by
Jean-Claude Garcia-Zamor

Westview Press / Boulder and London

A Westview Replica Edition

Copyright © 1985 by Westview Press, Inc.

Published in 1985 in the United States of America by Westview Press, Inc.,
5500 Central Avenue, Boulder, Colorado 80301; Frederick A. Praeger,
Publisher

Library of Congress Cataloging in Publication Data
Main entry under title:
Public participation in development planning and
    management.
    (A Westview replica edition)
    Bibliography: p.
    Includes index.
    1.Economic development projects--Africa--Addresses,
essays, lectures. 2. Rural development projects--
Africa--Addresses, essays, lectures. 3. Economic
development projects--Asia--addresses, essays, lectures.
4. Rural development projects--Asia--Addresses, essays,
lectures. I. García Zamor, Jean Claude.
HC800.P83 1985   338.96   84-15222
ISBN 0-86531-874-3

Printed and bound in the United States of America

10 9 8 7 6 5 4 3 2 1

To Harlan H. Hobgood
with admiration and gratitude

Contents

Preface

The idea for this volume was originally conceived by my dear friend, Harlan H. Hobgood. He asked me in 1981 to be on a panel on Participative Planning and Management that he was organizing for the annual meeting of the American Society for Public Administration (ASPA) in Honolulu, Hawaii, in March 1982. The purpose of the panel was to examine the assumption that unless the people affected participate directly in the planning and management of development projects and programs, these projects won't have a lasting success. The method of examination suggested by Harlan was a case study approach presenting what has been learned from both successes and failures in specific efforts to create a participatory process of project planning and management. Three of the chapters in this volume, by Derick W. Brinkerhoff, Richard W. Ryan, and Frances F. Korten, were written for the 1982 meeting in Hawaii.*

Immediately after the Hawaii conference, Harlan invited me to join him in co-chairing a panel on the same subject at the 1983 ASPA conference in New York City, and in co-editing the papers from the two panels into a volume on participative planning and management. Harlan, who was the director of the United States Agency for International Development (AID) Mission to Haiti, subsequently found himself unable to attend the New York meeting. The four chapters by David J. Gould, James B. Mayfield, Norman Uphoff, and Sheila Carapico were prepared for that conference.

During several visits to Port-au-Prince, I met with Harlan, and we both became increasingly aware that because of the responsibilities of his position, it

---

* My paper at the Hawaii meeting was on "Participative Management in Chilean Industries Under Allende" and is not included in this volume.

would be difficult for us to co-edit the book. I
decided to go ahead with the project, and invited
Theodore Thomas and Mohammad Mohabbat Khan to submit
their chapters to complete the volume.

Therefore, the person most responsible for the
idea of this work is Harlan H. Hobgood. I have known
Harlan since 1967 when we met in Rio de Janeiro,
Brazil, at a conference sponsored by the Comparative
Administration Group of ASPA. Over the years, I have
learned to appreciate not only his stimulating intel-
lect but also his sincere concern for the developing
countries. After I was elected chairman of the Section
on International and Comparative Administration (SICA)
of ASPA in 1978, Harlan, who was serving on the Executive Committee of SICA, became a most reliable collaborator. I was pleased to see him elected chairman of
SICA three years later.

It was a happy coincidence that Harlan was appointed director of the U.S. AID Mission in my own
country, Haiti. I feel that no one else was better
equipped to work with the Haitians on their challenging
developmental efforts. It is with deep gratitude and
affection that this volume is dedicated to him.

Jean-Claude Garcia-Zamor
Washington, D.C.
November, 1984

Introduction to Part I

Jean-Claude Garcia-Zamor

The introduction of this book is comprised of two chapters. The first, by the editor, defines the conceptual framework in which participative planning and management (PPM) is examined. Several requirements for successful PPM are enumerated. But PPM is also described as a difficult practice subject to failure when poorly applied, and some of the major constraints to genuine PPM are reviewed.

The chapter by Theodore Thomas argues that development objectives have been hampered by serious failures in the implementation process. Assistance agencies often fail to provide effective services, and clients often fail to sustain "delivered" development activity. Thomas states that considerable promise for more effective, sustainable development activity exists in engaging intended beneficiaries in project planning and in their continued active participation throughout the implementation stages. Client communities that have shared in planning and implementing development projects maintain and extend development activity more effectively than those that have not. According to Thomas, client-centered development strategies require new administrative response capabilities, unlike the normal bureaucratic, control-oriented procedures of most existing central governments. The challenge for the development planner therefore is reorienting the behavior of both technical and administrative personnel in central government agencies toward collaborative planning with development clients, toward responding to rather than directing or planning for those clients.

1

1. An Introduction to Participative Planning and Management

Jean-Claude Garcia-Zamor

An examination of the development strategies of several developing countries reveals that most plans are formalistic documents that are totally ignored by the agencies responsible for implementing them. The planning ministries of these countries generally pursue a "project-by-project" approach with several of the projects related neither to the national development plan nor to each other. Furthermore, most of the technical ministries do not have personnel who are qualified to identify, evaluate, and implement projects. In addition, resource utilization is not usually specified by development planners at the national level. They identify resources only indirectly in their national plans. At the project level, where funding is mostly assured by foreign donors or international lending institutions, planning may by necessity be more specific about resource allocation. Thus, the entire planning process in developing countries is not yet perfected and depends on the continuous technical assistance of external advisers.

Despite the obvious deficiency of the national planning agencies, "bottom up" planning is advocated as an ideal approach to development in these same countries. This approach is encouraged by foreign donors and international lending agencies in the hope that grassroots participation in the projects they finance will increase their success. Academicians have recently joined them in advocating some type of people-centered planning and a reorganization of bureaucracies to carry out more effectively special development projects. The theory and practice of empowering people and communities to participate in development projects have advanced in recent years. However, as Theodore Thomas points out in the following chapter, less attention and, consequently, less progress are evident in perfecting the linkages between empowered communities and existing government structures. The community empowerment process, according to Thomas, appears to be

3

aided substantially by external assistance provided
through newer social intervention methodologies.

Although the concepts of participation have been
around for quite some time, little is known about real
participatory public program management. This book is
an attempt to explore, research, and document cases of
participatory public program planning and management
and to relate program outcomes to such managerial practices. Numerous scholars have been studying and reporting on participation in planning and management,
but their works deal primarily with labor management in
industrialized societies and their findings are not
always relevant to developing countries.[1] This book
was written by people who have themselves participated
in the development of the projects about which they
write and in many instances have initiated the participatory approach in the implementation of these projects. Most of them view participation as the involvement of the projects' beneficiaries in decision-making,
implementation, and evaluation.

An international training handbook published in
1976 identified two basic kinds of delivery systems: a
"push" system and a "pull" system. By the "push" system the deliverer of the product or service triggers
the delivery; in the "pull" system the recipients of
the goods or services seek out and trigger the delivery. The "push" system requires less effort on the
part of the beneficiaries and more effort on the part
of the program deliverer, since the deliver must seek
out the people to whom to give the service or product.
The "pull" system implies that the beneficiaries must
seek out the service or product and do whatever is
necessary (travel, complete forms, etc.) to receive the
product; hence they have manifest interest in it.[2]
Similarly, there are two forms of participative planning and management; one induces participation and the
other merely encourages that suggestions for program
operations be expressed. Participation can be induced
formally through committee or boards, who encourage
local community people to make known their views on
policy issues that affect their work and welfare. Project managers can also enlist local involvement in
defining the objectives of the project, determining the
methods taken to reach objectives, and seeing and participating in the results.

The other form of participative planning and management merely encourages suggestions without insti-
tutionalizing participation.

Participative planning and management often results in a complex scale of activities and organization, so that people without sophisticated management
training can work together. Despite the complexity,
PPM's potential benefits merit consideration.

This introductory chapter will analyze the concept of participation by reviewing both its positive and negative implications in the context of development projects in the Third World.

The notion of participation was brought into focus in the 1930s. The idea was that the more involved people were in the challenges of production, the more productive they would be. Since then, a burgeoning literature on participation has developed in the United States and abroad. But the term "participation" continued to gain currency primarily in decision-making processes in industrialized societies. It is only since the late 1960s and the 1970s that the concept started to be used in the context of the newly developed subdiscipline of "development administration."

At the International Conference on Improving Public Management and Performance, held in Washington in 1979, one of the discussion groups accepted the notion that to manage a program is to make things happen through people. Therefore, management involves human as well as technical systems. The human systems extend well beyond the human resources available to the program manager to include the recipients of program benefits. The issue of internal and external participation became central to the group's discussions. Participation was viewed as helpful to managers in validating the premises on which programs rested and thus contributing to program effectiveness. With the emergence of the issue of participation, the group moved away from an input orientation to program management and towards an output emphasis, where the recipient of program benefits occupies a focal role. It was suggested that managerial sciences traditionally focused on the input side of program management, the improvement of which is invariably associated with upgrading input components. The focus on the outputs and the relationships with the recipients of program services, according to the group, posed a new question for which the established notions of management sciences were inappropriate. The group's discussion concluded with the realization that participatory requirements of public program management called for a body of theory and informed practice yet to be fully developed.[3]

But the limited timespan of the international gathering and the diversity of the topics discussed there did not permit an in-depth look at participation in project planning and management. However, enough was said to point out that the term "participation" needed to be more broadly defined in such a context. The following is an attempt to come up with several definitions that could redefine and expand the boundaries of participative planning and management (PPM). Although the following definitions of PPM are not exhaustive they do cover the main objectives of project promoters (both international and bilateral donors) who have been trying to implement the concept.

1. PPM promotes integration. It is important that the beneficiaries understand their roles and the objectives of the projects and that they receive sufficient information on which to base their decisions. As a form of communication, PPM helps prevent misunderstanding and provides for the discussion of various points of view that must be accounted for if integration is to exist. PPM is a practical way of integrating local communities' interests and development project goals.

2. PPM increases performance and stimulates a greater acceptance of performance criteria. Beneficiaries become emotionally involved and gain feelings of pride and accomplishment from the projects and become committed to their goals and standards. PPM also increases job satisfaction because, as the beneficiaries become committed, they naturally derive more satisfaction. Research by early social scientists has concluded that satisfied workers are productive workers and are far more prone than others to generate ideas that can benefit their projects. PPM also leads the beneficiaries to stronger perceptions of shared characteristics with project managers, generating further commitment to the projects' objectives. In this context they more readily accept final decisions, feel more responsibility for carrying them out, and exhibit less resistance to change. PPM motivates beneficiaries to contribute. They are given the opportunity to release their own resources of initiative and creativity toward the objectives of the project. It serves to clarify the effort/performance linkage and generates clear and effective action plans for task performance. Finally, by encouraging PPM, donors can increase both the probability that change will be accepted and the overall effectiveness of that change. PPM also increases the beneficiaries' motivation to implement the project managers' decisions, since they feel that their collective voice is heard before the decisions that affect them are made.

3. PPM helps deal with the significant problem of the lack of sensitivity and effective response to local community feelings, needs, problems, and views, which often characterize the relationship between donors and beneficiaries in developing countries. PPM may require time for the beneficiaries to learn to handle their newly found responsibility and time for the project managers to learn to trust the beneficiaries. In the

end however, PPM will help to establish a self-sustaining and expanding reservoir of skills in the community, as well as improve the local people by helping them become more productive and more creative. PPM permits local needs to be met more effectively, because local people are involved in identifying and working to address these needs. One possible effect of PPM could be the creation of new objectives for the projects which fit the needs and objectives of the beneficiaries. PPM prevents alienation, dissatisfaction, and the possibility of opposition to the project, which deflects time and energy from the pursuit of shared objectives to the waging of local conflict. The opportunity to participate in the planning and management of the projects might prevent minor irritations from developing into major incidents by providing occasions for individuals to express minor forms of conflict. PPM could change the total atmosphere so that people share their concerns about the projects, allowing grievances to be aired and discussed openly. It may also reduce conflict and mitigate many of the unintended and dysfunctional results of hierarchy. While in certain cases the conflicts may not necessarily be reduced, PPM will tend to move them from latent to overt and will stimulate efforts to deal with them. PPM is particularly appropriate when the nature of certain decisions requires substantial local input, when a decision will have broad impact in the community, or when there is a known divergence of opinion on the issues among local residents. Furthermore, the fear of insecurity felt by local residents when outsiders move in dissipates as the interpersonal trust increases between residents and project managers.

4. PPM brings higher and better-quality output. In certain types of projects the quality of improvement alone is worth the time invested in participation. Beneficiaries often make suggestions for both the quality and quantity of improvements. Although not all the ideas might be useful, there would be enough valuable ones to produce genuine long-range improvements. PPM helps develop better action plans by increasing the input of ideas which will lead to better decisions. Actual task success is enhanced when the total amount of participation is increased and when that participation comes from all or most of the potential communicators. The built-in feedback mechanism of PPM will translate broad goals into criteria that are meaningful and operational for local residents.

5. PPM increases the amount and the accuracy of information that project managers have about work practices and the environmental contingencies associated

with them. It also increases the beneficiaries' positive feelings toward their work practices by developing a network of support for these practices.

6. Finally, PPM allows a more economical operation
by permitting a greater use of local human resources
and eliminating many expensive transportation and management that outside services require. It also provides the community with a cushion against the effects
of externally induced economic changes. It helps to
reduce economic, social, and political dependency between individuals and between regions by recognizing
that people can and still will do things for themselves. Of course, the complexity of a particular project and the personality orientation of local residents
will contribute to determine the degree to which a participative approach is functional.

PPM is now widely advocated as a management technique by donors and recipients, both on ideological
grounds and as a direct means of increasing project effectiveness. PPM is often necessary because local residents have information that is more useful in making
decisions than that of the international and bilateral
donors. While PPM has excellent potential for building
teamwork, it is a difficult practice and can fail if
poorly applied. Four major obstacles to genuine PPM
described below are: 1. the dominance of one group over
the others; 2. the lack of interest of potential participants; 3. the lack of sufficient time; and 4. restrictions generated by present structures and systems.

1. The Dominance of One Group Over Others.
The application of PPM may shift from result-
oriented goals to securing prestige or wealth for a few
prominent members of a local community with a few of
them firmly in control and with most other participants
only moderately involved. PPM may record only the
views of those who can articulate them in an open forum
and eliminate the majority's views. It may give differ-
ential access to certain groups, giving way for them to
further the pursuit of special narrow interests. It can
easily be argued that PPM will always over-represent
the interests of the more powerful since participants
invariably differ in their respective power positions.
A serious issue with PPM may be that situations can be
used to manipulate local residents. This manipulation
may not necessarily be by project managers but by narrow local interest representatives. Emphasis on group
rather than individual suggestions may reduce the
accent on personal interests at the expense of more
general community interests. Still, even giving everyone an opportunity to participate may not produce equal

distribution of benefits but simply oligarchical dominance. Real power could be grabbed by the more educated and articulate. This factor is pointed out by Mohammad Mohabbat Khan, in "Experiences of Rural Development Programs in Bangladesh," as the major reason for nonparticipation in rural development programs.

2. Lack of Interest of Potential Participants.
It is often very difficult for the poorest of the local residents to understand why they should participate since this approach usually fails to give them any immediate financial rewards. Thus, the participative approach, potentially successful when people who desire participation are involved, does not address the question of how to motivate people who are not interested in participation. Such people feel a strong need for security and protection and usually make excellent salaried field workers since they can relate their input into the projects to a regular income. They feel content to let the more educated local elite negotiate with the donors. Soon, to project managers, it appears that direct participation of individual local residents may not be as important as their perception of the group's participation in these discussions. The international training handbook mentioned earlier points out that projects which for success, require explicit action by the beneficiaries, are probably the most difficult to plan and manage. This is particularly so if the beneficiaries are at or near the subsistence level and significant behavioral alterations on their part are required. Obviously, in many cases, the majority of the poor local residents may find it difficult to assimilate effectively the range of decision-making opportunities with which they are faced. Furthermore, those with an authoritarian orientation and need for dependence react positively where little participation is used, and they usually perform better in a nonparticipative situation.

3. Lack of Sufficient Time.
A real participatory approach often requires an educational campaign to gain the confidence of the local residents and to educate the poorest, and usually, more apathetic ones, of the importance of their participation. This is a time-consuming procedure that often threatens to over-extend the deadlines set by both the donors and the national governments to start and complete the projects. Even theorists who normally advocate greater participation have often argued that in a crisis, it is simply impossible to go around consulting people. All those familiar with the working of projects in developing nations can attest to the fact that usually project managers run crisis centers where

the combination of pressures from headquarters (usually located far away in Washington, D.C.) and the national governments contribute to push them towards a more pragmatic approach to participation (e.g., limited debate with the most educated ones, as exposed earlier). Any sophisticated theory of participation advocating otherwise may seem right when expounded in the sanctuary of a classroom or a conference room at headquarters, but it is diluted considerably in the real-life situation of working in the developing countries.

   4.   Restrictions Generated by the Present Structures and Systems.
   One of the dangers of PPM is that, if fully executed, it triggers institutional restructuring that is exogenous to most political and administrative systems that exist in the developing countries. Thus, a major obstacle to applying PPM is the conflict it might create with the national authorities. PPM represents a threat to central government officials who often view negatively any trends toward decentralization. Curiously enough, this is true even in countries where governments officially endorse decentralization schemes that have been suggested by some donor agencies. National authorities view PPM as a process that would not only permit the full benefits of the projects to remain in a remote community but something that could trigger a certain awareness and contribute to a loss of political control over the rural communities.
   An additional conflict, in certain cases, may be that any increased involvement of local community residents in development projects may hurt the vested local interests of those who dominate the existing local socio-politico-economic structures. In small communities of developing countries, there are often antithetical or conflicting interest groups that attempt to influence the planning and management of a project to get the most out of it. The existing systems in small communities can be even more rigidly stratified than in the urban context. The picture can still become more complex in situations in which the ethnic or tribal background of local residents vary considerably. In such cases, what is needed is some kind of formalistic participation from the bottom to insure that local projects will earn widespread support for the overall program of economic development.
   Some of the other problems that PPM creates will be reviewed in the last chapter, which also examines why the different theories of PPM are difficult to institutionalize in developing countries.

NOTES

1. See Chapter 12, "A Selected Bibliography on Participative Planning and Management."
2. Elements of Project Management. A publication of the Development Project Management Center, U.S. Department of Agriculture, in cooperation with the Agency for International Development. June 3, 1976, 100-101.
3. The proceedings of the International Conference on Improving Public Management and Performance were compiled and edited by O. Glenn Stahl, assisted by Gregory D. Foster and were published in 1979 by the Agency for International Development. The landmark conference, sponsored by the American Consortium of International Public Administration had 377 registered participants from seventy countries and thirty-one international organizations.
4. Elements of Project Management, p. 104.

2. Reorienting Bureaucratic Performance: A Social Learning Approach to Development Action

Theodore Thomas

A new implementation strategy in international development is emerging from field experience in development projects, encouraged by advances in social science concepts and methodology. Traditionally, development strategies have been based on economic criteria, centralized plans, and center-to-field (top-down) action orientations. The new trend is to incorporate human-oriented concerns, transactive planning and field-with-center collaborative action into development strategies. Various labels have been used for the new concept, but for present purposes the phrase <u>people-centered</u>[1] may best serve. Innovations in social science research methods, in combination with a theory of social action, influence the basic value orientation and the methodological approach. The underlying concept has been called <u>social learning</u>.

People-centered development is an action research methodology requiring collaborative planning between the government sponsored agency carrying out the program and the beneficiaries of government action. The primary strategic intervention required for achieving effective collaboration between communities and governments depends on reorienting central agency bureaucracies toward planning <u>with</u> rather than <u>for</u> development clients.

This chapter summarizes the primary components of the social learning concept and its contribution to international development strategy. It also examines two implementation strategies called community empowerment and bureaucratic reorientation. Included is an examination of possible constraints on people-centered development and an agenda for research and implementation.

BACKGROUND

People-centered development action designed to give primary attention to the management and implementation issue is new to the development profession in several distinct ways. First, until recently, development has been defined in economic growth terms and development strategy guided by centralized concepts of planning. Management and implementation concerns were pushed into secondary status at best. Attention to implementation issues is only now emerging.

Second, management-oriented professionals have not traditionally participated directly in policy formulation or in the implementation of economic development programs. New opportunities for management specialists are now appearing.

Third, management structures and practices, whenever explicitly included in development projects in the past, have been centrally designed and imposed on subordinate administrative agencies and on their clients. Even more commonly, management structures and practices based on centralized organizing concepts have been implicitly assumed in development project designs. Functional experts in health, agriculture, engineering or economics, were assumed to be experts in organizing and managing development projects as well. These assumptions are now being challenged.

A people-centered planning and implementation strategy is substantially different from past practice in that implementation issues and the essential role of management professionals as central to development action are explicitly recognized.

There are three sources for the new development strategy. They are: 1) the implementation gap; 2) social learning theory; and 3) a new concept of social development.

1. The Implementation Gap

Development objectives, both in individual projects and national goals, have been illusive targets. Many nations have failed to achieve even modest growth objectives, while others have achieved overall growth objectives at the time of[2] increasing inequalities rather than balanced growth. A few examples of success in economic growth combined with reduced inequality provide potential lessons,[3] but the overall picture remains as complex and as frustrating as ever.

Development planners are increasingly aware that development objectives are thwarted by serious and continuing failures in the implementation process.[4] Ineffective implementation is to be seen in the absence of needed coordination among international, national and sub-national agencies; in a variety of well-known bureaupathologies; in the absence of trained personnel; and, in an inflexibility of organizational form resulting largely from central agency requirements for control, orderliness, and standard procedure.

Failure of development projects to meet their objectives is also caused by unstable and shifting political support, by the absence of sustained or cohesive leadership from development donors or national governments, and by the inability of service delivery agencies to provide effective (i.e., trained and committed) implementation teams.

Another source of implementation failure, sometimes overlooked, is the absence of sustainability in projects.[5] Irrigation and tube well systems, transportation systems, and technical support systems for schools and training institutes require sustained maintenance programs not often achieved. Similarly, indigenous teachers, trainers, agricultural advisers and health professionals trained for service in new development institutions do not return from training or soon leave their assigned posts. The institutions often disintegrate after external development experts complete and leave the projects.

Recognition of these and other sources of implementation failure is now common in international development agencies and is increasingly documented in project evaluations.

2. Social Learning Theory

People-centered development is strengthened by recent action research experiments combining social science knowledge with action. These experiments are labeled differently as "the learning process",[6] "engaged planning",[7] or "transactive planning".[8] As the implementation gap is better understood, development practitioners are applying new understandings in social science methodology to improve the linkages between the development agency and client. New learning based on case examples shows impressive potential for improving the implementation process and for more effectively sustaining development projects.

Social learning theory provides a significant change from current practice in social science research. Its basic tenets, in the present context at least, derive from the work of Edgar Dunn[9] and are being interpreted by several others including David Korten and John Friedmann. Some would claim that a paradigm shift is implicit in social learning theory -- that a "scientific" revolution of no small consequence is in the making.[10]

Social learning is based on an expanded understanding of knowledge, which differs from objectives knowledge used so successfully in understanding the

physical evironment.[11] Objective knowledge of our
physical environment has been developed by primary
reliance on tools of logic and empirical analysis, with
the researcher or scientist separated from the subject
of the research at a neutral and unbiased distance from
the object of attention. Scientific knowledge acquired
by a neutral observer (researcher) is utilized in ex-
pert-designed plans (often called blueprint planning)
and is implemented by "experts" through modern organizational systems and procedures we now call bureaucracy. For many tasks in the modern world, scientific
knowledge and bureaucracies have proven to be effective
instruments. For other tasks, however, they have not
been effective.

Social reality is allegedly different from physical reality, requiring a different research strategy
for the discovery of social knowledge. Social reality
is deeply embedded in customs, traditions,[12] and beliefs
of human beings in social communities, is not fixed[13]
or unchanging as allegedly are physical phenomena,
and is dependent on value and action commitments of
individuals who make up societies. Social realities
are created and can be changed, and are influenced by[14]
any and all research interventions. The researcher
therefore is not neutral in relation to the research
object as in the standard scientific design.

Social knowledge is derived from social realities
and from the value commitments of both the researcher
and the researched through a learning process in which
research and social action take place simultaneously.
Action research is an interactive or transactive dialogue in which the researcher is engaged in a mutual
learning experience with the subject(s) of the experiment. The researcher contributes knowledge derived
from professional training and personal value commitments, while research subjects contribute the data of
personal and communal realities of which they are the
sole and expert possessors.

Social learning alters the traditional roles of
researcher/planner/manager and the traditional roles of
the clients of change activity. The researcher is no
longer a neutral observer of distant facts but is an
active contributor to the formulation of new social
knowledge. The planner no longer designs only with
scientific data and professional expertise but collabo-
rates actively with clients in the formulation of human
-scale plans. The manager no longer acts neutrally to
deliver units of service defined from above but actively negotiates human-defined service units acceptable both to clients and to central representatives of
the larger political unit.

The subject of research, the client of the planner
/manager, is no longer a passive bureaucratic object

required only to contribute neutral data but rather is recognized as an expert capable of and expected to participate actively in choices about future life styles.

When social learning theory is applied to international development work, the development agent, whether donor or LDC government agent, is no longer the deliverer of development to the poor recipient. The agent rather is the possessor of professional expert knowledge which requires joining in a collaborative planning process with social expert knowledge in the possession of the so-called clients of development. Both types of knowledge are valid. Both are required for effective social change.

Social learning theory and the renewed emphasis on management and implementation strategies pointed out earlier relate directly to a third stimulus supporting a new development strategy, a new concept of social development centered on human values and equity.

3. Social Development

Definitions of development have undergone significant change during the past decade.[15] Original concepts of development couched in primarily economic terms (GNP and per capita growth) became increasingly inadequate for the complexities of national aspirations. Economic growth often resulted in maldistribution of basic resources and industrial output. Intractable poverty afflicting significant numbers of nations and people remained.

More recently, economic development goals have been refined to focus attention on the poorest majorities, on unequal distribution within successfully growing nations, and on basic needs in specific functional areas such as health, housing, education, population, agriculture and rural development.[16]

During this period of change, attention was directed toward the participation of beneficiaries in development programs -- often with little accomplishment and a considerable sense of "lip service" for what many considered a controversial and time consuming diversion from real needs.

From the point of view of social learning theory, this shift of concern toward the poorest peoples and basic needs, laudable as it was, still left the clients of development in the role of passive recipients. To alter that role, it is necessary to go one step farther by adding a human value component to the definition of basic needs. The added component is a sense of self-worth and a personal capacity for actively participating in life's important decisions. Basic needs as redefined must encompass a sense of political efficacy

which, when realized, converts passive, reactive recipients into active, contributing participants in the
development process.

Social development becomes the liberation of human
beings and communities _from_ passive recipients _toward_ a
developed, active citizenry capable of participating in
choices about community issues.

The concept of social development enlarges earlier
conceptions of economic development or development
goals in other ways as well. Social development is not
to be interpreted as a prescriptive ideal to be imposed
on the poor and poor nations of the world by the allegedly developed; rather it is an ideological commitment to the goals of social change for the rich, developed West/North as well as the previously defined
underdeveloped South/East. The goal of social development is that of enhancing the capacity of peoples and
communities to manage the environments in which they
live regardless of which corner of the earth might be
the domicile.

Modern (i.e. present and future) life is now described as a continuing condition of rapid change
within turbulent environments.[17] Seemingly intractable
conditions of crime, pockets of poverty and inequality,
unemployment, resource scarcities, and elements of
social challenges are not dissimilar in severity from
conditions of underdevelopment, poverty, political instability, and the absence of human rights among the
unenfranchised of the world. Perhaps now the image of
"spaceship earth" sharpens our understanding of the
challenges we all face and of the opportunity presented
for mutual learning while engaged in the search for
resolution of these challenges. As the specter of
nuclear holocaust generated by Western technology im-
pinges on present social reality, the dominant vision
of the civilized, progressive West as better and as the
model for the poorer, ignorant, backward communities of
the non-West, loses all its power.

Social learning as new social action theory and
method and social development as an enlarged conception
of social change offer new value premises for the international development strategist. For change agents
concerned with development (as redefined) in the Third
and Fourth Worlds, new intervention strategies are
necessary. Community empowerment and the reorienting
of development bureaucracies are two such strategies
introduced below.

COMMUNITY EMPOWERMENT

There is nothing new about the objective of
seeking effective participation of poor communities in
political and economic systems. Economic development

specialists have long expected the rewards of growth to diffuse (some say "trickle down") through developing societies to engage the productive and participative capacities of all peoples. The results however have been unsatisfactory.

Limited success in achieving participation has been found through direct intervention in poor communities by using community organizing and community development strategies.[18] Though organized communities have sometimes resulted, the integration of these communities into wider political and economic structures has been less evident. Despite some successes in economic growth objectives and in micro-level community development projects, these achievements have not yet been translated into effective general strategies for sustained development.

A social learning approach offers the potential for improving development program implementation by empowering communities for active participation in development programs and simultaneously linking those communities to the political and administrative structures of the larger society. Thus the development effort is not solely that of organizing client communities as an end in itself, but rather is the empowering of persons and communities for effective participation in the broader political and economic community. The empowering of communities is an integral and essential part of development programs designed in the long term to achieve more general regional and national goals.

Empowering people and communities for self-sustaining activity is not a mysterious process. One development strategist often uses the first proverb to illustrate the empowerment process.[19] "Give a man a fish and he eats today; teach a man to fish and he can eat every day." But it is said the proverb begs the question of who owns the fish. Ownership offers a sharing of the rewards of life among the members of a community. Equitable ownership and accessibility to physical and economic resources continues to be a major challenge for many of the world's people.

But of equal importance in interpreting the proverb is the action statement "to fish," implying a capacity to act. The physical or technical capacity to fish is perhaps readily understood, based on well-known technology. Less evident but perhaps more critical to effective social development is the psycho-social capacity "to fish." Combating the alienation and anomie characteristic of powerlessness may well be the more difficult requirement in enabling or empowering the "poorest majorities" in the world to first believe it possible, then to seek actively, and only finally to acquire ownership of life-sustaining tangible resources.

This emphasis on the psychological concept of empowerment should not however divert attention from the continuing and serious question of access to tangible resources (who owns the fish).

Community empowerment then is that process of learning how to fish. The first step in learning is psychic ownership of the self and of personal potential (owning the capacity to act, rather than to be acted on). A second step is the acquisition of resources in the environment, including developing a capacity to be active, cohesive and effective as communities.

Assisting development clients to assume ownership of themselves and their resources is a first stage in people-centered development action. Self-managed communities have enhanced their capacity to receive and utilize new resources from the external world. Organized communities of farmers can assist in planning and building local irrigation systems and then assume responsibility for operating and maintaining them. Organized communities can assist in building and operating community health centers and can respond to and maintain preventive medicine as well as positive health programs.

Community empowerment strategies need not be restricted to traditional village boundaries or established political entities. Empowerment of development clients can be effectively built on specific resource bases available to the clients -- agricultural produce farms, livestock farms, forestry resources, cottage industries -- or particular infrastructure requirements such as irrigation services, water systems, or farm-to-market transportation systems. Resource centered community organizations can provide effective linkages between development clients and their development service agencies.[20]

Community empowerment has even broader potential as a strategy for improving the implementation of development projects. The term community is normally used in the context of rural village dwellers or urban neighborhoods, emphasizing the primary living group and geographic locality.[21] Another way to identify community is to emphasize the interrelatedness of groups of people, even though widely dispersed, who perceive common needs and problems, acquire a sense of identity and have a common set of objectives.[22] A profession may be a community. An administrative cadre or a bureaucratic sub-system devoted to health or to agriculture, for example, could be defined as community. If professional groups, bureaucracies, or even would-be

business entrepreneurs in any society exhibit characteristics similar to those of more traditionally defined development clients (e.g., passive acceptance of
external action), then the "empowerment" of newly defined development communities such as these may be a
required and appropriate strategy.

REORIENTING BUREAUCRACIES

Little attention and consequently little progress
is evident in perfecting the linkages between empowered
communities and existing governmental structures.[23]
Central government agencies have been demonstrably
unsuccessful in engaging clients in self-sustaining
development programs. There is substantial evidence
that centrally dominated governmental agencies, designed to deliver services from the top down, are ill-
adapted to understand and serve the needs of empowered
communities capable of managing their own resources.

It is not enough then merely to assist development
communities in achieving the capacity to manage personal and community resources. The people-centered
development strategist is challenged both to help empower development communities and simultaneously to
work at reorienting governmental bureaucracies toward[24]
more effective linkages with client communities. The
former may indeed not be possible without the latter.
Reorienting bureaucratic performance may well be the
critical intervention in sustaining community empowerment.

It is possible to examine the question of bureaucratic reorientation in the development context by
looking at both the nature of bureaucracy itself and
the specific manifestations of bureaucratic performance
in development agencies. Modern organizations are complex social instruments designed to coordinate the efforts of large numbers of people toward specific and
commonly recognized, at least in highly generalized
terms, objectives; i.e., to produce autos, deliver welfare, control crime, deliver electric power, make a
profit, maintain the peace, wage war, etc.

Bureaucracy is the term most often used to describe an idealized form of modern organization (although, of course, we are also familiar with the term
bureaucracy used as a rubric for dysfunctional performance, sometimes nonperformance). Students of modern
organizations regularly describe the bureaucratic
organization as effective when operating in stable and
relatively unchanging environments where required procedures can be made routine, control over personnel and
service delivery units can be maintained, and both activity and end product can be standardized. In contrast, routine, control, and standardization are far

less possible and organizational performance less effective in turbulent environments.[25] Research and
experimentation are underway in organization theory and
practice to invent nonbureaucratic responses for ir-
regular, rapidly changing, turbulent environments.

A different perspective for matching formal organizations to their environments suggests that bureaucracies perform effectively when their clients know how to
"queue" -- i.e., understand the rationale and the procedure for claiming services.[26] Not only must members
of the bureaucratic organization be educated to the
requirements for legal, routine, standardized performance, but the clients of those organizations must
understand and then conform substantially to bureaucratic norms.

A third characteristic of effectively functioning
bureaucracies is the imperative for centralized or top-
down command and planning functions. This characteristic is supported in both public and private bureaucracies by the principle of separating policy formulation from implementation and delivery activities --
in public organizations, policies are to be adopted by
political representatives of the people and implemented
efficiently through the organization by professional
personnel; in private organizations, the owners have
the right of policy choices, with professionals once
again the vehicle for efficient delivery of the
product.

Bureaucracy norms for organizational performance
are known to all who have Western-oriented educations
and work experience in modern institutions. These
include legal and political hierarchical control exer-
cised in a pyramidal structure, specialization of
functions, standardized rules and procedures, merit for
job placement and promotion, and efficiency and economy
as effectiveness criteria.[27]

The characteristics noted above represent norms or
idealized prescriptions for bureaucratic performance,
i.e., how bureaucracies should operate. On the other
hand, experience and empirical analysis yield an alternative set of performance characteristics. Donor
agencies and LDC government bureaucracies, at least as
often as other organizations, are described in terms
quite at variance from the effective and efficient
performance expected of the good bureaucracy. Included
in these descriptions are traits such as slowness and
inflexibility in performance; degrading treatment of
clients, and to a certain degree, subordinates; dispa-
rity of service toward the rich and away from the poor;
and professional staffs "cognitively distant" from
their clients in attitude, culture and often language.

An additional troublesome characteristic of development agencies is the direction of response capability. Rewards for performance, including decision power, pay and promotion are in the hands of "higher" levels of authority. Decisions about what service is to be delivered and the effectiveness of delivered service are channeled from the top. It is to be expected, therefore, that responsiveness flows upward in the organization while decisions and policy choices flow downward.

The contrast between the requirements for bureaucratic performance including the actual performance characteristics of development agencies as compared to the needs among development clients and communities could not be more striking. Large segments of LDC societies and virtually entire populations do not know how to "queue," that is, they do not know and do not understand the norms and the procedures for modern organizational performance. We on the so-called developed side tend to "blame the victim" by assuming that the deficiency is theirs; that instability, ignorance and resistance to change are faults of theirs, and that the change required for "progress" is solely theirs to make.

The conditions of "underdevelopment," however, might rather be described only as different rather than backward. Poverty, high birth rates, low life expectancy, illiteracy, alienation and anomie, as examples of these conditions, can be defined as characteristics of unstable or turbulent environments in which bureaucracies are not effective. Changing or reorienting bureaucracies may therefore be a more effective strategy for achieving development than attempting only to change the victim. A mutual learning process may ensue in which both parties achieve a desired growth and development. Reorienting bureaucracies toward a more flexible, responsive capacity to plan collaboratively with clients is therefore the second stage of a people-oriented development strategy.

The following characteristics are to be sought in reorienting bureaucratic performance to social development objectives:

- the ability to plan collaboratively with clients by sharing expertise with non-experts and by listening effectively to client definitions of needs and facts;

- the ability to link client communities with government agencies in collaborative action by means of nonbureaucratic control (authority) mechanisms that allow for equalized, two-way communication channels;

- the capacity to increase bureaucrats' responsiveness to clients and to their superiors through the use of incentive mechanisms;

- the capacity to empower clients to share in the planning and implementation of projects, evaluating organizational performance based on the responsiveness and participation of those clients.

A new set of norms for reoriented bureaucracies suggests reciprocal rather than hierarchical controls; flexible, temporary (perhaps amoebic-like) structures rather than fixed pyramids; specializations tempered by extensive intraorganizational communication, especially with client groups; flexibility and discretion in the application of rules and procedures as determined by task group negotiations and sub-organizational contract devices; and, equity as a primary evaluation criteria followed by efficiency measures.[28]

The change agent who promotes bureaucratic reorientation may be any of several actors in the development process -- a skilled community leader, a professional of a private, voluntary organization, a government officer, a donor agency officer, or an external development consultant. The identification and training of the social development agent may well be a first step in introducing and encouraging collaborative action among diverse parties unaccustomed to relating to each other in other than formalized, legalized, "bureaucratic" patterns.

Task force teams of development agency personnel, donor agency personnel, specialists in community organizing, and "outside" action research oriented consultants (from universities or management institutes, for example) have been helpful in guiding the early experimentation in linking development communities more effectively to "reoriented" development agencies. A task force team along these lines was called a working group in one instance.[29]

The theory of people-centered, participative action is widely accepted. And now field experience, documenting effective implementation of projects is slowly accumulating to give credence to a people-centered development strategy. An initial, promising beginning has been made.

CONSTRAINTS

The achievement of effective people-centered development action based on empowering communities and reoriented development agencies is constrained by several factors.

1. The generation of power by communities and citizens' groups is frightening to political and administrative leaders. The idea of "empowering" communities, regardless of the intentions or the anticipated development consequences, is received with skepticism or fear. Many national governments are struggling to

achieve and maintain political control amidst conditions of general social unrest. In the face of such
conditions, political leaders are unlikely to welcome
empowerment strategies.

2. Related to the specter of power is a more complex constraint identifiable as an absence of political
will in national government leadership. Ruling elites
do not want, in effect, to encourage change or the empowerment of local communities. Established political
and economic interests are adequately, at least in the
short run, served by existing conditions. Even professionals in government service find their own self-
interest working to deter a wider distribution of resources and political participation. General conditions of disorder, civil strife, or insurgency make
political commitments to effective development actions
in local communities difficult if not impossible.

3. A third factor constraining new approaches to
reorienting bureaucracies is a deeply embedded, self-
perceived and socially reinforced need for certainty
among planners and managers of government agencies.
Many government agents are unable to tolerate the absence of direct control, of clear measures of efficiency, and of rationally planned outcomes. A well-
documented requirement for a new personal skill in
organizational performance, for example, is a tolerance
for ambiguity, a behavioral objective that is far more
difficult to achieve in practice than to define. Virtually all of us -- university professors, development
consultants, donor agency professionals, and Third
World professionals -- are emotionally and intellectu-
ally compelled toward certainty, control, and anticipated outcomes.

The power of this drive toward certainty and away
from serendipity is a dominating constraint to the
achievement of people-centered, as opposed to bureaucratic, action.

4. Closely related to a continuing need for
certainty is the incapacity of schools, universities
and training institutes to "teach" social learning and
collaborative planning. The fundamental pedagogical
style of the modern school is one of transmitting
objective knowledge to the uninitiated learner. To
educate a new kind of governmental development agent
requires a reorientation of educational institutions
and training approaches. The pervasiveness of the
current pedagogical model impedes movement toward
collaborative, mutual learning styles.

5. The final constraint is rather more difficult
to define. Its source is the extreme diversity in culturally mixed organizational systems around the world.
When colloquia of development specialists gather to
evaluate old and create new development strategies, we

do so from a relatively homogeneous understanding of
social and organizational norms and values. We can
talk with each other with a moderate degree of understanding. We can even function together with relative
ease in coordinated action toward common objectives.
Problems quickly become apparent when one attempts
to communicate with diverse social and political communities. Many social communities in various parts of
the world are unassimilated to currently dominant
social and organizational forms. Further, significant
numbers of communities have "mixed model" acculturation
patterns: Western-oriented educations and modern organizational norms mixed with non-Western social norms and
values. A stimulating organization development challenge, for example, is represented in Middle Eastern
oil-producing countries where large staffs of expatriate professionals have been recruited from such diverse
cultures as Korea, the Philippines, Sri Lanka, India,
Pakistan, Britain, the United States and European
countries. Interdepartmental coordination and task
force management is a perplexing challenge, in such a
multicultural organizational setting. Even though communication takes place within a single language, coordinating behavior toward common objectives in multicultural organizational teams is extremely difficult.
A similar constraint faces attempts at people-centered
development action in largely mixed model, multicultural environments.

AGENDA

The constraints identified above outline an agenda
for a new social development approach to management.
1. It should be obvious that additional research
and, even more importantly, new action experiments in
empowering communities and reorienting bureaucracies
must be undertaken. As promising as current experience
is, the ultimate test of people-centered strategies
will be their effectiveness in diverse situations.
2. A part of the research and experimentation
agenda must reach the macro-level of organizational
analysis and practice. It is not enough to deal only
with the linkages at the bureaucracy-community nexus.
The implications for national level and international
organizations are yet to be examined in substantive
detail.[30]
3. The phrase mutual learning has been both explicit and implicit throughout this paper. One person
calls it the "process of grafting personal on processed
knowledge."[31] Mutual learning obviously engages highly
diverse people of differing abilities and cultural
realities in cooperative endeavors. Do we know enough
about this process? How close are we to being able to

diffuse mutual learning skills and practice to ever enlarging numbers of development professionals and development clients?

4. Another agenda item is the challenge to avoid "artifacting" people-centered development action strategies. To see "social learning" and the "reorienting of bureaucracies" as technological tools which development agents must give to their clients without changing their own behavior or reorienting the performance of their own organizations would miss the critical element of social learning theory. It would then be one more development technique or artifact stored on the warehouse shelf from which it might on occasion be retrieved to fill in time at a dreary and routine training session. How do we reorient values and behavioral responses while avoiding artifacting?

5. The most significant and longest range agenda for development agents is the ultimate relevance of social learning-based strategies and social development objectives for a more generalized societal transformation process.[32] Social learning, it has been alleged, enlarges and improves the power of social science research methods, opening new possibilities for resolving seemingly intractable human problems. Social development as redefined reorients the criteria for progress toward more human oriented, equity-focused measures of achievement. Together these redefinitions suggest the necessity of significant adjustments in the values and structures of modern institutions.

Modern institutions and modern technology have molded our interdependent world community, holding out the promise of longer and enriched lives. They have also accentuated human poverty, inequality and the specters of technological destruction and nuclear holocaust. Reorienting modern institutions to enhance the former while curtaining the latter is a worthwhile human goal.

NOTES

This paper was originally written as background for the Social Development Management Workshop sponsored by the National Association of Schools of Public Affairs and Administration held at the World Conference of the Society for International Development (SID), Baltimore, Maryland, July 18, 1982.

The paper is a synthesis of ideas from multiple contributors and a personal interpretation of those contributions based on my own earlier work. I have been interested in people-centered strategies for development since the late 1960s and have proposed some revolutionary, perhaps "reorienting," strategies for development agencies.

This present analysis has been substantially informed by the field work and published reports of several development analysts, principally John Friedmann, George Honadle, David Korten and Jon Moris. In this analysis I have relied on some of their terminology, phrases and conceptual "hooks." But the intellectual debt goes much deeper. The theoretical underpinnings are extensive, only partially identified in the notes and references of the publications cited in the text.

The analysis itself has been shaped to some extent through the active engagement of a growing number of Social Development Management Network associates who contributed to the SID Workshop and to two previous workshops. Principal among these have been Derick Brinkerhoff, Coralie Bryant, Edwin Connerley, Marcus Ingle, Leonard Joy, Rudi Klauss, Frances Korten, Catherine Lovell, and Philip Morgan.

1. The human focus to development objectives has multiple sources, but my use of the term here builds on several earlier references including Theodore H. Thomas, "People Strategies for International Development: Administrative Alternatives to National Administration Vol. 5, No. 1, pp. 87-107; James P. Grant, "Development: The End of Trickle Down?", Foreign Policy, 12, Fall; also published as "Growth from Below: A People-Oriented Development Strategy", Overseas Development Council, Development Paper No. 16, December 1973; and George Carner and David C. Korten, "People Centered Planning: The USAID Philippines Experience," Working Paper No. 2, Washington, D.C.: NASPAA, 1982. See also Raymond Apthorpe, People Planning and Development Studies, (London: Frank Cass, 1970), for use of the term "people planning." Continuing use of the term is evident in forthcoming World Bank publications, including William Baum and Arturo Israel, "Reorienting Donor Bureaucracies for People-Centered Development: Experience of the World Bank," a paper delivered at the 1983 Conference of the American Society for Public Administration, New York; and the initial drafts of the 1984 World Development Report.

2. Hollis Chenery, Redistribution for Growth, (London: Oxford University Press, 1974); Ozay Mehmet, Economic Planning and Social Justice in Developing Countries, (New York: St. Martin's Press, 1978); and Barbara Ward, Lenore d'Anjou and J. D. Runnalls, eds., The Widening Gap: Development in the 1970s, (New York: Columbia University Press, 1971).

3. Robert E. Hunter, James P. Grant and William Richard, "A New Development Strategy? Greater Equity, Faster Growth, and Small Families," Overseas Development Council, Development Paper No. 11, October 1972.

4. Milton J. Esman and John D. Montgomery, "The Administration of Human Development," in Implementing Programs of Human Development, Staff Working Paper No. 403, Part III, Washington, D. C.: The World Bank, 1980.

5. George Honadle, "Fishing for Sustainability: The Role of Capacity Building in Development Administration." IRD Working Paper No. 8, Washington, D. C.: Development Alternatives, Inc., 1981.

6. David C. Korten, "Community Organization and Rural Development: A Learning Process Approach." Public Administration Review, Vol. 40, No. 5, September-October 1980, 480-511.

7. Jon R. Moris, "Administrative Authority and the Problem of Effective Agricultural Administration in East Africa: African Review, Vol. 2, No. 2, June 1972.

8. John Friedmann, Retracting America: A Theory of Transactive Planning, (Emmaus, Pa.: Rodale Press, 1973), reissue 1981.

9. Edgar S. Dunn, Economic and Social Development: A Process of Social Learning, (Baltimore: The Johns Hopkins Press, 1971).

10. David C. Korten, "The Management of Social Transformation," Public Administration Review, November-December 1981, 609--618; and Friedman.

11. In addition to Dunn, and other references already indicated, the reader is referred to Peter Berger and Thomas Luckman, The Social Construction of Reality, (New York: Doubleday, 1966), Theodore Roszak, The Making of the Counter-Culture, (New York: Doubleday, 1969); and Henry Cochran, "Society as Emergent and More Than Rational: An Essay on the Inappropriateness of Program Evaluation," Policy Sciences, 12 (1980), 113-119.

12. Berger and Luckman.

13. There is evidence that "good" science does not in fact proceed from this assumption about physical phenomena. See, for example, the work of Fritjof Capra, The Tao of Physics, Boulder: Shambhala, 1975, and The Turning Point, (New York: Simon and Schuster, 1982).

14. Cochran.

15. Chenery; The Brandt Report, North-South: A Programme for Survival, (London: Pan Books Ltd., 1980); and Mehmet.

16. Grant and Hunter, Grant and Rich and a New Development Strategy.

17. Alvin Toffler, Future Shock (New York: Random House, 1970).

18. Lane E. Holdcroft, The Rise and Fall of Community Development in Developing Countries, 1950-65: A Critical Analysis and an Annotated Bibliography, MSU Rural Development Papers, East Lansing, Department of Agricultural Economics, Michigan State University, 1977; and Mary Hollnsteiner, "Mobilizing the Rural Poor Through Community Organization", Philippines Studies, 27: 387-416.

19. Honadle.

20. Carner and Korten.

21. Hayden Roberts, Community Development: Learning and Action, (Toronto: University of Toronto Press, 1982), 25-33.

22. Ibid., 27.

23. John D. Montgomery, "The Populist Front of Rural Development: Or, Shall we Eliminate the Bureaucrats and Get on with the Job?", Public Administration Review, 39 (January-February, 1979), 58-64.

24. David C. Korten and Norman T. Uphoff, "Bureaucratic Reorientation for Participatory Rural Development," Working Paper No. 1, Washington, D. C.: NASPAA, 1981.

25. Donald Schon, Beyond the Stable State, (New York: Norton, 1971).

26. Bernard Schaffer, "Deadlock in Development Administration," in Collin Leys (ed.), Politics and Change in Developing Countries, (Cambridge University Press, 1969).

27. Theodore H. Thomas and Derick Brinkerhoff, "Revolutionary Strategies for Development Administration," SICA Occasional Papers, American Society for Public Administration, Washington, D. C., 1978.

28. Ibid, and Korten and Uphoff.

29. David C. Korten, "The Working Group as a Mechanism for Managing Bureaucratic Reorientation: Experience from the Philippines", Working Paper No. 4, Washington, D.C.: NASPAA, 1982.

30. A beginning was made at a recent panel presentation at the New York Conference of the American Society for Public Administration, April 1983. Included was a paper referenced above by William Baum and Arturo Israel, both of the World Bank.

31. Friedman.

32. Korten, 1981.

Introduction to Part II

Jean-Claude Garcia-Zamor

Part II has four chapters. In chapter 3, David J. Gould analyzes popular participation in African development planning and management. Popular participation is defined by Gould in terms of those policies and practices which facilitate citizen access to decision-making and are embodied in the administrative system and process. Inadequate popular participation is seen as a component of a larger problem: ineffective management, planning and policy performance in Africa. As such lack of participation is viewed as a result of poor management rather than the cause of it. The problem of nonexistent popular participation is heightened further by the colonial heritage of African countries. Administration's role under colonial rule was to subjugate citizens and exclude them from participation. The post-colonial administration's elite lifestyle and the political regimentation prevailing in most countries encourages citizens to withdraw from an active role in government.

The study by Gould finds a degree of variation in popular participation depending on the regime's ideology. The market-economy states surveyed (e.g., Ivory Coast, Nigeria, and Kenya), do not encourage citizens to participate in development management and planning. This is thought to be in part a carry-over from their bureaucratic, and authoritarian colonial past, and a reflection of the greater tolerance for inequality inherent in capitalism. At the opposite end of the ideological spectrum, an Afro-Marxist regime had only a slightly better record in popular participation. In countries such as Congo-Brazzaville, Mozambique and Madagascar, the Leninist model demands that the ruling party be led undemocratically by a "revolutionary vanguard of the ideologically select," in the context of strong centralization. Despite this participation-discouraging ideological freight, Madagascar had in the 1970s managed to develop an interesting and effective popular participatory scheme in the rural sector.

Still, Afro-Marxists' overall record in popular participation is not good. The best popular participation record is sported by populist-socialist states such as Tanzania and Algeria, where, despite some flaws and setbacks, the nationalistic, egalitarian, non-Leninist ideology finds some echo in measures enhancing popular participation in planning and management.

The second chapter, by Derick W. Brinkerhoff, provides a case study of a participatory strategic and evaluation exercise undertaken by an international donor agency in collaboration with the host country government. This joint assessment of U.S. development assistance to Senegal, carried out by the U.S. Agency for International Development (USAID) and the Government of Senegal (GOS) in 1980, is analyzed in terms of: (a) the links between participation and the results achieved, and (b) the elements of the assessment as an organizational change intervention that contributed to its success.

The joint assessment consisted of four project evaluations and a macro-economic analysis of the constraints to development faced by Senegal. A joint working group managed the process of conducting the field evaluations, discussing the results with AID and GOS personnel, and producing the final documents acceptable to both parties. The joint assessment formed the foundation for a collaborative mode of program planning between AID and the GOS for future use of U.S. assistance funds in Senegal.

Participation contributed to the success of the joint assessment in several ways. Beneficiary and other local level input improved the quality of information obtained by the evaluations. Involvement of GOS officials in the evaluation process made it easier for the GOS to accept the findings as valid. GOS participation improved the policy environment for AID projects, and facilitated the resolution of implementation problems. Also, some GOS participants acquired evaluation and planning skills.

However, Brinkerhoff argues that participation is not without its costs. The involvement of a range of actors in the joint assessment was time-consuming and increased the management load on the working group in charge of the evaluations. Because of the time demands and the scarcity of resources, GOS members of the working group were forced to reduce their level of involvement. The assessment required process skills as well as technical skills. Further, the results of the assessment entailed risks for both AID and GOS; negative findings posed a potential bureaucratic threat.

As an example of an organizational change intervention, the joint assessment illustrated the impact of certain facilitating conditions on the probability of

success. These include: (a) pressure for change from
key actors, (b) commitment to change leading to allocation of resources, (c) participation of organization
members from multiple levels, (d) organizational receptivity to innovation, (e) mechanisms for follow-up,
and (f) a minimum level of stability in the organization and in its environment. The question of incentives to operate in a participatory manner in an
organizational environment where participation carries
a high cost is particularly salient. Several of these
facilitating conditions will emerge only if there are
incentives for someone to institute change.
     The third chapter by Richard W. Ryan is on local
participation in food and nutrition programs in Upper
Volta and Togo. From 1978 to 1980 Ryan was involved in
managing nutritional health programs sponsored by the
Catholic Relief Services (CRS) in Upper Volta and Togo.
The programs are aimed at improving and monitoring the
nutritional health of women of child-bearing age and
children to 5 years. A key aspect of the programs is
the participation of the beneficiaries in financing and
implementing village center operations. The mothers
assist the auxiliaries in weighing babies, distributing
food, and generally maintaining to center. Village
authorities are involved from the program's inception
since they are responsible for providing a sheltered
meeting place and a secure warehouse.
     Ryan notes that the high degree of local involve-
ment in CRS programs is not so much a conscious application of participation strategy as it is the result of
the economics of a private, voluntary organization
(PVO) and a fairly uncomplicated self-image. However,
the PVO as well as its supporters frequently point to
these programs as examples of grassroots participation.
This chapter examines this claim. Judith Tendler's
classification of PVO participation is utilized: top-
down decision-making, decentralized decision-making
involving local elites, and genuine representative or
grassroots participation by beneficiaries. Beneficiary
and PVO staff participation are analyzed. The CRS
programs are found to incorporate each of Tendler's
types in varying degrees. The greatest incidence of
grassroots participation is expected to be found in
mature food and nutrition programs where secondary projects (agricultural, health, etc.) are organized by the
beneficiaries. The involvement of the local elite may
diminish at mature food and nutrition village centers,
but is is always present. Ryan offers eleven lessons
from experience, following a description and analysis
of the case study. These lessons emphasize the importance of local ownership of programs, finding a fit
between program goals and local resources, and the key

role of local and international PVO staff in nurturing participatory management.

The fourth and last chapter of this part, written by James B. Mayfield, discusses the Egyptian Basic Village Service program as a new strategy for local government capacity building. The Basic Village Service program recently established in the villages of rural Egypt provides an extremely interesting case study which can enhance our awareness of the theoretical and operational issues related to the process of local government development, decentralization and management and administrative capacity building for rural development in a Third World setting. A review of recent shifts in Egyptian local government and the Egyptian government's commitment to decentralization dramatizes the significant relationships that exist between the need for local revenues and financial resources, the need for increased management skills in program design, implementation and evaluation, and the need for increased local participator initiatives through locally-established village institutions.

3. Popular Participation in African Development Planning and Management

David J. Gould

What are the realistic prospects of popular participation making an impact on development planning and management in Africa? The advantages which enhanced participation should engender make the question relevant. These include strengthened institutions, greater legitimacy, better accountability and perhaps even -- though it remains to be proved -- improved policy performance. To address the question properly, however, it is first necessary to take stock of the African experience with popular participation to date.

By popular participation we are not referring to the entire spectrum of conceivable devices facilitating citizen access to and involvement in planning and management. That range of techniques might encompass activities of the party, local government, presidential dialogue, mass media, etc., including such activities as elections. Societal participation in that broad sense would consider the membership, and access patterns thereto, of those groups that determine ideological options, define the public interest, and share in the managing of collective resources and goods. Our focus is somewhat narrower for the purposes of this study, emphasizing ways of facilitating citizen involvement as may be lodged in the administrative system and process. This requires going beyond the claim a regime may make about its participation record to examine actual performance. Before reviewing the popular participation experiences of a number of representative African countries, some context setting is appropriate. The degree to which a given regime succeeds or fails to achieve popular participation in development planning or management is but one component of a larger problem: that of ineffective management, planning and policy performance in Africa. This result has been noted by virtually every expert who has observed African planning and management first hand.[1] Some specialists have considered popular participation to be a key variable in explaining development administration's widespread

35

deficiencies.[2] Others have considered popular participation in program project design and implementation to
be an important, if not the most significant, variable
determining ultimate success in attaining the hoped-for
results.[3] Still others, while recognizing popular participation as a factor, tend to play down its signifi-
cance in the face of more technocratic considerations
in development planning and management.[4] Inadequate
popular participation is seen here as a symptom rather
than as a fundamental problem of African underdevelopment. The structures, processes and behaviors of a
country's administrative system are derived from and
dependent on basic causal factors, including ideology,
social class mobilization, economic forces, political
imperatives and commitments, and technological level
(including managerial skills and competence).[5]

Popular participation is a part of the rules,
behaviors, structures, and processes, formal and informal, that the external environment of the administrative system assigns to its internal environment
instrumentally so as to enhance the likelihood of the
system performing and achieving the policy goals. Popular participation is a creation of the internal environment of the society. Its nature and chances for
success will depend on considerations of policy in the
external environment of the administrative system. To
the extent that a commitment to encourage popular participation emerges, it is the result of force that the
administrative system does not control, but rather by
which it is shaped.

A number of factors affect popular participation
in Africa. Historically the African colonial state was
an intrusive, authoritarian conqueror with an administration that was essentially an alien element grafted
onto, and disrupting forever, the patterns of traditional African society. Popular participation had no
place in such a state. One the contrary, the administrative system was often designed to subjugate the
population. Unquestioning compliance or punishment was
the lot of the administered. This heritage has proved
difficult to overcome in the post-colonial era. Indeed,
few post-colonial African regimes have made destruction[6]
of the strong centralizing behemoth of the state a
priority.

Strike two involves technology and human resources. In most African countries, functional or real
adult illiteracy in the language of the administration
(English, French, Portuguese, etc.) is the rule rather
than the exception. The number of college-educated
people, even high school diploma-holders, is normally
infinitesimal. In most countries, members of this
elite minority are called "intellectuals," whether they
are so endowed or not. They tend to relate to each

other rather than to those below their station. They
are set apart from the population by education, aspirations, income, lifestyle, etc. They are dispropor-
tionately employed in the public sector. Indeed, in
some countries (e.g., Congo and Mali), college graduates are automatically assured a comparatively high-
ranking position in the public service. College graduates concentrated in the public sector are commonly
called "technocrats," virtually no matter how appropriate their studies were in preparing them technically to
assume planning, policy-analytic or managerial responsibilities. The group is sometimes called, less chari-
tably, "administrative elite" or even less so, "bureaucratic bourgeoisie." However it may be called, a group
or class is ubiquitously identifiable, more or less
without regard for ideology.[7] Sociologically, this
group is inherently unlikely to relish sharing its pre-
rogatives with the population, absent an extremely
strong commitment from higher up.

Strike three encompasses the political dimensions
of post-colonial African states. With few exceptions,
(e.g., Senegal, Nigeria, Botswana, Mauritius) African
regimes are one-party affairs. This is the case regardless of ideology. Where they do occur, elections
take place in a single-party framework. Candidacies
must be approved by the supreme authority before being
fielded. Varying degrees of internal democracy prevail
within such parties. Occasionally there are surprises.
But candidates or ideas in general are never tolerated
when posing a challenge to the regime's ideological
options and scarcely ever when challenging a regime's
fundamental policy options.[8] Except for the countries
cited, opposition newspapers are not tolerated. Public
criticism of the regime in most countries is a dangerous activity. Such regimentation is normally justified
in terms of "raison d'etat." Such control is also allegedly needed to permit the needed "mobilization" of
the population in order to accomplish societal goals in
the face of a hostile environment, turmoil and crisis.
Regimes that view challenging people and ideas as disruptive and threatening in the political sphere are ill
-disposed to promote popular participation in the politically charged areas of planning and administration.
Put another way, the prospect of popular participation
in planning and administration is not encouraged by
such a regime. The observer may legitimately wonder
whether any commitment made by a regime to popular participation is not done for the consumption of external
technical aid agencies which insist thereon rather than
being a sincere reflection of governmental policy.

Faced with the additional, innumerable difficulties of nation-building and multiple exigencies of
statecraft in crisis,[9] there is little wonder that the

scope of political participation has actually been diminishing since independence. In his classic 1976 study, Kasfir coined the term "departicipation" to cover the lessened scope of participation due to governmental policy that he had found in his own East African fieldwork and throughout the literature covering other countries in Africa.[10] Hence, while enhanced popular participation may be a stated goal, departicipation remains the norm, the unfortunate reality in many, if not most, African countries. For all of the above reasons, enhanced popular participation planning and management is posited as inimical to most African regimes' self-interest.

Is the outlook for participation equally negative throughout Africa? We are going to suggest, hypothetically, that the degree of popular participation planning and management will generally vary depending on the regime's ideology. For analytic purposes, it is possible to place African regimes into three categories with respect to their "ideological commitment."[11] The forty-nine countries in Africa are extremely diverse and any effort at generalization is hazardous.[12] To simplify the task, African regimes may be conveniently categorized under three distinct ideological labels:[13]

1. Capitalist, in which the regime pursues a market-economy policy, whether admitted or not (African capitalist regimes are sometimes diffident about so labeling themselves);

2. Populist-Socialist, in which the people are celebrated in nationalistic, egalitarian opposition to colonialism and capitalism; and

3. Afro-Marxist, in which, without following any other country's model, Marxism-Leninism is the avowed ideology.

Following is a sample characterization of some African regimes with respect to these categories:

Capitalist	Populist-Socialist	Marxist-Leninist
Gabon	Algeria	Angola
Ghana (1966-82)	Ghana (1957-66)	Benin
Ivory Coast	Guinea-Bissau	Congo
Kenya	Guinea-Conakry	Ethiopia
Nigeria	Tanzania	(post-1974)
Zaire	Zambia	Madagascar
		Mozambique

CAPITALIST REGIMES

Capitalist market-oriented regimes are characterized by a more or less operationalized commitment to the following values:

1. Private markets as a positive good and allocator of resources;

2. Capital as the crucial factor of production;
3. An open economy;
4. Pro-Western relations in training, technology and investments;
5. Greater tolerance for inequality.

Although Lindblom has stated that "only within market-oriented systems does political democracy occur,"[14] others specialized in Third World studies suggest[15] that capitalism can best be preserved through the creation of a bureaucratic-authoritarian state. Indeed, a form of capitalism that some call "peripheral capitalism" but that is nonetheless capitalist[16] was the condition of all African countries on the eve of their independence. Twenty-six years ago, all African countries (including already-independent Liberia, Egypt, Morocco, Ethiopia and South Africa) were market-oriented and had been so in one form or another since the beginnings of colonialism. Capitalism had thus coincided with bureaucratic authoritarianism. These considerations are heightened in regarding the post-colonial state as a carry over from the colonial capitalist state: an intrusive instrument for domination, mercantilist-capitalist in orientation, authoritarian in structure and in administrative behavior.[17]

Already there have been major changes of orientation, style, tone and policy emphasis as between colonial and post-colonial African states. Whether these changes are so profound as to represent a transformation of the pre-existing ideology, goals, structures and behavior is another question.[18] Several authors have found substantial convergence. To what extent has the colonial legacy with respect to popular participation been carried over to post-colonial-capitalist states?

None of market economy states surveyed has distinguished itself with an outstanding record in the promotion of popular participation and development management planning. Ivory Coast is considered by many the "economic miracle" of West Africa. In Young's words, this country is "by some distance the most influential exemplary state on the African capitalist pathway."[19] It has achieved remarkable growth, averaging seven to eight percent in GNP annually since the 1950s, and and annual per capita growth rate of 3.3 percent from 1960-1976. The agricultural sector has grown substantially, and a dynamic industrial sector has been built up. At the same time, the price paid[20] has been great in terms of dependency and inequality. With respect to participation, on the plus side is the intraparty competition which the regime allowed in the 1981 elections, resulting in a degree of electoral participation, arguably constituting a political opening. However, the carryover to administration and planning of this recent political innovation has yet to be observed. Cohen makes a case that the "presidential dialogues" with the people constitute meaningful participation. However, if this is the best case that can be made for participation in planning and administration in the Ivory Coast, then opportunities for popular participation in administration and planning must be severely limited in this authoritarian, centralized state. Kenya flirted with socialism in the early years following independence, but has for at least fifteen years been confidently and assertively pursuing a capitalist strategy. The productivity-centered approach has resulted in "major innovations" and steady gains,[21] with an average GNP growth rate of 5.9 percent from 1964 through 1977.[22] Several critics have, however, pointed to the dependency and inequality-widening consequences of the capitalist strategy pursued.[23] With respect to participation, the record of citizen involvement in planning and management is not outstanding. It is true that the administration has been effective in delivering services and amenities to the rural sector.[24] Indeed, Bienen presents the argument that local administration constitutes the prime agency for political participation because it serves as the major contact point between the state and the citizenry charged with explicit social and economic transformation tasks and instructed to serve as the channel for local government and demands.[25] However, the limits of this wish are observable in practice. A convincing study[26] presents solid evidence as to the difficulties of achieving even citizen understanding and compliance with centrally determined policies, let alone meaningful participation in developing these policies.

Nigeria, Africa's most populist country, is a case of "capitalism run riot," in Young's blunt characterization.[27] Oil-driven prosperity was combined with indigenous entrepreneurship and corruption-stimulated bursts of growth to allow the country to overcome a wrenching civil war and achieve Africa's largest economy. The consequence was a GNP and PCI so high as to make the country too rich to qualify for US foreign aid. Agriculture was seriously neglected, however, as the country pursued "nurture capitalism," focusing on the urban mercantile and industrial sectors, the ruling class having no rural origins or outlet.[28] The overall impact has certainly been to promote inequality.[29] There have been impressive developments in the political sphere, including a refreshing civilianization of what had been a military government, reframing of a new constitution embodying civil liberties and human rights quarantees, and a multiparty electoral system. Political decentralization has led to deconcentration of authority in numerous social and economic areas, i.e., the twenty-two state governments. This has brought government theoretically closer to the 90 million people. However, in the specific domain of development planning and management, there is little evidence that the authoritarian structures, procedures and attitudes characterizing the administrative system have been overcome to create operational citizen access. A recent study of the workings of the Citizen Public Complaint Commission suggests that opportunities to complain provide outlets for frustration as opposed to input into planning-management.[30]

MARXIST-LENINIST REGIMES

Marxist-Leninist regimes are at the opposite end of the spectrum from market-oriented capitalist regimes. There are many differences from country to country within this category, and considerable differences between Afro-Marxist and Marxist-Leninist states elsewhere in the world. Nonetheless, Afro-Marxist regimes may be said to have:
1. A leading party that is Leninist, i.e., manned undemocratically by a "revolutionary vanguard of the ideologically select," supposedly not to represent but to incarnate the will of the workers and peasants,[31] to which all state organs (political branches, military, bureaucracy) and social formations are deemed subordinate;
2. A permanent drive to create a "socialist sector" and gain control of the "commanding heights" of the economy.
3. Comprehensive central planning as an ideal. Clearly, the ambition of the Afro-Marxists, upon taking over the colonial or early or post-colonial governments, was to deploy a Marxist-Leninist "mobilization strategy" so as to effect a radical structural transformation of society. However, their origins are primarily in military cliques or liberation armies, whose social base lies with "revolutionary democrats" -- political figures, intellectuals, teachers, with a strong cohort of well-educated urban youth. Workers and peasants tend to have little to do with this elite group, although it is in their name that the latter governs. Although Afro-Marxist states generally seek to pursue close ties with Communist countries and sometimes adopt similar positions on international issues, even Afro-Marxist regimes call themselves non-aligned. Moreover, East Bloc and Chinese trade and aid links have in no Afro-Marxist country displaced or even come close to equal the continued weight of Western economic ties. In areas of technology, resource development,

capital and in many respects lifestyle, the West remains the "necessary evil" to which Afro-Marxist regimes refer. With respect to popular participation, orthodox Marxism suggest the existence of an organized group of workers, with a strong class identity, a working class "struggling" for establishment of the regime, as well as its effective participation in the conduct of strategy. In practice, however, workers have tended to be turbulent and refractory.[32] A major area of skepticism relates to the Afro-Marxists' theoretical bias in favor of the masses. In principal, the Marxist-Leninist model pursues a "democratic centralism" line, which means that important decisions are made at the top, with input based on discussion from below; in practice, the insistence on a "correct line" determined on high, ineluctably precludes open democracy in the party as a dangerous luxury. It is not surprising that most Afro-Marxist regimes have highly centralized government and administration, wherein planning and top management functions are reserved for a highly educated, if "revolutionary," elite. These factors do not bode well for popular participation.

Congo-Brazzaville returned to Marxism-Leninism officially in 1969, with a proclamation by then leader Marien Ngouabi (assassinated in 1977) of a people's republic. Many significant achievements were registered, namely some initial increases in minimum wages, per capita income and GNP.[33] The public sector was dramatically expanded from 3,500 to 25,000 employees from 1960 to 1970.[34] On the downside the public sector was viewed, even by sympathetic scholars such as Bertrand and others, to be a major drain.[35] Four billion CFA in annual subsidies had to be provided in the 1970s to keep the failing public enterprises from going bankrupt. Agricultural productivity also faltered. Only the Congo's oil revenue allowed for such liberality. The Congolese economy was characterized by continued Western involvement in the country (e.g., 80 percent of the productive sector remained in the hands of Western owners as of early 1983).

A remarkable feature of the Congo has been the leadership's openness to self-criticism, at several junctures indicting itself severely for such ills as "weak party leadership," lack of liaison between the leadership of the party and the masses, the inflexibility of the "state apparatus," etc.[36] Since that indictment was formulated (1975), two presidents have been removed, one by assassination, another by internal shuffle, in large part over issues of state policy, planning and management strategies. Within Congolese public enterprises, a "tripartite" decisional system exists whereby representatives of the state, the party, and the workers' union must be given the opportunity to discuss decisions before they are reached. This innovation is worth noting. However, in practice it does not always work as a theory. Many observers believe that the excessive time spent on such discussions, and the generally refractory demands made by workers, constitute a drain on productivity; technocratic pressures for reducing the participatory nature of this innovation may be instated, given the strong pressures that exist for increasing public enterprises' productivity.

Madagascar has gone through a significant amount of internal strife, with frequent changes at the top since the early 1970s. Its Marxist-Leninist character emerged in 1973-74 in reaction to the earlier so-called "democratic socialism" of the 1960s, which had been characterized by "the very close ties" that then President Tsiranana had "retained with the former metropole and South Africa and by the unchallenged predominance of French interests on the island."[37] Major acts of expropriation took place, and the regime by 1976 had expanded the socialized sector from fifteen to sixty percent of the economy.[38] Financial prudence and real concern for rural welfare were said to characterize the regime.[39] An interesting experiment in popular participation, begun by Tsiranana, was _Fokonolona_: the basic cell of self-reliant and decentralized rural society. However, the subsequent leader, President Ratsiraka, began transforming them into more state-oriented operations, believing that they had been dominated by local notables and prosperous farmers and that these village units had had too much power placed in their hands. "Firm state supervision and discipline and intensive ideological instruction were required. Thus conceived, _Fokonolona_ would seem destined for departicipation and bureaucratization."[40] Nonetheless, this interesting innovation is worth noting.

Mozambique's, gaining of independence (1975), and its continued structural dependence in many economic respects on South Africa, make any assessment of its development performance difficult. However, despite Marxist-Leninist centralism, "dynamizing groups" were formed by the regime throughout the country shortly after independence. Their mission was to politically indoctrinate the rural population. A novel experiment, these popular consultations appear to have brought about a degree of significant participation. "Mass involvement, however, does not extend to debate over the basic options or policy orientations of the regime."[41]

In general, we see that the performance of Marxist-Leninist regimes in the area of participation is mixed, constrained by an emphasis on the "centralism" in "democratic centralism," but with considerable effort nonetheless to involve the population at some level in the process of planning and management.

POPULIST-SOCIALIST REGIMES

Populist-socialist regimes are perhaps the most amorphous. They stand at midpoint between market-oriented/capitalist and Afro-Marxist. Indeed, several countries have passed through a populist-socialist stage en route to one extreme or another (e.g. Nkrumahs Ghana, Tsiranana's Madagascar). They may be characterized as being:

1) Strongly nationalistic in orientation;
2) Radically confrontational in style;
3) Anti-capitalist in pronouncement and, to some extent, in doctrine;
4) Celebratory of the masses; and
5) Marxist in orientation, if not Marxist-Leninist in structure.

Participation by elements of the nonelite population in planning and management has a somewhat greater chance of occurring in the populist-socialist context in so far as it constitutes a high theoretical priority in terms of the regime's self description, nor is it subject to the doctrinaire exclusionary prejudices against popular participation embodied in capitalist or Afro-Marxist sister regime values.

Tanzania is generally the first socialist country to which admirers and detractors point when seeking to make their "case" for or against socialism. Since the 1967 Arush Declaration, the ruling party in Tanzania has been governing on the basis of a powerful set of radical norms. A "truly socialist society" was envisioned, "where all people were workers," where no one lived on the work of others, "where all major means of production and exchange were controlled and owned by the peasants through the machinery of their government and their cooperatives," and where the ruling party was "a party of peasants and workers."[42] Tanzania has encountered various difficulties in achieving its development goals, in fact in the 1970s the net growth rate was negative.[43] Several authors have pointed to the limitations in the party's operational capacity to serve as a vehicle for rural participation.[44] Authors such as Fortman have identified establishment of participation as incompatible with the internal demands of a rigid structured and centralized organization.[44] Capitalists and pragmatists were disappointed because CCM stuck to collectivist strategies while Marxist-Leninists (including some outspoken academics at Dar es Salaam University advocated the party's transformation into a vanguard party. The latter concept was rejected "precisely because (President Nyerere) wanted a mass party for Tanzania, avoiding ideological elitism, and providing for accountability of the leadership to the masses."[45] Indeed, despite difficulties in promoting

economic growth, Tanzania has been one of the leading
African countries in featuring significant participation. "In both ethos and structure," Young wrote,
"the party provided elements of access to the citizenry
at large that were substantially greater than in most
African parties."[46]

Algeria is a country literally born in a national
liberation struggle waged for nearly a decade against
France. The party which led Algeria to independence in
1962, the FLN, has been governing it ever since, and
doing so under a socialist ideology. <u>Auto-Gestion</u>
(self-management) was a linchpin of regime ideology in
its early years. "Worker power" did not become easily
institutionalized, and in the late 1960s concepts of
efficiency melded with worker control. This coincided
with the dramatic expansion of the public sector: more
nationalizations and new industrial ventures, fueled by
gas and oil finds. In 1971, "socialist management"
decrees rejuvenated and subsumed self-management in the
public sector. Although not strictly speaking the more
radical self-management ("neither <u>Auto-Gestion</u> nor
<u>Co-Gestion</u>" as some have put it), <u>still</u> means that
elected worker assemblies in each production until
exercise meaningful inputs. True, ultimate authority
resides with the (technocratic) managers, and beyond
them the state tutelary authority.[47] According to
Nellis, these assemblies reflect the permeation of
policy choice by the underlying populist-socialist perspectives.[48] Young also contends that "the powers of
the elected workers' assemblies ... are not trivial and
do offer potentially meaningful leverage."[49]

Guinea-Conakry may have begun swerving somewhat
from the defiant socialist path laid out by President
Sekow Toure when breaking with France and President
DeGaulle and "going it alone" in 1958. Although the
"neo-colonial bauxite enclave" (concessions which were
then parceled out to American, French, Swiss, and
Soviet companies) provided some foreign currency, the
socialist sector failed to achieve productivity, manu-
facturing activities had dwindled to almost nothing
(2.6 percent of GNP in 1968) and agriculture had
achieved a negative growth rate in the 1970s.[50] In
lieu of economic decay and repression, a poor human
rights record, a massive exodus (twenty percent of the
population), deprived the country of skilled human
resources. Unlike the other two socialist regimes
surveyed, Guinea does not have impressive achievements
in popular participation. "Human investment" in agriculture production cooperatives (CAP) failed by the mid
1960s; a new set of cooperatives initiated in 1965 had
failed in 1972. Derman observed here that:

"cooperative facilities were also offered to buy tomatoes, mangoes, and oranges; in reality these were simply forced deliveries to the state priced below the market level. The peasants tended to view them as versions of forced labor for the personal enrichment of state officials."[51]

When in 1974 Toure initiated a new set of cooperatives, he criticized past efforts as having been based in capitalist concepts. Derman wryly opined:

"to explain the failure of the past on incorrect ideas of the population, without asking where they got them, why they maintain them and what will lead them to change these ideas, is inadequate."[52]

CONCLUSIONS

We have been reviewing the records of three different ideological regime types to search for insight into the determinants of effective popular participation in development planning and management. We have lingered over ideology and external environmental forces -- external to the administrative system. We have found that populist-socialist regimes tend to achieve the most innovation and success in providing meaningful citizen access to development, planning and management, with Afro-Marxist and capitalist regimes finishing second and third, respectively. Explanations as to why this is so are not self-evident. But we suggest that the relative success of socialist regimes is due, at least in part, to the conscious effort that they undertake to break radically from the colonial structural model of top-down central policy making, planning and management.

Afro-Marxist regimes may also wish to carry out a major break with the past, but do so via an instrument -- the Leninist vanguard party -- which tends in practice to be heavily centralized and elitist. Capitalist regimes have made the least efforts to tinker with the colonial legacy, apparently applying the maxim, "If it works don't fix it." Although that model may provide some other benefits, including, in a few cases, a degree of multiparty electoral competition, it is not well disposed to citizen access for development planning and management.

It is not asserted that ideology constitutes a decisive variable for determining development policy performance in general. In a convincing study, Young[53] has demonstrated that, if development policy performance can be measured against six criteria (growth, equity, relative autonomy, preservation of human dignity, popular participation, and expansion of societal capacity), no single type of ideological regime is demonstratively superior. Indeed he found that capitalist regimes tend to excel in growth; socialist and Marxist regimes in distributional equity; and the record on the other criteria was mixed. Further research could explore the interrelations among these variables and, specifically, the impact of greater popular participation in actually achieving societal development.

NOTES

1. International Bank for Reconstruction and Development, Accelerated Development in Sub-Saharan Africa: An Agenda for Action (Washington: IBRD, 1981).
2. See Rural Development Participation Review, published at Cornell University since 1979, for a continued stream of studies reflecting this viewpoint.
3. George Honadle, "Development Administration in the Eighties: New Agenda or Old Perspectives?," Public Administration Review, March/April 1982. See, e.g., the work by David Korten, et. al., which stresses both "social learning" by peasants in a project's ambit and, based on the latters' wishes and needs, "bureaucratic reorientation" by host-country and donor agencies. David Korten and Felipe Alfonso, eds., Bureaucracy and the Poor: Closing the Gap (West Hartford, CT: Kumarian Press, 1983). See also the work by George Honadle, et. al., at Development Alternatives, Inc., emphasizing local "capacity-building" as a project management enhancement strategy. In a recent essay on development administration, Honadle stresses participation expansion as a key criterion for assessing the value of prospective contributions to the development administration literature; likewise the work of the Development Project Management Center, U.S. Department of Agriculture, which stresses user-centered strategies for project design and management. See also the African case study by David Leonard, Reaching the Peasant Farmer, (Chicago: University of Chicago Press, 1979).
4. For example, one of the field's most eminent specialists, Dennis Rondinelli, does not even include popular participation as a principal problem of development project management in a widely used and even translated study, "Nine Problems in Development Project Management," Project Management Quarterly, 1976, although it may be subsumed under problem #9, "general inadaptation to milieu."
5. These views are set out in more detail, and illustrative case studies provided, in Gould, Law and the Administrative Process: Analytic Framework for

Understanding Public Policy-Making (Washington: University Press of America, 1979), and Bureaucratic Corruption and Underdevelopment in the Third World: The Case of Zaire (Elmsford, NY: Pergamon, 1980).

6. Bula matare, or rock-crusher, in the words used by Lingala-speaking Zairians to characterize the impact on them of the Belgian colonial state. (The phrase was widely used in 1974 by Mohammed Ali fans to characterize his awesome fighting prowess in contradistinction to that of George Foreman; their world title bout took place in Kinshasa, Zaire, in that year.) I am indebted to Crawford Young for the historical reference.

7. See I. L. Markovitz, African Politics and Society. (New York: Free Press, 1977).

8. Crawford Young, Ideology and Development in Africa (New Haven: Yale University Press, 1982), 319.

9. Leonard Binder, James Coleman et. al., Crises and Sequences in Political Development (Princeton: Princeton University Press, 1971).

10. Nelson Kasfir, The Shrinking Political Arena (Berkeley: University of California, 1976).

11. Young, Ideology and Development.

12. They include: Angola, Algeria, Benin, Botswana, Burundi, Cameroon, Cape Verde, Central African Republic, Chad, Comoros, Congo, Djibouti, Egypt, Ethiopia, Gabon, Gambia, Ghana, Guinea-Bissau, Guinea-Conakry, Guinea-Equatorial, Kenya, Lesotho, Liberia, Libya, Madagascar, Malawi, Mali, Mauritius, Morocco, Mozambique, Namibia, Niger, Nigeria, Rwanda, Senegal, Seychelles, Sierra Leone, Somalia, South Africa, Sudan, Swaziland, Tanzania, Togo, Tunisia, Uganda, Upper Volta, Zaire, Zambia, Zimbabwe (n.b., counting South Africa and Namibia, but not including Western Sahara).

13. Young, Ideology and Development.

14. Politics and Markets (New York: Basic Books, 1977), 116. Cited in Young.

15. Samuel Huntington, Political Order in Changing Societies (New Haven: Yale University Press, 1968); Guillermo O'Donnell, Modernization and Bureau-Authoritarianism (Berkely: University of California, Institute of International Studies, 1973).

16. See, e.g., Samir Amin, Unequal Development (New York: MR Press, 1976), and Markovitz.

17. Young, Ideology and Development, 187-188.

18. Several authors have found substantial correspondence. See Bonnie Campbell, "The Ivory Coast," in John Dunn, ed., West African States (New York: Cambridge University Press, 1978); Colin Leys, Underdevelopment in Kenya (Berkeley: University of California, 1976); Robin Cohen, Labor and Politics in Nigeria, 1948-1971 (London: Heinemann, 1974); Gould, Bureaucratic Corruption.

19. Young, Ideology and Development, 190.

20. Ibid., 202. See also Campbell, "Ivory Coast;" and Michael A. Cohen, Urban Policy and Political Conflict in the Ivory Coast. Chicago: University of Chicago, 1974).
21. Young, Ideology, 212.
22. Joel D. Barkan, "Comparing Politics and Public Policy in Kenya and Tanzania," in Politics and Public Policy, Joel D. Barkan and John J. Okumu, eds. (New York: Praeger, 1979), 16-17, cited by Young 217.
23. See Leys, Underdevelopment in Kenya.
24. Young, Ideology, 244.
25. Henry Bienen, Kenya: The Politics of Participation and Control (Princeton: Princeton University Press, 1974).
26. Leonard, Reaching the Peasant Farmer.
27. Young, Ideology, 219.
28. Ibid., 237.
29. Sayre Schatz, Nigerian Capitalism (Berkeley: University of California, 1977). Gavin Williams and Terisa Turner, "Nigeria," in Dunn, West African States.
30. Ibrahim Omale, "When Nigerians Complain: An Assessment of the Rationale for, and the Functions of, the Public Complaints Commission," Ph.D. Dissertation, University of Pittsburgh, 1981.
31. Young, Ideology, 27.
32. Ibid., 29.
33. International Bank, Accelerated Development, 143-144.
34. Hugues Bertrand, Le Congo (Paris: Maspero, 1975), 255.
35. Samuel Decalo, "Ideological Rhetoric and Scientific Socialism in Benin and Congo-Brazzaville," in Socialism in Sub-Saharan Africa, Carl Rosberg and Thomas Callaghy, eds., (Berkeley: University of California Institute of International Studies, 1980), 260.
36. Africa Contemporary Record, 1975-76, B477; Young, Ideology, 42.
37. Ibid., 53.
38. Africa Contemporary Record, 1976-77, B251; Young, Ibid., 59.
39. Ibid.
40. Ibid. See also Robert Archer, Madagascar Depuis 1972 (Paris: Harmattan, 1976), and Philipee Leymarie, "Le Fonkonolona: la voie malgache vers le socialisme?," Revue francaise d'etudes politiques, Vol. 116, August 1975.
41. James S. Mittleman, "Mozambique: The Political Economy of Underdevelopment," Journal of Southern African Affairs, Volume 3, No. 1, January 1978; Young, 92. In "Revolutionary Participation in Ethiopia," Rural Development Participation Review, Volume 2, No. 1, Fall

50

1980, John Harbeson observes that post-1975 Marxist-Leninist Ethiopia has succeeded, despite numerous obstacles, in "empowering" substantial numbers of peasants.

42. Young, Ibid., 104-5.
43. International Bank, Accelerated Development.
44. Henry Bienen, Tanzania: Party Transformation and Economic Development (Princeton: Princeton University Press, 1970); Joel Samoff, Tanzania: Local Politics and the Structure of Power (Madison: University of Wisconsin, 1974); Issa Shivji, Class Struggles in Tanzania (London: Heinemann, 1976); L o u i s e Fortman, "Pitfalls in Implementing Participation: An African Example," Rural Development Participation Review, Volume 1, Number 1, Summer 1979.
45. Young, Ideology, 110.
46. Ibid., 109-110.
47. Ibid., 133.
48. John R. Nellis, "Socialist Management in Algeria," Journal of Modern African Studies, Volume 15, Number 4, December 1977.
49. Young, Ideology, 133.
50. International Bank, Accelerated Development, 141-186. Other data come from Claude Riviere, Guinea: The Mobilization of a People (Ithaca: Cornell University, 1977); William Derman, "Cooperatives in the Republic of Guinea: Problems of Revolutionary Transformation," in Popular Participation in Social Change: Cooperatives, Collectives and Nationalized Industry. June Nash, Jorge Dandler and Nicholas Hopkins, eds. (Hague: Mouton, 1976).
51. Derman, Ibid., 420; also Young, Ideology, 169-178.
52. Derman, Ibid., 427.
53. Young, Ideology.

4. Strategic Planning Through Participation: Joint Program Evaluation in the Sahel

Derick W. Brinkerhoff

INTRODUCTION

Expanding the scope of participation in international donor agency projects and programs has been discussed from a variety of perspectives. Most analyses have focused upon beneficiary involvement in rural development projects designed and funded by donor agencies. A few studies have addressed participation issues within the donor organization itself, seeking for the most part to explain why so little participation has taken place. Research on participation for development, and recommendations for practice based on that research, have suffered from definitional and methodological problems. This feature has generated considerable debate on the topic.[1]

Similar problems and debate have affected the study of participation in the field of management and organizations.[2] Few analyses have sought to merge these two research and experience bases, though recently the situation has begun to change. Among the reasons for this change are: (a) increasing concern with facilitating development processes, particularly at the local level, that can become self-sustaining without continuous injection of external resources; and (b) growing awareness of the critical role of management in making effective use of resources, whether indigenous or donor-provided.[3] Pockets of applied research activity on participation and management in developing country settings are emerging to form some initial precepts for action. Without a broader empirical base of experience against which to test and refine these precepts, though, they will remain tentative.

This chapter contributes to this experience base a case study of a participatory strategic planning and evaluation exercise undertaken by a donor agency in collaboration with the host country government. Examples of evaluations that actively seek to maximize participation are few. The joint assessment of U.S.

51

development assistance to Senegal by the U.S. Agency
for International Development (USAID) and the Government of Senegal (GOS) during 1980 represents a rare
instance of an evaluation carried out by a donor agency
with the active participation of host country people,
from the local to the central levels.[4]

The chapter begins with a section that describes
the joint assessment, providing background on its be-
ginnings, the activities involved, the participants,
and its mode of operations; and the results achieved.
The second section offers an analysis of the case,
focusing upon the links between participation and the
achievements of the joint assessment. The third looks
at the lessons learned, and examines the assessment in
terms of the characteristics of successful organizational innovation. The final section provides some
concluding remarks.

THE USAID/GOVERNMENT OF SENEGAL JOINT ASSESSMENT

The impetus behind the USAID/GOS joint assessment
was the desire of the USAID mission director, new to
Senegal in 1979, to obtain an objective analytical ap-
praisal of the AID program and of the GOS situation.
The antecedents of the AID program at that time had
emerged from the response to the Sahelian drought of
1973. Food to avert mass starvation was Senegal's
central need; and AID became the major food donor,
supplying 50,000 metric tons of sorghum on a bilateral
basis and 4,000 tons through the World Food Program.
In addition to relief efforts, AID identified short-
term needs directly related to the effects of the
drought and designed a project portfolio that concentrated upon village well construction, reforestation,
rehabilitation of livestock watering points, and provision of farming inputs.

With immediate and short-term needs addressed, AID
turned its attention in collaboration with the GOS to
medium and long-range development strategy. Based on
two overarching objectives -- achieving food self-
sufficiency and stimulating development in rural
regions of the country -- the USAID mission targeted
four areas for attention. These included improved
agricultural technology for dry-land farming in
Senegal's peanut growing region, irrigated agriculture
in the Senegal and Casamance River basins, livestock
and range management in the north and east, and rural
primary health care. By 1979, projects in these four
target areas had been in operation for four years.

On the Senegalese side during this period, government concern over the steadily deteriorating economic

condition of the country was growing. External borrowing and resulting debt service had reached potentially overwhelming proportions; and the parastatal infrastructure set up to facilitate agricultural production had eroded to where it produced few but costly services, alienated peasant farmers, and had minimal impact on production. The then Prime Minister Abodu Diouf (later President) presented to the Senegalese National Assembly a preliminary reform plan (Plan de Redressment) in December 1979 to respond to the economic crisis facing the country.

Soon after his arrival in Senegal, the USAID Director approached the minister of planning and coordination with a proposal for the formation of a joint analytical group to carry out an evaluation of the AID program of the last five years. The proposed program assessment was intended not only to evaluate past progress in achieving development objectives, but also to establish the basis for joint US/GOS strategic planning of foreign assistance for 1981-1986. The minister accepted the proposal and a joint management committee, co-chaired by the minister of planning and the U.S. ambassador, was established to provide oversight and supervision for the evaluation.

Below the management committee, a working group was constituted to manage the actual conduct of the evaluation. This group was comprised of two USAID staff members assigned full-time, a consultant, two GOS members from the Ministry of Planning and Cooperation (MOP), an administrative assistant, a translator and a secretary. On a day-to-day basis, the AID members of the working group were the most active. The GOS members, though technically seconded to the joint assessment for its duration, had to split their time between their regular duties and the work of managing the evaluation. One of these, the director of the MOP's planning division, ended up with only a minimum amount of time to participate in the group. The bulk of GOS participation in the working group fell to his deputy, the other MOP staff member nominate to serve.

The plan for the joint assessment consisted of two related sets of activities. The first encompassed evaluations of four of AID's oldest projects that represented the mission's major programmatic emphases in Senegal: dry-land cropping, irrigated agriculture, livestock, and rural primary health.[5] The second set of activities included an analysis of the macroeconomic environment and the constraints to development faced by Senegal.

In planning and managing the evaluation process, the working group explicitly sought to maximize participation in the assessment at as many levels as possible. At the grassroots level, beneficiary surveys

were carried out as part of each of the four project
evaluations by staff and students of the GOS National
School of Applied Economics (ENEA). With assistance
from a U.S. Census Bureau methodologist and an AID/
Washington sociologist, ENEA professors and students
developed an evaluation methodology that melded social
anthropological investigation with survey research
techniques. Based on this methodology a set of ques-
tionnaires and a research guide was developed for each
of the four projects to be evaluated. ENEA students,
under the supervision of their professors and the joint
assessment consultants, chose a sample of potential
beneficiaries in the four project target areas and
carried out$_6$ the surveys through group and individual
interviews. In total, over 1,000 responses were collected and analyzed. The beneficiary surveys, because
of their breadth and scope and the logistics required
to carry them out, represented approximately half the
time of the entire joint assessment, according to the
coordinator.

Also at the field level, the expatriate AID project manager and his Senegalese counterpart participated as full members of the teams evaluating the livestock, irrigated agriculture, and rural health care
projects. Central level participants in the evaluation
teams consisted of AID consultants and GOS technical
personnel from the appropriate ministries. During the
conduct of these evaluations, the teams sought the participation of other GOS and AID officials, both at the
central and local levels, whose knowledge of the projects being evaluated made them useful sources of
information.

The macroanalysis representing the other portion
of the joint assessment was conducted by a USAID consultant with MOP and other GOS informants. Because of
time and resource limitations, the planned constrained
analysis was carried out in a more simplified format
than originally intended.

The four field evaluations of the projects took
place during March and April of 1980, following several
months of preparatory effort by the joint working
group. Procedurally as well as conceptually the evaluations were joint undertakings. The MOP informed its
field offices and those of the line ministries concerned of the arrival of the teams through GOS official
channels. These local personnel facilitated logistical
arrangements for the teams and contact with informants.
The evaluation teams prepared reports which were first
reviewed internally by the USAID mission and then
passed on to the joint assessment working group. The
working group presided over a series of intensive
meetings in May between U.S. and GOS personnel in which
the evaluation results were presented, revised, and

synthesized. Participating were the members of the joint working group, the technical divisions of the USAID mission, and the various line ministries and technical agencies of the GOS.

Sensitivities concerning negative results uncovered by the evaluations occasionally ran high on both sides. These meetings provided a forum for negotiations and consensus-building around what would appear in official documents, as both AID and the GOS wrestled with the possible political implications of the evaluations' findings.

Following this series of meetings the working group prepared a preliminary version of the final report and presented it to the management committee, who discussed and commented on the findings. The group, with guidance from the USAID mission director, then prepared a revised final report.

The general recommendations of the joint assessment were approved by the management committee in July 1980, and an aid-memoir was signed by the minister of planning and cooperation and the U.S. ambassador. At this point the Joint Assessment Management Committee was reconstituted as the Joint Planning and Evaluation Committee. Under this committee a standing working group, composed of the MOP's director of planning and his deputy plus USAID mission program and project development staff, was formed to operationalize the ongoing collaborative planning process the joint assessment initiated. This working group was charged with assembling multiministerial ad hoc committees to develop a joint strategy for U.S. development assistance to Senegal over the next five years.

PARTICIPATION AND THE RESULTS OF THE JOINT ASSESSMENT

In the eyes of observers and participants alike, both on the USAID and GOS sides, the joint assessment was a successful operation. The consensus is that the assessment succeeded not only in terms of the products generated, i.e., valid findings and analyses useful to inform strategic planning, policy and program formulation, but also, and according to some more importantly, in terms of the process that the evaluation established. The participatory nature of the joint assessment is credited with contributing to both these aspects of its success.

The participation in the project evaluations of local residents and of local-level GOS and project personnel contributed to technically valid findings that aided in modifying ongoing project activities and provided input to future project design and sectorial programming. Such benefits are among the more frequently cited reasons for advocating local level

participation -- better information leading to better
decisions in the use of scarce development resources.[7]
The desire to acquire such information was behind
the beneficiary survey component of the joint assessment. While from a methodological perspective, according to the USAID coordinator, the surveys could
have been more rigorous, they were successful in providing both AID and the GOS with information on the
results of development efforts that had previously been
unavailable.

On the process side, the participatory nature of
the joint assessment that brought together U.S. and GOS
personnel in candid discussions of development issues
and opportunities established a new kind of relationship between a donor agency and a host government. This
new relationship had both a technical and a political
component. GOS personnel who participated in the joint
assessment, either as members of an evaluation team or
as reviewers of findings, etc., acquired new technical
skills in interacting with the USAID consultants and
staff members to accomplish the evaluation. Participation here resulted in GOS capacity-building in the
areas of data collection, analysis, and development
programming. While this was a secondary purpose of the
joint assessment's agenda, it is nonetheless important
particularly in the African context where skilled manpower constraints continue to reduce the effectiveness[8]
of indigenous public and private sector organizations.

The contribution of participation to the political
component of this new relationship has to do with
generating agreement and commitment. Senegalese participation in the evaluation provided a mechanism by
which the GOS could accept and "own" the findings of
the joint assessment. Building acceptance and "ownership" of the evaluation results was a ticklish process
because of the potential bureaucratic and political
repercussions of the failings and shortcomings uncovered by the evaluations. The bulk of these negative
findings revolved around lack of impact and inadequate
institutional support of project activities. Both AID
and the GOS felt vulnerable to criticism, and the joint
working group's guidance of the discussion and negotiation process was crucial to generating a final product
that both reflected the findings and was palatable to
the two parties.

The political commitment fostered by participation
in the joint assessment and reflected in the signed
aid-memoir contributed to the success of the joint
planning effort that has followed the evaluation. The
experience of the joint assessment shows that a participatory process can help to establish an effective
donor agency-host government collaboration at several
levels. According to USAID staff, the participatory

mode of strategic planning at the central level has facilitated the resolution of operational problems with particular projects in the field.

This outcome highlights the importance of viewing strategic planning as integral to operational management.[9] Through the participatory evaluation process, the joint assessment provided an opportunity to develop a shared understanding of: (a) the nature and scope of project implementation in the field, and (b) the constraints imposed by the USAID and the GOS operating systems. This mutual understanding has been incorporated into AID and GOS policy decisions leading to an increase in the quality of both the mission's strategic plan (the Country Development Strategy Statement, or CDSS) and collaboration between AID and the various GOS ministries during project implementation.

The joint assessment, by improving AID's planning process through increased participation, has contributed to AID's producing a better "product," i.e., more successful development outcomes. This demonstrates that project effectiveness is influenced not only by local-level participation in design and implementation, but by the configuration of central-level participation that shapes the policy environment in which a project functions.

So far, the analysis has concentrated upon the positive contributions of participation to the USAID/GOS joint assessment. However, it is also important to note not just the benefits, but the costs and constraints.

One cost has to do with the impact of "bad news." Relatively open, participatory evaluations entail risks for the organizations involved in that if negative results are uncovered, the organizations have less control over who has access to the information. Especially in public sector organizations, with norms of accountability to groups of external clients, officials are very aware of the nontechnical uses of evaluation results.[10]

Several of the findings of the joint assessment were negative, both from the USAID mission's and the GOS' perspective. Bureaucratic and political pressures often push toward suppression and restriction of information in such situations, creating the opposite atmosphere needed for an effective participatory process. Such suppression and restriction did not take place in the case of the joint assessment, but some pressures in that direction had to be faced. As noted by members of the working group, the successful negotiation of the wording of the jointly signed aid-memoir resulted from the more open relationship between AID and the GOS that the joint assessment helped to establish.

On the operational side, a participatory mode of operations is time-consuming. Participants in the joint assessment acknowledged the substantial amount of time required to bring about widespread involvement in the evaluation. Despite the gains in technical quality of evaluation results obtained and the improvement in the policy dialogue, the joint assessment confronted pressures to "get on with the job." In the eyes of the USAID coordinator, the assessment periodically ran the risk of degenerating into a "paper exercise" given the bureaucratic push to show results. Being participatory slows down organizational operations. Gathering information from many sources, writing joint reports, coordinating the efforts of participants, holding review and discussion meetings, obtaining consensus among the various actors, and keeping superiors and other interested parties informed are all time-intensive activities. Some research indicates that these kinds of time costs help explain why organizations are often reluctant to undertake participatory strategic planning.[11]

Participation, besides being time consuming, is people-intensive as well. The beneficiary surveys in particular required the coordinated efforts of large numbers of people, as did the project evaluations. In the case of the beneficiary surveys, rural residents were involved as informants; and, in the case of the project evaluations, project staff and other GOS personnel provided information. Participation can entail people costs not just for organization members, but for outsiders too.

The bulk of the people costs of the joint assessment, however, fell to the two organizations that carried it out: AID and the MOP. The USAID mission was able to undertake the participatory evaluation and planning process because it possessed some slack resources of its own -- most importantly someone to take on the coordinator role -- and access to others through AID/Washington. Organizations vary in the amount of slack resources they have; how much or how little slack is available defines an organization's discretionary capacity.[12] A major defining feature of public sector organizations in developing countries is their lack of slack and resultant inability to channel resources to unforeseen needs.[13]

The Senegalese MOP was no exception to this situation, and GOS personnel from the MOP were unable to participate in the working group as fully as initially planned because of conflicting work demands from which they could not be released. Due to the periodic unavailability of the GOS members of the working group, the USAID members had to take on the major responsibility for keeping the evaluation "on track." Faced with the GOS constraints and the workload demands of the assessment, the working group arrived at, in the words of the coordinator, "an eighty (AID) - twenty (MOP) split" in the division of labor.

An additional aspect of the people constraint to participatory evaluation, or other kinds of participatory processes for that matter, relates to the individual characteristics of the participants themselves. Several persons interviewed stated that many of the results of the joint assessment hinged upon the personalities of those involved. Examples cited of characteristics of various actors that contributed to the success of the assessment were: the personal commitment and political savvy of the USAID mission director, the management skills and value orientation toward participation of the working group coordinator, and the interest and competence of the Senegalese deputy director of the MOP planning division who participated in the working group.

Some research attention has been directed toward exploring the motivational, emotional, and perceptual aspects of participants, both in terms of limitations to participation and outcomes of participation. This research has been relatively fragmented, however, and hypotheses advanced are narrow and unrelated.[14] It is apparent that successful application of participatory methodologies within organizations depends partially upon personal characteristics of the people concerned, and that incentives to participate are an especially significant element in the participation equation. This latter point will be touched on below. One potentially promising avenue of investigation looks at how internal organizational structures and practices affect members' ability and willingness to operate in a participatory mode.[15]

LESSONS LEARNED FROM THE JOINT ASSESSMENT

The case of the USAID/GOS joint assessment demonstrates that it is possible to operate in a participatory fashion in AID, given a certain set of conditions. It also shows that there are tangible benefits to this kind of a participatory activity both to the donor agency and the host country government, though the two parties acknowledged that these benefits were not costless.

Several other USAID missions have expressed interest in experimenting with the joint assessment model as a way of improving their strategic planning for development assistance. In examining the joint assessment's potential as a model for collaborative donor agency-host country strategic management useful in other settings, it is important to try to identify prerequisites and/or necessary conditions for success.

Looking at the joint assessment as an attempt to introduce organizational change is a useful way of pursuing this analysis. Much has been written about the characteristics of the change process, the factors that influence change, and how to successfully bring about change in organizations.[16] It is beyond the scope of this chapter to review the voluminous literature on the topic. Recent applied research and practice incorporating the best of what is known about organizational change, however, provide a framework in which[17] to place the joint assessment case.

Organizational change interventions, this experience suggests, have a higher probability of lasting success when the following facilitating conditions are present or can be created:

1. Pressure for change both from within the organization and from key actors in the organization's external environment.
2. Commitment to change that leads to allocation of resources in support of the intervention.
3. Participation by organization members at various levels in the planning and implementation of the intervention.
4. Receptivity within the organization to innovation, change, and learning.
5. Organizational mechanisms for follow-up and review of the results of the interventions.
6. A minimum level of stability and continuity in the[18] organization and its external environment.

The joint assessment, viewed in the context of these facilitating conditions, emerges as an example of an organizational change intervention that "did things right." As the case discussion indicates, the joint assessment was characterized by the existence, or development, of each of these conditions.

Pressure for change came in the form of the USAID mission director's desire to evaluate the results of the U.S. assistance program, and was strengthened by the GOS concern with its deteriorating economic situation. Both AID and the GOS were sufficiently committed to the idea of a collaborative program evaluation to allocate resources to carry it out. Multilevel participation by both AID and GOS personnel was a defining feature of the assessment. Both organizations were willing to experiment with a joint operating mode in carrying out the evaluation, and both were open to dealing with the results uncovered, despite the bureaucratic "pain" involved. In the course of the assessment, the joint planning mechanism was designed and put in place to permit continuing collaboration in strategic planning for the future U.S. assistance program in Senegal. Finally, sufficient continuity of organizational actors and procedures in AID and the GOS existed to ensure that the results of the evaluation were used to make changes in the content of the aid program and in the ongoing strategic management process.

Successful replication of the joint assessment model, this analysis indicates, is to some extent contingent upon either having in place or generating the facilitating conditions that experience, including the joint assessment's, has shown are linked with effective organizational change. Obviously, other factors are important as well; direct cause and effect relationships cannot be easily drawn in the case of complex social phenomena. The extent of the relative impact of any of the conditions is ultimately the product of a particular situation. The simplification inherent in abstracting from reality to develop a model with generalizable potential necessarily reduces its explanatory power. Nonetheless, the results of the joint assessment, when coupled with experience with similar interventions, supports the validity of the claim that the facilitating conditions described above played a significant role in the assessment's success.

A further set of concerns comes to mind, however, if the question is asked, what led to the presence of the facilitating conditions in the case of the joint assessment? These concerns relate to prerequisites for such a participatory evaluation and planning exercise. Perhaps the most important of any prerequisites that could be identified deal with incentives. Participants in the assessment mentioned several. First, good relations between the donor country and the host country are needed in order for a joint evaluation to be feasible. Incentives for a participatory mode of operations are minimal in an adversarial and conflictual environment. Second, there needs to be some sense on the part of the host government that engaging in a joint evaluation and committing scarce resources to such an activity has a reasonable probability of leading to additional resources. In the GOS case, AID's portfolio has doubled, standing currently at close to forty million dollars.[19] This first prerequisite, then, is a relative absence of negative incentives to participate, and the second involves having positive incentives.

A third prerequisite is implicit, though no less important for not having been cited by those involved. Someone within the donor agency in a position to act must want to do things differently. This also relates to incentives. For joint participation in donor agency program evaluation and strategic planning to become more than an isolated occurrence requires modification of the agency's internal structures and procedures so that incentives to "swim upstream," to use Bryant's term, are increased.[20] Without such changes, participatory innovations will remain the province of organizational mavericks and will stand little chance of becoming institutionalized.

CONCLUSIONS

The USAID/GOS joint assessment is a significant example of an organizational intervention explicitly incorporating a participatory approach to one element of the management task: strategic planning. It is significant because it illuminates several key questions that confront the management of development assistance. First, how can information on development results be more effectively collected and channeled into donor agency and host government strategic planning and programming? Second, how can the benefits of participation across organizational boundaries be captured without incurring excessive costs to those involved? Third, what are effective ways of introducing more participatory operating procedures into both donor and host country bureaucracies?

The joint assessment poses one set of responses to these questions, and further, provides some supporting evidence for an emerging model for addressing them in other contexts. It is also important to keep in mind the limitations of the assessment, and recognize that its major focus in terms of participation was on involvement of host government personnel in a donor agency's operations. Intended beneficiaries of donor-funded projects participated solely as providers of information. Generating self-sustaining development requires building the capacities of rural residents as well as of public sector organizations to do things on their own. Engaging people in a dialogue about their experiences with development efforts designed to benefit them is one way to improve the quality of those efforts through feedback from those intimately acquainted with the results, and simultaneously to increase local capacity of people to help themselves.[21] The joint assessment did the former, but not the latter. Ironically, one of the recommendations of the assessment was that local residents should participate more actively in the design and management of development projects.

The joint assessment initiated a good, continuing information and communication flow with government officials, which has had an important impact on the quality of AID strategic planning and on the relationship with the GOS. It is equally important to establish such a flow with members of the "target groups"

development assistance is aimed at benefiting. Better-
ing their lives is, after all, the ultimate purpose of
donor activity in the Third World.

NOTES

1. See John M. Cohen and Norman T. Uphoff,
"Par-ticipation's Place in Rural Development: Seeking
Clarity through Specificity," World Development, Vol.
8, 1980, pp. 213-235. This article reviews the major
issues relating to rural development participation and
elaborates a framework for analyzing participation
along three dimensions: what kinds of participation
take place, who participates in them, and how the
process of participation operates. The article is a
distillation of the research carried out by Cornell
University's Rural Development Committee through an
AID-funded cooperative agreement to study rural development participation.
2. See H. Peter Dachler and Bernhard Wilpert,
"Conceptual Dimensions and Boundaries of Participation
in Organizations: A Critical Evaluation, "Administrative Science Quarterly, Vol. 23, No. 1, March 1978,
pp. 1-39.
3. Several U.S. Agency for International Development documents discuss the role of management in development. See: "Management Development Strategy Paper:
AID's Response to the Implementation Needs of the
1980s," Washington, D.C.: USAID, Office of Rural Development and Development Administration, June 1981;
and AID Policy Paper: Institutional Development, Washington, D.C.: USAID, Bureau for Program and Policy
Coordination, March 1983. Management concerns are also
highlighted in World Bank, World Development Report
1983, Washington, D.C." World Bank, c.1983. See
especially, Part II, " Management in Development," pp.
41-135.
4. Research for this case study was carried out
in Senegal and Washington, D.C. through interviews and
review of published and unpublished USAID reports,
documents, memoranda, and files. The author would
particularly like to thank David Shear, Donald Brown,
Malick Sow, and Cheikh Tidiane Sy for their cooperation
and assistance.
5. The four projects evaluated were: Cereals
Production I (SODEVA), Bakel Small Irrigated Peri-
meters, Eastern Senegal Livestock, and Sine Saloum
Rural Health Services Delivery. For summaries of the
results of these evaluations, see: USAID/GOS, Joint
Assessment of U.S. Assistance Programs in Senegal,
Annex 1980, Dakar, Senegal: USAID, 1980.

6. For more detail on the joint assessment's research methodology, see USAID/GOS, op. cit., "Beneficiary Survey Methodology and Attachments." AID's approach to project evaluation is discussed in USAID, Design and Evaluation of AID-Assisted Projects, Washington, D.C.: USAID, Office of Personnel Management, Training and Development Division, November 1980. Francis W. Hoole analyzes evaluation research issues that arise in the field of socio-economic development; see his Evaluation Research and Development Activities, Beverly Hills: Sage Publications, c.1978. For a discussion of evaluation and its relevance for decision-makers and stakeholders see Michael Q. Patton, Utilization-Focused Evaluation, Beverly Hills: Sage Publications, c.1981.

7. See Cohen and Uphoff, op. cit.

8. See, for example, World Bank, Accelerated Development in Sub-Saharan Africa: An Agenda for Action," Washington, D.C.: World Bank, c.1981; especially Chapter 2, "Basic Constraints," the section on underdeveloped human resources, pp. 9-11; and Chapter 4, "Policy and Administrative Framework," the sections on economic decision-making, policymaking capacity, and organization and management, pp. 31-45.

9. See Thomas H. Naylor, "How to Integrate Strategic Planning into Your Management Process," Long Range Planning, Vol. 14, No. 5, 1981, pp. 56-61.

10. Eleanor Chelimsky notes that public sector agency evaluation systems often become "hostage" to other agency needs, such as defending budget requests, justifying programs, and showing results. See her, "Program Evaluation and Appropriate Governmental Change," The Annals, Vol. 466, March 1983, pp. 103-118. See also Carol H. Weiss' classic, Evaluation Research, Englewood Cliffs: Prentice-Hall, Inc., c.1972; especially Chapter 2, "Purposes of Evaluation," pp. 10-24, where she discusses overt and covert purposes, differences in expectations about intended uses of evaluation findings, etc. Chapters 5 and 6, "The Turbulent Setting of the Action Program" and "Utilization of Evaluation Results," also touch upon many of the issues faced by the joint assessment.

11. See R.G. Dyson and M.J. Foster, "The Relationship of Participation and Effectiveness in Strategic Planning," Strategic Management Journal, Vol. 13, No. 2, 1978, pp. 77-83.

12. James G. March and Herbert A. Simon, Organizations, New York: John Wiley and Sons, Inc., c.1958.

13. Naomi Caiden and Aaron Wildavsky, Planning and Budgeting in Poor Countries, New York: John Wiley and Sons, c.1974.

14. Dachler and Wilpert, op. cit.

15. See, for example, Derick W. Brinkerhoff, "Inside Public Bureaucracy: Empowering Managers to Empower Clients," Rural Development Participation Review, Vol. 1, No. 1, Summer 1979, pp. 7-9; Coralie Bryant, "Organizational Impediments to Making Participation a Reality: 'Swimming Upstream' in AID," Rural Development Participation Review, Vol. 1, No. 3, Spring 1980, pp. 8-11; Judith Tendler, Inside Foreign Aid, Baltimore: The Johns Hopkins University Press, c.1975; and Harry W. Strachan, "Side-Effects of Planning in the Aid Control System," World Development, Vol. 6, No. 4, April 1978, pp. 467-478.

16. The literature in this area is vast. Two useful collections of articles are: Warren G. Bennis et al, The Planning of Change, New York: Holt, Rinehart and Winston, c.1976; and Michael L. Tushman and William L. Moore, eds., Readings in the Management of Innovation, Boston: Pitman Publishing, Inc., c.1982. Also of interest because of the applications in developing countries is: Robert Abramson, An Integrated Approach to Organization Development and Performance Improvement Planning: Experiences from America, Asia, and Africa, West Hartford: Kumarian Press, 1978.

17. Much of this work as applied to the Third World has been pioneered by the staff of the U.S. Department of Agriculture's Development Project Management Center (DPMC), located in Washington, D.C. The DPMC is partly supported by USAID's Office of Multisectoral Development, formerly the Office of Rural Development and Development Administration, though an applied research project on methods for the improvement of organizational performance in developing country public sector agencies.

18. Inter-American Institute for Cooperation on Agriculture, Planning and Project Management Division, Improving Rural Development Planning and Management: Proceedings of IICA-PROPLAN/USDA-DPMC Seminar, San Jose, Costa Rica: IICA, December 1981, pp. 107-108. These proceedings contain a good discussion of CPMC's approach to organizational change.

19. The AID appropriation for Senegal for the 1985 fiscal year, combined Development Assistance and Economic Support Fund, totals $39.2 million. This figure comes from: USAID/Senegal, Annual Budget Submission FY 1985, Senegal, June 1983.

20. Bryant, op. cit.

21. Two analyses that look at the question of involving local residents more actively in evaluation are: Marie Therese Feuerstein, "Evaluation as Education -- An Appropriate Technology for a Rural Health Program," Community Development Journal, Vol. 13, No..

2, 1978, pp. 99-105; and Louise Fortmann, "Taking the Data Back to the Village," Rural Development Participation Review, Vol. 3, No. 2, Winter 1982, pp. 13-16. Establishing a process by which both organizations and local people can learn is seen by a growing number of researchers and practitioners as central to effective development. Coralie Bryant and her co-authors propose an "integrated participatory evaluation process" as a means to facilitate learning by both development organizations and the people the organizations' projects aim to benefit. See Coralie Bryant, Therese Borden, Elisabeth Shields, and Louise White, "Research in Development Management: Learning About the Effectiveness of Management Interventions," Washington, D.C." National Association of Schools of Public Affairs and Administration, unpublished workshop background paper, April 1983. See also David Korten, "Community Organization and Rural Development: A Learning Process Approach," Public Administration Review, Vol. 40, No. 5, September/October 1980, pp. 480-513.

5. Participation in National Food and Nutrition Programs: Some Lessons from West Africa

Richard W. Ryan

INTRODUCTION

During the mid-1970s, private voluntary organizations (PVOs) were publicly praised as examples of how international development agencies could aid the rural poor. PVO supporters in Congress credited them with managing development projects with a minimum of agency overhead and a maximum amount of beneficiary participation. Catholic Relief Services (CRS), the overseas development agency of the U.S. Catholic Bishops, boasted of a project overhead cost of under ten percent. As a result of this politically favorable image and Congress's emphasis on insuring high levels of community participation, PVOs began receiving larger amounts of project funds from the U.S. Agency for International Development (USAID). Consequently, their role in U.S. development efforts has broadened and intensified.

Yet, PVO activities may not prove to be participatory if we define participation as bottom-up project formulation and direction by intended beneficiaries. Frequently, what is cited as participation by the poor in PVO projects is more accurately described as engagement, the result of successful and sustained outreach to the poorer members of rural communities. This is no small accomplishment, but in terms of participation, it is better described as a top-down intervention that allows for decentralized decision-making by a small number of local elites.[1]

The literature on U.S. PVOs involved in international development is sparse, and little is written by those who have worked in PVOs. This is unfortunate since valuable experience remains unmined on issues of organization and project design, evolution of nationwide health programs, interface between the PVO, villages and government bureaucracies, and the degree to which the poor actually participate in programs.[2] What

67

is available are outside critiques of PVO food assistance efforts and USAID program evaluations.[3]

It is the purpose of this paper to help bridge the gap between the rich experience of PVOs and the poverty of PVO analyses. Our focal point will be beneficiary participation in two Food and Nutrition Programs conducted by Catholic Relief Services. There are unique characteristics of CRS development efforts that create a high degree of dependency on the community and that present opportunities for the realization of participation representative of beneficiary interests. The poor conduct many of the program functions because the PVO operates on a low budget and must depend on local personnel to carry out service delivery. Thus, participatory implementation becomes a mainstay of the program. When a program operates in this manner over two decades, the community develops a sense of ownership of and commitment to the program unusual in donor-assisted development. In these cases, participation takes on a representative nature.

This PVO dependency on the community and beneficiary-ownership is typical of the Food and Nutrition Programs in which CRS has been involved in establishing in some twenty sub-Saharan African countries. Many of these were begun at the outset of national independence. The program operations are marked by a small expatriate staff, an emphasis on utilizing indigenous resources, especially personnel, and program office autonomy. The major change during the last ten years has been an evolution in orientation from relief to development. (The name, Catholic Relief Services, is misleading on two counts: the agency conducts development programs and projects on a nondenominational basis.)

The objective of this paper is to examine CRS program operations in Upper Volta and Togo to determine the degree and types of participation present. The author worked in these programs between 1978 and 1980. Program goals will be described along with the functional roles involved in program implementation. This will be followed by a discussion of obstacles to grassroots participation and suggestions for overcoming these. Clearly, the lessons will not be applicable to all voluntary or public agencies, but they may shed some light on long-term PVO programs and how they compare to current thinking on the participation of the poor in the development process.

I. FOOD AND NUTRITION PROGRAM DESCRIPTION AND GOALS

The single abundant resource of many African countries is the people. However, without sufficient food available to feed increasing populations, nutritional health becomes a critical problem. Kwashiorkor and marasmus represent the more advanced stages of nutritional deficiency, but even simple undernourishment takes its toll on a nation's productivity by preventing normal growth in the young. Brain damage, stunted growth, and acute susceptibility to disease are usual outcomes of untreated nutritional deficiencies. Malnourished infants and children grow into under-productive and, in more serious cases, physically dependent adults.

The primary goal of Food and Nutrition Programs is to reduce the incidence of malnutrition. Stated formally, the goal of Food and Nutrition Programs is to assist food deficit nations in long-term human resource development. The goal must be operationalized within policy guidelines set by the national government and in keeping with CRS's low overhead, local reliance approach. An implicit goal in CRS development activities is to assist those who are committed to self-help. Poorer regions generally have more incentive to invest time and labor in program service delivery, and this fits well with the PVO's mission of reaching the poorest of the poor without importing the necessary program infrastructure.

Participation of the poor in Food and Nutrition Programs has not been a primary or explicit PVO goal related to congressional mandates of the 1970s. Rather, grassroots participation, at least in service delivery, has been a feature of programs since they were initiated over twenty years ago. Limited PVO resources and a religious philosophy of helping those who help themselves combine to make CRS locally dependent for program success. Clearly, CRS forfeits a degree of centralized control for local support. Grassroots service delivery achieves participation in implementation but not necessarily in goal setting. However, when participation is more closely examined later in this section, it can be seen that decades of local responsibility for service delivery lead to a sense of program ownership. In active and well run nutrition centers, ancillary projects become formulated by beneficiaries through bottom-up participation. So while CRS has not necessarily made beneficiary participation an intended goal, its reliance on local infrastructure has fostered beneficiary direction of evolving program activities.

Establishing a system to operationalize the program's principal goal of nutritional health is fairly simple although achieving that goal is not. The program beneficiaries are children and women. The nutritionally vulnerable, high-risk group is children from birth to five years of age. Also, women of child bearing age are included as food ration recipients to insure their health and the prenatal health of their fetuses. Including women as recipients augments the economic value of the food supplement package going to a family and thus increases the possibility that children will receive adequate nourishment. The "risk" of malnourishment can be reduced if subsistence farming families can be offered food supplements as "con-tractual assistance" and not simply as food aid.[5] Securing agreement of the family to insure that children receive increased and proper food is a key facet of these programs. Nutritional monitoring of each child is conducted at the village nutritional center with the use of standard weight-for-age charts to see to it that the family is upholding its end of the agreement.

In Upper Volta, 130,000 women and children were estimated to receive food supplements during FY 1984. Commodities in that program included corn meal, non-fat dry milk, and soy bean oil totaling 7,797 metric tons and valued at $2,788,000 (the value does not include ocean transport costs). The number of beneficiaries in neighboring Togo was sent at 93,000. Their commodity package was composed of bulgur, non-fat dry milk, and soy bean oil. The commodity value is $1,980,000 for 5,579 metric tons. On an average, there are[6] two children for each woman receiving food allotments.

Nutrition program activity is non-dramatic. The results are long-term (generational) and bear an indirect relation to how most development projects and programs are defined: short term, measurable increased outputs. These donor yardsticks work against Food and Nutrition Programs which are aimed at prevention. However, as nutritional monitoring systems become more widely implemented, the element of measurable impact is enhanced.

The National Policy Framework
The Food and Nutrition Programs in Upper Volta and Togo, like those in other sub-Sahara African countries, are national in scope. They were established under a country agreement and implemented in cooperation with a sponsoring ministry, commonly the social welfare or health ministry.

Nutritional surveys have been conducted in most countries by the government frequently in cooperation with a donor country agency or university. This baseline survey information is used to determine the regions that require the most food aid. The sponsoring ministry updates information about crop failures in sections of the country, and these become priority areas. Program location, however, is significantly influenced by national politics and logistical factors such as proximity to main roads and warehouses.

The World Bank Development Reports, published
yearly, give some indication of the level of poverty
and lack of medical services in Upper Volta and Togo.
The World Bank publishes these indicators and advises
that the data is frequently inadequate. These, then,
should be considered rough comparative measures of
development. However, based on these and other indicators and my own travels in the area, it is safe to
say that most of Upper Volta and northern Togo experience harsh poverty. They are situated in the midst of
the Sahelian drought area and are marked by an absence
of natural resources.

The scope of the food deficit problem escapes individual or village solution. It can, however, be
addressed at the national level with international assistance. National leaders can make improved nutritional health a goal particularly when a donor, USAID,
Food for Peace, is willing to supply food commodities.
The sponsoring ministry provides warehousing, some
truck and rail transport, and limited personnel support
throughout the country.

The public health director of CRS for sub-Saharan
Africa points out that, "Risk of malnutrition and
underweight are not recognized concerns in subsistence
economics."[7] Responses to a pilot health training program for Ghanaian traditional healers lend support to
this conclusion. Learning about basic nutrition was
ranked fifth in popularity out of six training sessions
in basic health attended by indigenous healers in
Ghana's Techiman District.[8] It is senseless to worry
about a health condition if it is common and if there
is a lack of local resources for its treatment. Therefore, the impetus for a policy response in the case of
nutritional health comes from the national level.

Local-level Reliance
       U.S. PVOs such as CARE and CRS have realized some
success at village-level development, because they have
assumed that the final responsibility for program delivery is local. The accomplishments of these PVOs are
due in large part to the indigenization of program and
project service delivery structures. In the capital
city or port, the PVO employs local staff many of whom
remain with the agency for decades. At the village
level, the PVO is dependent upon residents for program
support and control. The longevity of the Food and
Nutrition Programs in Upper Volta and Togo has permane-
ntized the relationship among the PVO, its local hired
staff, village health auxiliaries, peasants, village
elites, and government bureaucrats. In effect, local,
and not international, personnel have been developed to
manage foreign assistance resources. This provides

programs with stability and institutional memory despite a high turnover rate among expatriate personnel.
It also creates a pool of experienced villagers and
trained staff to undertake development efforts in the
PVO's absence.

This legacy of local infrastructure development is
rarely discussed within CRS, because reliance upon
local personnel is assumed since the PVO has been operating this way for decades. The potential of CRS's
program infrastructure for consciously promoting local
participation is given little consideration, nor are
training programs for strengthening this potential much
explored.

Classifying Participation

Before proceeding with a detailed look at program
implementation and the role participation plays in program functions, it is useful first to clarify what is
meant by participation. For this purpose, participation is analyzed according to Judith Tendler's classification of decision-making in PVO projects.

Tendler conducted an evaluation of numerous PVO
projects for USAID in part to redefine what PVOs mean
by participation. Her three categories of participation in decision-making are: 1) "genuine representative participation where 'the poorest groups are fully
represented in decision-making'" (also referred to in
this paper as bottom-up participation); 2) "top-down
'sensitive'", where the PVO consults with those to
benefit from the project but dominates service delivery
decisions; and 3) "local elite decision-making" that
allows for local tailoring of projects by a limited
few.[9] Tendler notes that this last category represents
decentralized rather than participatory project management. She also points out that there was little evidence of representative participation in the projects
she studied.

However, Tendler is not recommending the use of
participatory structures in every instance. She notes
that project success is not correlated with a particular category, and that there appears to be an inevitable conflict between broad participation and technical
tasks. The two simply do not fit together well.
Tendler advises that participatory approaches need to
be evaluated "according to their suitability for the
task at hand."[10]

Tendler concludes that the PVO projects reviewed
can often be best characterized as top-down or outside-
in, although PVOs label them participatory.[11] This
assessment can be applied to CRS Food and Nutrition
Programs at least during their early years. Their
planning, in particular, can be classified as top-down,
sensitive. Also, at the outset it can usually be said,

as Tendler does, that beneficiaries "joined the village group to get access to services, but were not participating in decision-making nor interested in doing so."¹² As was pointed out earlier in this section, most rural inhabitants would not choose nutritional health as an achievable development goal. There is a dependence upon outside resources, and technical knowledge is necessary for establishing a nutrition monitoring system.

However, this top-down classification does not adequately explain participation once nutrition programs are established and conducted over a number of years. Beneficiary responsibility for the program steadily increases along with a sense of local "ownership." The percentage of those who want to participate in decision-making is also likely to increase in those Food and Nutrition centers where the mothers play an active role in program implementation. The core functions of the nutrition program remain fixed, but opportunities for representative participation emerge in ancillary projects chosen by the beneficiaries. These are generally health or agricultural projects related to reducing nutritional or other risks common in subsistence societies. They differ from the core program in that they are locally initiated and planned. The PVO may provide matching funds, for example, for a well digging project, but control remains at the local level. (Ancillary projects are discussed further in Section 2.)

There is value for beneficiaries in the evolution of programs toward ancillary projects. However, program maturation poses a challenge for CRS, because: 1) the nutrition programs are basically organized as top-down "sensitive" in their planning of services; 2) the programs are becoming somewhat more technical as the nutritional monitoring system is disseminated; and 3) a limited number of CRS staff are skilled at facilitating the more participatory ancillary projects. These obstacles to participation will be referred to throughout the remainder of this paper.

II. PROGRAM IMPLEMENTATION AND FUNCTIONAL ROLES

An indication of Food and Nutrition Program capabilities emerges from a description of the roles of infrastructure members. The types of participation and potential for broadening representative participation also become clear. The first part of the discussion examines the roles played by nutrition center auxiliaries and beneficiaries. Second, the influence of local elites and checks on their power are weighed. Third, the functions of PVO field and office staff are described.

1. Village Food and Nutrition Center Functions

Once a month mothers bring their pre-school age children to village centers for weighing and to pick up food rations. Visits generally occupy half a day. In that time the mother is counseled concerning the child's nutritional health. The child's progress or decline is indicated on the individual weight chart. If decline is evident or if the child remains stable but underweight, the mother is reminded of the contract the family has entered into: in return for the food supplement, the family is supposed to insure that the child receives enough food for proper growth.

Peer pressure plays a significant role since children are weighed at the front of meeting areas in full view of others. A child's chart will be handled by several persons, and the child's status is also plotted on the master chart reflecting the nutritional health of all the children of that center. The master chart affords a village or sub-regional indicator of the nutritional status of young children, the group most vulnerable to shortfalls in food supply. Thus, the master charts serve as early warnings of famine conditions (in the absence of reliable local food production statistics).

During their time at the center, the mothers attend cooking demonstrations on the preparation of the imported foods. Generally, a meal is prepared and fed to the children and mothers. Educational sessions are also conducted on the nutritional value of local foods, and food groups are explained using visual aids. Information on proper birthing techniques, post-natal care, family health, and village sanitation is presented at different sessions throughout the year.

Center maintenance activities include the collection of the mothers' contribution or "cotisation" which pays for trucking, auxiliary worker salaries, and medicines or other items the mothers want purchased. The measuring and distribution of food also falls into the areas of maintenance tasks.

The variety and quality of center activities are affected by the following factors: 1) the number of years the center has been in operation and its reputation in the community; 2) the educational level of the village auxiliaries, and the frequency of training they receive from PVO staff; 3) the commitment of the mothers to the program; and 4) the ability of the PVO and the government in insuring regular delivery of food, scales, charts and other resources. The influence of these factors are best explained by focusing on specific roles.

A. Village Health Auxiliaries

Responsibility for the coordination of center activities rests with the health auxiliaries. The auxiliaries are local women who may have a background of nursing or para-medical training in addition to the preparation provided by the PVO in nutrition, village health, and center operations.[13]

In Upper Volta the auxiliaries are paid directly by the villagers, and in Togo CRS administers their salaries and benefits through a centralized system. There is more of a likelihood of missionaries functioning as village auxiliaries in Upper Volta than in Togo. Togo has a higher proportion of government health and social welfare workers (replacing missionaries), and infirmaries and other modest government facilities serve as sites for nutrition centers.

Center auxiliaries are the information link between village needs and PVO resources. Auxiliaries calculate the size and frequency of food shipments necessary to provide all attending mothers with complete food supplement rations, and they manage the center's finances under varying degrees of PVO supervision. In Togo, CRS staff collect the mother's contributions and pay for trucking and auxiliary salaries from the Lome office. Expenditures are made locally in Upper Volta.

Auxiliaries organize instructional sessions, complete the master weight charts and fulfill the key function of "enforcing" the family's contract with the center through verbal persuasion. Since one center may be responsible for serving several hundred women and double or more the number of children each month, the two centers' auxiliaries are clearly overtaxed in the performance of minimally necessary tasks.

B. Village Beneficiaries

From the experience I had of directing the CRS Togo program office and assisting in Upper Volta's program, I would relate the probability of a center's success to its initial image in the community. If the center is viewed as an undertaking of capital city bureaucracies to be managed and supplied by their agents, then the local women will adopt the role of passive recipients. Alternatively, if village support (i.e., labor, storage and meeting facilities) is agreed upon as a necessary element to a center's operation, then an active role is more likely.

This appears elementary, but in the rush to establish new centers (or any other rural development project) the securing of local inputs is often deferred. Once villagers are introduced to the idea of external responsibility for service delivery, it is difficult to change-over to shared responsibility. It is as though the PVO has turned back from its original plan, is withdrawing previously committed resources, and is unfairly demanding that the village take up the slack. Thus, initial image is critical to the program's engendering beneficiary participatory implementation or passivity. Other factors involved in engaging beneficiaries are local leadership and local attitudes about cooperation and self-help.

The easiest tasks for mothers to assume are maintenance functions: the collection of contributions, cooking, distribution of food rations, and offloading of trucks. After some experience with the weight monitoring process, mothers are able to assist auxiliaries in weighing children, and if literate, recording weights on charts.

There is considerable opportunity for mothers to influence center activities especially where there is a close working relationship between beneficiaries and auxiliaries. This is how participatory implementation occurs. Instead of being passive recipients of services, beneficiaries, by assisting in service delivery, come to influence the type and form of services offered. The basic program elements of weight monitoring and food distribution remain fairly constant (although distribution schedules have been revised to suit local demands). Type and frequency of instruction in pre- and post-natal care, household and village sanitation, nutritional information - food values and preparation - are strongly influenced by mothers in beneficiary-active centers.

More significantly, in the area of resource use, mothers can vote on the disbursion of center funds remaining after auxiliary salaries and truck transport are paid. The purchase of medicines for the treatment of malaria, worms, and simple infections may be approved. If medicines are already available, funds may be directed toward a well digging project or the purchase of seeds and cultivating tools. Communal acreage for raising cash crops are commonly planted near Food and Nutrition Centers.

The expansion of Food and Nutrition Center services and activities into areas of beneficiary financed medicines and cash crop farming changes the nature of program participation from top-down "sensitive" to bottom-up decision-making. This more representative type of participation takes place in ancillary projects growing out of the Food and Nutrition Program structure. Before we explore this further as a means of enabling beneficiaries to participate in resource use planning, a word needs to be said about the origin of these self-help funds.

C. Beneficiary Contributions

During each monthly visit, the mothers make a contribution toward the cost of trucking food from the capital city and for auxiliary salaries. Their contributions are in the range of ten to twenty-five cents per beneficiary per month. Food rations are allotted for each mother and child in attendance, and the value of each food package is approximately one hundred times the nominal contribution.

Some centers are able to build a surplus fund after expenses are paid. Honest bookkeeping by the auxiliaries and regular year-around contributions by mothers will permit a "caisse" to grow. Competition among truckers and controls on national gasoline prices will often make the difference between surplus or none.

CRS regional Food and Nutrition Program supervisors attempt to visit their centers monthly, but this is impossible for distant regions and for other areas during the rainy season when dirt roads are impassable. A greater check, however, on the misuse of beneficiary contributions and the illegal distribution of food are active beneficiaries. If village women understand center functions through participatory program implementation, embezzlement of contributions or sale of food by auxiliaries will be difficult to cover-up. More investigations of program abuses are instigated by beneficiaries than by CRS staff or government officials. This, in itself, is a strong argument against the over-professionalization of village-level service delivery in these and other decentralized programs. There is a high degree of accountability within Food and Nutrition Programs, more than if a government bureaucracy or local private contractor had sole responsibility for collecting funds and paying for truck transport. Because beneficiaries are directly contributing to service delivery costs with money and labor, they are attentive to the manner in which their resources are used. If their investment was removed, program corruption would be tolerated because wasting public funds carries little risk of public condemnation. It would be interesting to compare levels of corruption in CRS coordinated programs and projects where beneficiaries contribute money and labor with projects where all services and resources are provided by the PVO.

There are to be sure, problems with distributing large quantities of imported food in infrastructure-poor countries. However, as imperfect as it is, the system works. The PVO plays a bookkeeping role, albeit from afar, but the beneficiaries provide daily oversight in that the auxiliaries live among them. In Upper Volta, the auxiliaries and villagers have more

direct responsibility for managing their finances -
paying for salaries and trucking locally. Both functions are more centralized in Togo, and I am uncon-
vinced that this deters corruption better than direct,
local accountability.

D. Toward Representative Participation in Ancillary Projects

Earlier it was pointed out that the description of
Food and Nutrition Program decision-making as top-down
"sensitive" applies best to new centers. It also applies to older centers with low rates of participatory
implementation due to program disorganization (logistical) or low community interest (lack of shared responsibility). It was pointed out that where participatory
implementation is high and a surplus of center contributions exists, an opportunity is present for bottom-up
participation. The PVO goal of human resources development through self-help is realized.

Village women experienced in Food and Nutrition
Center functions and accustomed to working together are
well prepared for initiating their own projects. Representative participation in project design and implementation can be aided by auxiliaries, village elites,
or CRS staff skilled in facilitating group decision-
making. The combination of 1) skilled facilitators, 2)
beneficiary assistance in program implementation, and
3) a surplus of contributions is not universal. However, the existence of these factors at some centers in
both Upper Volta and Togo allow for opportunities to
promote bottom-up participation that have rarely been
explored.

A problem of scale emerges in large centers serving hundreds of women. This and the lack of communications facilities, as pointed out by Frances Korten,
present obstacles to representative participation.
Korten suggests that tasks may be broken down to permit
smaller groups to meet where they live. This necessitates the creation of a rudimentary communications[14]
system to notify participants of local meetings.

CRS program offices need to take scale into consideration when deliberating over the opening of new
village centers. The more centers, the greater the
opportunity for beneficiary participation in ancillary
projects. Multiplication of centers, however, creates
problems for PVO logistics and supervision which are
already inadequate in both countries.

PVO program offices support center projects
through the provision of supplementary resources.
Micro-project funds assist nutrition center-initiated
well digging, school construction, or agricultural
endeavors. The program office also distributes annual
shipments of medical supplies suitable for infirmaries

as well as large quantities of garden seeds. These are not resources of the scale commanded by major donors, but they nicely fit the needs and absorption capacities of villagers.

Perhaps the most promising ancillary project conceived by CRS is the "oil seed module." Unlike the large-scale water and agriculturally related projects that CRS is managing in Upper Volta, the oil seed module requires a minimum of PVO and AID resources. Families would be encouraged to grow indigenous or locally adaptable oil seed crops (e.g., sunflowers or sesame) as a supplement to existing staple crops. The families could consume this protein-rich product or sell the oil thus improving their income in one form or another.[15] The CRS Upper Volta office was considering a scheme to purchase locally produced vegetable oil, substituting it for imported oil distributed at Food and Nutrition Centers.

CRS would play a catalyst role providing initial supplies of seeds, technical advice, and imported Chinese or Indian oil seed decorticators. Although there is top-down, PVO intervention at the outset, crop production, sale or other use would be locally managed.

2.   The Influence of Local Elites
Elites at the village level include traditional chiefs, school teachers, traditional healers and paramedic personnel, minor government bureaucrats fulfilling symbolic roles, missionaries, donor government representatives (including Peace Corp Volunteers), merchants, and party cadre members. Other elites have means of making their presence known throughout the PVO's service delivery structure at the port, warehouses, and government offices in the capital city. The PVO, having little political clout, must come to terms with their influence.

However, it is the local elites who have a direct bearing on the operations of village Food and Nutrition Programs. Their command of physical resources, technical expertise, and authority make it essential for the PVO to include them in discussions of opening a village center or expanding existing program activities into ancillary areas. The power of traditional rulers, for example, is still quite strong at the local level in Upper Volta. They are key to settling local disputes and in bringing wrong-doers to justice.

It is not surprising then that in Tendler's analysis of PVO projects she found a high degree of decentralized decision-making by these elites. They represent local, established interests and need to be reckoned with. The degree to which they can control center activities for their own benefit is what concerns us here.

There are varied incentives for local elites to become involved in pressuring the PVO for a nutrition program in their area. First, there is often genuine concern for the welfare of the inhabitants of an area. The chief, school teacher, or missionary may see the program as a means of cushioning the poorer residents from shortfalls in food. Second, there is prestige connected with having a center in one's village, and elites can enhance their own power by playing a role in establishing a center. Plus, the program can be a conduit for the flow of additional resources increasing the wealth and importance of an area. The establishment of one program facilitates the introduction of others.[16] Third, the program creates several jobs and demands for services, and local elites will likely be involved in suggesting employees and service providers.

The power of local elites should not be viewed as static and unchallengeable. Personalities, variations in resource bases, national politics, and bureaucratic interventions all combine to create fluid situations quite the opposite of how Westerners tend to view traditional, rural societies.[17] The PVO needs to have current information about local elites when it is conducting discussions about opening a new village center. The village is expected to provide a secure building for the storage of food, scales, charts and other materials. Also necessary is a shaded meeting area and perhaps additional land for farming or poultry raising. PVO staff should have information on the seriousness of the village's commitment to the program and which of the elites can guarantee resource support.

The general cycle of events begins with frequent visits by several village elites to the PVO office to lobby for a nutrition center. Or if the village is far up-country, local elites will contact PVO staff when they are in the vicinity. Frequently, a delegation of mothers headed by a government employed mid-wife or a successful market woman will visit the PVO office to appeal for a center, citing the seriousness of malnutrition in the area.

Continuous pressure by village representatives can force the PVO's decision particularly if it is known to be seeking to expand the number of centers in the country. There is the danger that local elite pressure will dictate the location of new centers regardless of more serious malnutrition in other parts of the country. The geographical advantage is with those who live not too distant from the capital city and PVO headquarters. A check of PVO maps indicating operating centers attests to the influence of proximate elites as well as to the PVO's desire to minimize logistical problems.

The situation of the PVO being captured by proximate elites is a mutually beneficial arrangement. It lends further support to Robert Chambers' warning about the spatial bias of rural development tourists. Visits by PVO agents and donor agency representatives are concentrated around urban areas. Routes are set by good roads, and the areas observed are invariably more developed than what lies beyond those roads.[18]

Once a village is chosen as the site of a new center, elites are likely to nominate the auxiliaries who will manage the program. A local trucker may also be suggested as the transporter for the food. Their influence may also be present when an established center is in the midst of deciding what to do with surplus funds. Ancillary projects hold more opportunity for personal gain by elites than does the nutrition program. The village chief or a farmer with extensive land holdings may agree to contribute use of land in return for a percentage of cash crop profits. Or it may be decided to establish a village birthing clinic employing the services of the local mid-wife and creating a centralized outlet for the area's herbalist.

The PVO can also be convinced to work with exogenous elites - missionaries or Peace Corps Volunteers (PCVs) - simply because these persons appear more rational or organized from a Western perspective. The problem is that an exogenous definition of order and control may carry through to all center activities with the missionaries or PCVs directing center functions. This may stunt participatory implementation and initiative and inhibit beneficiaries from developing a sense of program ownership. The same atmosphere of control and dependency would carry over to ancillary projects.

Again, much depends on the status of the elites involved and their intentions. However, it is clear that elite involvement in center organization will be strongly influential, and the PVO must be prepared to deal with this.

A. Checks on Local Elites

While it is imperative for the PVO to be well informed about the intentions of local elites, it is difficult for expatriate staff to decipher power structures of unfamiliar cultures. They are simply poorly prepared to do so. This is where CRS, CARE and other established PVOs excel. They can rely on loyal, experienced local staff to sort out the players and to provide the information necessary to sensible program expansion. The advantages of depending on local staff to do this should be obvious, but Americans have a propensity for ignoring cultural obstacles to perception.[19] The U.S. situated policymaking offices of both CRS and USAID think little about the information collection difficulties faced by the program staff in the field.[20] Reporting requirements are specified by stateside administrators many of whom have no experience working in rural Africa.

Indigenous staff speak the local and national languages. Second, they spend considerable time up-country visiting Food and Nutrition Centers and other PVO programs. They are in-tune with local politics and circulate regularly among their own network of elites. Third, each CRS program office has a core, indigenous staff that represents the field organization's institutional memory. Expatriate staff turnover is extremely high in Africa and record keeping is antiquated. Thus, the local personnel's recounting of program history is the primary source of information available to an in-coming program director. Information provided by the local staff assessing the intentions of local elites, relating incidents of past program abuses, and gauging the ability of villages to provide supporting resources proves, as the director gains experience, to be highly reliable. Their information is not as sound for use in prioritizing food shortage areas throughout the nation (their views tend to be regional and biased toward their ethnic groups) or in calculating leverage with ministries to get the promised program support. A more specific breakdown of PVO staff functions is presented below.

There are other checks on the power of local elites that are not as controllable by the PVO as is the informational role of the staff. These include the presence of effective government field personnel who can monitor local programs and projects and advocate representative decision-making. Also, the existence of diverse, competing elites may make it difficult for any one elite or clique to capture a program. This also presents the program with alternative local resource providers if the one chosen fails to fulfill his/her obligations.

3. PVO Staff Functions

A. Field Staff

CRS relies upon two categories of field staff to supervise Food and Nutrition Programs and other PVO supported activities. These are regional nutrition supervisors and end-use food checkers. Since the service delivery structure in Upper Volta, Togo and other countries is based on decentralization, supervisory staff spend the majority of their time visiting villages.

A. 1. Regional Nutrition Supervisors

The Food and Nutrition Program is divided into geographical regions, and a nutrition supervisor has responsibility for the centers within her area.[21] Regional supervisors are generally health professionals with nursing, public health, or nutritionist skills. They may be U.S. or European expatriates, local residents, or bureaucrats seconded from a social welfare or health ministry.

They fulfill multiple and not always complementary roles as the "linking pin" between the village centers and the PVO program office. At the village they train and supervise auxiliaries in center functions: use of weight charts, nutrition and health education, food distribution and preparation, transportation arrangements, and finances. The supervisor's interpersonal and group facilitator skills are critical in sustaining a spirit of participation at a center. The lack of such skills or lack of a commitment to beneficiary participation can open the gate to the domination of a center by local elites. A supervisor can strongly influence but cannot control local events. She is best described as a catalyst at the local level.

It is through regional supervisors that program office directors receive most of their information about center strengths and problems. This gives some indication of the importance of their organizational intelligence role. Their reports signal possibilities for increasing the number of beneficiaries, encouraging expansion into ancillary projects, or halting food shipments until a village can provide adequate storage facilities. Their discretional range of decision-making is only surpassed by the program director's.

A. 2. End-Use Food Checkers

These are unskilled PVO employees who inspect village facilities for proper and safe storage of PL 480 food. More food is lost to spoilage and infestation than to theft. End-use checkers are also responsible for seeing that local food receipt and distribution records balance. They report discrepancies and misuse of food to village authorities and to the PVO program director. In addition, they may collect beneficiary contributions if the regional nutrition supervisor so requests. However, this is usually the limit of their involvement with nutrition programs, outside of observation, since center oversight is regarded as the domain of the nutrition supervisors. Without a substantial upgrading of job skills through training or through the hiring of better educated employees, end-use checkers cannot be expected to play an expanded role in program support.

This does not presently pose a problem since their current functions are significant in themselves. Much like financial auditors, their impact in keeping people honest is greater than their numbers would indicate. Even the smaller programs employ two end-use checkers who spend most of their time on the road. In the course of fulfilling their primary role, end-use checkers gather information useful in broader program decision-making. They report on their impressions of overall center operations, the progress of other PVO funded projects in the area, new government activities, and general political news.

Although the positions are stable and held by one or more senior employees, end-use checkers are susceptible to the influence of local elites. End-use checkers are sometimes bribed or threatened not to reveal misuse of such food. In other circumstances, they may be disinclined to report on accountability problems of nutrition programs in villages where they have relatives and friends.

However, in the majority of cases, end-use checkers are loyal to program purposes and report accurately on field conditions. In both Upper Volta and Togo, local staff have argued convincingly to limit and eventually suspend corrupt programs. The job security they possess working with a U.S. PVO enables them to share in the responsibility for decision-making that regulated against abuses by local elites.

By virtue of their itinerant function separating them from the program office, field staff are regularly subjected to calculated appeals to their patriotism or ethnicity to quash critical reports of government and village elites misusing food commodities. After all, the food is supplied by the U.S. and more can always be sent. A surprising amount of national program loyalty has been internalized over the years that enables end-use checkers and other PVO employees to act in terms of the larger national interest. This is particularly striking in countries where the same can be said for a small percentage of civil servants.[22]

B. Program Office Staff

The final cluster of roles to be explored are those directly associated with top-down program planning and implementation. Whether or not the PVO program succeeds in warranting Tendler's designation of "top-down 'sensitive'" rests largely with the orientation of the program director, the assistant director, and project coordinators. These staff members perform two functions critical to program size and quality. First, they fulfill a communications or brokerage role in interpreting the requirements of the country program to PVO headquarters and donor organizations. Second,

they are responsible for top-down functions: implementing nutrition monitoring systems, commodity logistics and reporting, and project coordination. The program office staff also consists of the customs or port
representative, warehousemen, bookkeepers, and clerical
personnel closely duplicating the makeup of a commercial freight receiving office.

To illustrate the program office functions, the
roles of program director, project coordinator and support staff will be described.

B. 1. Program Director

With few exceptions, program directors are U.S.
expatriates hired through CRS's New York headquarters.
Local nationals are more often appointed as assistant
directors, but they are not provided with additional
training for them to assume directorships.

It is stressed that the program or field office is
the policymaking unit when it comes to channeling PVO
resources and establishing program priorities. Because
of the distance involved and the PVO's reliance on
slow, postal communications, considerable discretion is
vested in the program director. This discretion is a
positive facet from the point of view of decentralized
decision-making, enabling country programs to be shaped
according to local needs. Yet, if the program director
is disinclined toward certain PVO policies he/she can
easily thwart their implementation for a considerable
time. Program direction, project planning, and personnel actions are some of the areas over which the
director has major control. However, since the PVO
office is dependent upon sponsoring ministries, CRS
headquarters and donors for doling out operational resources such as food commodities, the director's immediate control over operations is lessened. In short,
the program director can choose to oppose or be inactive more than to initiate and control the timing of
activities.

This interdependency of action is evident in the
director's role of go-between with host government
officials, beneficiary representatives, and foreign
donors including USAID and PVO headquarters. There are,
indeed, competing demands for the resources at the
PVO's disposal while at the same time there may be conflicting requests for action from PVO and donor offices. The trick of the program director is to separate
out and act on legitimate demands for resources while,
for example, placating the local USAID mission about
high port food losses due to insufficient warehousing.

In analyzing the director's duties using Henry
Mitzberg's ten managerial roles, the following four
functions stand out.[25]

1. Leadership: a small staff and minimal overhead place added emphasis on the director's sorting out and prioritizing numerous resource and reporting demands. Means for accomplishing tasks must also be included in staff direction, and this is where the director has some choice between broader based participation or top-down management. Hiring is not delegated since each staff position assumes great importance in a labor-intensive, pretechnological office environment. Interviewing potential employees occupied an inordinate amount of my time.

2. Disseminator: The director must insure that PVO staff and sponsoring ministry officials are apprised of PVO and donor policies concerning project resources and food commodity handling and use. There are legal requirements to be followed and reported. Also, the director disseminates information concerning the availability of additional resources down to the village level.

3. Figurehead: Particularly in Africa where U.S. presence is minimal, U.S. citizens with titles are rare and thus accorded informal status as foreign policy spokespersons. The function of visiting villages and attending local dedications of new projects or facilities is as equally important as representing the PVO at host government and donor meetings. The importance attached to this role in traditional societies makes it more time consuming and more significant than most Americans would anticipate.

4. Disturbance handler: Every organization has its unanticipated crises and brush fires. However, due to the combination of an unpredictable operational environment and small PVO staff, the director's work schedule is dominated by responding to problems over which he/she has very little control but some influence. The program history in Togo eroded more current efforts at stabilizing program functions and ruled out anything as sophisticated as encouraging beneficiary participation in ancillary projects. Public administration education does little to prepare one for operating in such an environment. However, one quickly appreciates the necessity of a minimum level of bureaucracy$_{24}$for replicating and disseminating innovative policies.

B. 2. Project Coordinator

This is a professional level position occupied by either educated local personnel or U.S. expatriates. Project coordinators are often employed under specific project contracts which narrowly define their responsibilities and remove them from nutrition program functions. There is potential for this position to be used in matching projects more closely with food and nutrition center needs and in facilitating representative participation in PVO activities. Unfortunately, this is not the tendency where coordinators are responsible for large, USAID or European Economic Community projects. The job description is copied from USAID, and functions are seen as finding project coordinators, wherever they may be, and moving money. Much time is spent just getting the project underway: making contact with potential co-managers and seeking waivers for in-country purchase of vehicles and other key items.[25]

An alternative approach, and one that has been successfully tried, is permanentizing the project coordinator's position so that it does not depend on the existence of one project or is unduly influenced by the exigencies of one donor. This could reduce the rapid personnel turnover associated with single project coordinators, and it would provide the coordinator the opportunity to become familiar with the PVO's entire country program. There is more likelihood then of PVO channeled project funding being directly integrated with nutrition program activities. Project co-managers are also more easily identifiable, because the PVO project coordinator is familiar with nutrition program staff and beneficiaries. He/she spends more time in the field.

The drawbacks are that the coordinator's time must be shared among several smaller projects as well as the nutrition program. Also, the PVO has to assume part of the coordinator's salary and plan to support the position at least for several years.

There is an implicit argument here for the PVO to avoid large-scale, donor funded projects unless it consciously decides to continue to branch out in this direction. This, however, is not compatible with existing nutrition program capacities or structure.

B. 3. Support Staff
Several characteristics attributable to local staff have already been mentioned. Two of these, providing institutional (program) memory under conditions of high expatriate turnover and providing checks on program abuses by government bureaucrats, are particular strengths of program office support staff. A third is the stability of the relations they maintain with village representatives and government bureaucrats responsible for lending support to the food programs. They fulfill a wide range of functions from clearing food commodities and other imports through customs to interviewing village spokespersons and maintaining financial records.

By dint of their longevity and responsibilities, they influence PVO policy and are a contentious force for those seeking to change policies and procedures the staff has helped to mold. To be sure, implementing a

PVO directive is difficult to achieve without orientation and training for the core support staff. As CRS has evolved from a relief organization to a development oriented one in the 1970s and 1980s, it has found its more loyal and senior staff unequipped to deal with increasingly sophisticated job requirements. Project supervision and reporting, proposal writing, and an orientation toward integrating food programs and projects have required skills other than those for which staff members were originally hired. An unfortunate aspect of an organization tied to low-overhead service delivery is lack of training funds, particularly for local staff. They are viewed as an organizational economy not warranting a long-term personnel development investment. It is not as if there was a policy to underpay local personnel - in fact they are well paid according to government scales. There is simply little or no local personnel policy. Lacking resources to upgrade core staff capabilities, program directors have hired more educated employees to fill new project and program slots.

For the most part, support staff duties are performed in and around the capital city. This aids in their forming cooperative relationships with government customs agents, national railroad functionaries and warehouse supervisors. The drawback is that the PVO staff - local nationals and expatriates alike - take on the urban, bureaucratic perceptual biases of their host government counterparts.[26] This is inimical to a program committed to decentralized, rural service delivery. These biases favor contact with literate, middle class, organizational representatives and not the rural, illiterate subsistence families the PVO seeks to assist.

A solution is to insure frequent job rotation among office and field staff so that all personnel spend a month or more each year in the field. This is less possible in jobs requiring specialized skills or cultivated contacts such as bookkeeping and customs clearance. The expatriate members of the staff also require time up-country to observe first hand the difficulties and opportunities of rural development. There would be less resistance to such an idea if personnel were asked to prepare an annual work objectives plan to include periods of cross-training and rural travel.

4. Summary
This section has described the major infrastructure members of the Food and Nutrition Programs coordinated by CRS. Functional responsibilities have been outlined along with an assessment of the extent to

which representative participation is realizable in
current program activities.

The nutrition programs were found to be high in
participatory implementation although long-term policy
planning is top-down. At centers where the program is
viewed as beneficiary owned, ancillary projects provide
an opportunity for realizing representative participation if the PVO actively supports such a policy.

The power of local elites is seen as significant
and their involvement is considered necessary to the
inauguration and maintenance of village centers. There
are multiple checks on elites, the more effective being
regional supervisors skilled at facilitating beneficiary participation and information gathering by other
CRS staff.

Expatriate staff functions were also discussed.
Considerable discretion is vested in the program director, permitting him/her to encourage or oppose PVO
policies on participation or other issues. In the case
of the project coordinator, it was suggested that the
position be recast to achieve greater integration with
Food and Nutrition Program needs. Finally, local support staff were seen as providing program continuity.
A PVO policy for local staff development was urged.

III. LESSONS FROM EXPERIENCE

Key lessons derived from the examination of Food
and Nutrition Programs in Upper Volta and Togo will be
summarized. Many of these lessons merit attention as
subjects of further, more focused research.

Obstacles to Expanding Representative Participation in
Food and Nutrition Programs
    1. The influence of local elites has been acknow-
ledged. In resource scarce societies modest wealth,
formal education or rank provide individuals with dis-
proportionate amounts of power. However, due to the
variety of local elites and the even greater range of
attitudes they may hold toward Food and Nutrition Programs, it cannot be assumed that they will oppose participatory frameworks. Village auxiliaries and nutrition supervisors are the means by which the PVO can be
informed of local elites' motives vis-a-vis nutrition
programs and projects. These personnel are also well
situated to ascertain the level of beneficiary interest
in assuming responsibility for village project decision-making. A possibility exists, more likely in
Upper Volta, that beneficiaries will defer to those who
have traditionally made choices for the village. In
Togo, party cadre influence will be greater. Alternatively, it may be that a particular ethnic group or
area has a tradition of consensual decision-making or

cooperative type structures for agricultural endeavors. Again, PVO field personnel are in a good position to inform the program office of appropriate policies in each case.

The lesson here is that elite involvement with village programs is necessary and complex. Simplistic PVO and donor policies pitting exogenous strategies for participation against locally acceptable leadership are bound to fail.

2. A recurring point throughout the discussion of PVO functional roles is the scarcity of personnel skilled in designing participatory program frameworks or in facilitating group decision-making. Those that possess such skills have received their training prior to coming to CRS.

Sporadic training efforts have not kept pace with more sophisticated demands placed on local staff. As the PVO has progressed from a relief to a development agency, local employee modes of operation and interpretation of PVO goals have not changed. Many employees are still oriented toward a top-down relief operation. They have not been formally exposed to the rationale of nutrition monitoring and the need to integrate projects with the established nutrition program.

3. The membership at village nutrition centers may be too large to permit their functioning as representative decision-making bodies. It is not unusual for centers to receive several hundred women and children each month. Even if a third of these women are inclined to be active in ancillary projects, it would be a formidable task to coordinate their input. As it is, village auxiliaries are already overextended in providing services at larger, more active centers.

Also as Frances Korten points out, local decision-making can be obstructed by lack of communications and transportation between residences and central meeting locales.[27] These are common problems in Food and Nutrition Programs where women may walk long distances to a center only to learn that food commodities have not arrived. Representative participation would increase the frequency of meetings, and distance alone would become a key factor in determining who participated and who stayed home.

4. The final obstacle was not specifically mentioned in prior discussion, but it is inherent in programs benefiting women and children. Although the food package is an economic supplement to the entire family, men are not perceived to be benefiting. Also, despite the rhetoric about women in development, it is difficult to get donors to consider women as the focal group in development projects. The lack of political power accorded to peasant women and the bias that

donors and national bureaucracies have toward male farmers make it difficult to attract resources for ancillary projects. Considerable research has been conducted
on these biases and on the productive role[28] performed by
women in traditional, agrarian societies.

Recommendations for Improving PVOs' Capacities as Development Agencies

1. The PVOs need to dedicate resources to staff
training and development. The requirement is particularly urgent for local staff, but expatriate personnel
would also benefit from program-specific training and
organized language instruction. PVOs deserve credit
for their ability to deliver services at low operating
costs. However, capacity to manage sophisticated programs that include nutrition monitoring systems and
ability to promote beneficiary participation is undercut by lack of training. Training budgets could be calculated as a percentage of the value of the resources
being managed in a particular program or project. The
appeal to donors is that resources would be better
targeted and the chances of long-term program impact
improved.

2. Reverse the trend to expand the size and
number of national programs in Upper Volta, Togo, and
other African countries. Emphasis has been placed on
increasing tonnages in food commodity programs at the
expense of qualitative improvements. In the rush to
expand the nutrition program into new villages, the
necessary groundwork to build community support and
ownership is bypassed.

Program directors are encouraged to expand commodity programs annually, and the rewards system favors
rapid expansion over qualitative changes. Rewards and
resource support could be recalculated to favor nutrition monitoring improvements, enhancement of participation, and the linkage of projects to existing village
programs.

3. Insure that the scale and timing of donor
funded projects match local needs and infrastructure
capabilities. This requires a change in perspective
that necessitates fitting resources to local project
requests instead of overloading the limited absorption
capacities of most country programs.

Instead of seeking large USAID projects with narrow guidelines, endeavor to establish a mid-size version of the popular "micro-projects" fund. These funds
could be allocated by the program director or projects
coordinator in lump sums up to $1,000 with approval
required for larger requests. This is much closer to
the scale of resources needed in ancillary projects
emanating from village nutrition centers. The lack of
stringent reporting requirements and the limited,

matching nature of these funds make them more conducive
to village cooperative endeavors.

Also, the oil seeds project prototype requires
promotion and dissemination to Food and Nutrition Programs throughout Africa. It serves multiple purposes -
cash crop, nutritional by-products, import substitution
- and is easily tailored to different countries and
regions.

4. Continue to minimize the number of U.S. expatriate staff and avoid the tendency to centralize
decision-making. The training of local staff is a
substitutable policy for the hiring of additional expatriate managers or technicians in most cases. The
investment is thus made in personnel who are much more
likely to remain in the country and continue in development work as a career.

There are tradeoffs in permitting each country
program a large degree of discretion. It contradicts
headquarters' tendency to seek standardization and
control. Yet, a strength of PVO programs is in their
ability to respond to local needs and transmit these
requirements to potential donors. The flexible, brokerage role suits the PVO's program office capabilities
and keeps the program focused on local priorities.

5. Maintain the low-profile of PVOs in the field,
but educate host-country ministries and international
donors about the development orientations of PVOs. For
example, CRS's nutrition programs are already well
known at the village level, and the agency's low-profile assists the strategy of local responsibility for
program implementation since the program comes to be
seen as a local structure. However, there is much
confusion about the programs of U.S. PVOs at the level
of national development policy. Ministries and USAID
alike are frequently under the impression that PVOs are
more involved in relief efforts than in long-range development programs. The weight monitoring facet of the
nutrition programs and strategies to integrate programs
and oil seed projects require dissemination.

There is much to be learned from the decades of
experience of U.S. PVOs in sub-Sahara Africa. The
agencies have a responsibility, yet unfulfilled, to
share their knowledge with others seeking similar
objectives.

NOTES

1. Judith Tendler, Turning Private Voluntary
Organizations Into Development Agencies: Questions for
Evaluation. AID Program Evaluation Discussion Paper
No. 12 (Washington, D.C.: U.S. Agency for International
Development, April 1982).

2. "Project" refers to development efforts with specific objectives within a fixed time frame. "Program" indicates an ongoing and often institutionalized endeavor that may include complementary, shorter duration projects.

3. For a critique of food aid, see Frances Moore Lappe and Joseph Collins, Food First: Beyond the Myth of Scarcity, (New York: Balantine, 1979). For program assessments, see the USAID evaluation series which includes David E. Sahn and Robert M. Pestronk, A Review of Issues in Nutrition Program Evaluation. AID Program Evaluation Discussion Paper No. 10 (Washington, D.C.: U.S. Agency for International Development, July 1981).

4. Kwashiorkor is severe malnutrition in infants and children characterized by failure to grow and develop, changes in pigmentation of the skin and hair, degeneration of the liver and apathy. It is caused by a diet excessively high in carbohydrate and extremely low in protein. Marasmus is a condition of progressive emaciation due to malnutrition.

5. Rev. Carlo Capone, "A Review of an Experience with Food-Aided Nutrition Programs," reprinted from Nutrition Planning, Vol. 3, No. 2 (May 1980), pg. xxiii. Doctor Capone is the Public Health Director for CRS's Sub-Sahara Africa Region, and the architect   of the region's Food and Nutrition Programs.

6. This information, from the Annual Estimate of Requirements, was provided by Mike Kerst, Program Officer for West Africa, Food for Peace, U.S. Agency for International Development, Washington, D.C.

7. Capone pg. xxi.

8. D.M. Warren, G. Steven Bova, Sr. Mary Ann Tregoning, and Mark Kliewer, "Ghanaian National Health Policy Toward Indigenous Healers: The Case of Primary Health Training for Indigenous Healers (PRHETIH)". Revised version of a paper submitted to Social Science and Medicine, Ames: Iowa State University, January 1982.

9. Tendler, pg. 15.

10. Tendler, pp. 21, 24.

11. Tendler, pg. 19

12. Tendler, pg. 20.

13. A complete discussion of the roles of auxiliary workers is found in Doris M. Storms, Training and Use of Auxiliary Health Workers: Lessons from Developing Countries (Washington, D.C.: American Public Health Association, Monograph Series, No. 3, 1979).

14. Frances F. Korten, "Community Participation: A Management Perspective on Obstacles and Options," in David C. Korten and Felipe B. Alfonso (eds.), Bureaucracy and the Poor: Closing the Gap (Singapore: McGraw -Hill International Book Co., 1981).

15. Capone, pp. xxiv-xxv.

16. CRS also conducts national school lunch programs in most countries where it has program offices.

17. Change in peasant societies is examined by Judith Heyer, Pepe Roberts and Gavin Williams (eds.), Rural Development in Tropical Africa (New York: St. Martin's Press, 1981); Donal B. Cruis O'Brien, Saints and Politicians: Essays in the Organization of a Sengalese Peasant Society (London: Cambridge University Press, 1975); and by Kenneth Evan Sharpe, Peasant Politics: Struggle in a Dominican Village (Baltimore: Johns Hopkins University Press, 1977).

18. Robert Chambers, Rural Poverty Unperceived: Problems and Remedies. World Bank Staff Working Paper No. 400 (Washington, D.C.: World Bank, 1980).

19. Edward T. Hall examines culture's impact on perception and communication in The Silent Language (Garden City, New York: Anchor Press/Doubleday, 1973), and in Beyond Culture (Garden City, New York: Anchor Press/Doubleday, 1977).

20. Jon Moris critiques information demands on field personnel in "Information for Design, Management and Evaluation" in his Managing Induced Rural Development (Bloomington, Indiana: International Development Institute, Indiana University, 1981).

21. Nutrition supervisor and village auxiliary positions are generally occupied by women due to their greater acceptance by program beneficiaries.

22. For a vivid description of the behavioral pressures at work in African bureaucracies, see Jon Moris, "The Transferability of Western Management Concepts and Programs, an East African Perspective," in Joseph E. Black, et al. (eds.), Education and Training for Public Sector Management in the Developing Countries (New York: Rockefeller Foundation, 1977).

23. Henry Mintzberg, "The Manager's Job: Folklore and Fact,"Harvard Business Review 53 (July-August 1975): 49-61.

24. David C. Korten addresses these issues in his discussion of program learning in "Community Organization and Rural Development: A Learning Process Approach," Public Administration Review 40 (Sept.- Oct. 1980): 480-511. See also Rushikesh Maru, "Organizing for Rural Health" in Korten and Alfonso (eds.), Bureaucracy and the Poor.

25. Jon Moris elaborates on the infrastructural preliminaries of donor funded projects in "A Case in Rural Development: The Masai Range Development Project," in Managing Induced Rural Development.

26. Chambers, Rural Poverty Unperceived.

27. Frances Korten, "Community Participation."

28. See, for example, Ruth Dixon, Rural Women at
Work: Strategies for Development in South Asia (Baltimore: Johns Hopkins University Press for Resources for
the Future, 1978); Institute of Social Studies, Women
in Development: A Bibliography (The Hague: Institute
of Social Studies, 1978); and Kathleen Staudt, "Administrative Resources, Political Patrons and Redressing
Sex Inequities: A Case from Western Kenya," Journal of
Developing Areas 12 (no. 4, 1978): 399-414.

6. The Egyptian Basic Village Service Program: A New Strategy for Local Government Capacity Building

James B. Mayfield

In the past thirty years, our understanding of how rural development can best be implemented has been both expanded and deepened. The notion of development has broadened from the narrow, largely economic focus of increased GNP (through extended industrialization and broadened savings and investment) toward a far-reaching socio-politico-economic orientation that emphasizes an integrated multisectoral approach to development. Development initiatives have become more sophisticated in the level of analysis used to understand how people in villages and rural communities engage in self-sustaining activities. Often these activities are stimulated by and linked to the central government agencies, but still defined and made meaningful through social and cultural experiences quite independent of a government's administrative systems.

During the first two decades after World War II, the process of implementation was defined, by development theorists, in very simplistic terms using a model of administration largely articulated and developed in Western Europe and the United States. This "Western" model, based upon the Weberian ideal-type model of bureaucracy, Frederick Taylor's notion of efficiency and scientific management, and the basic "principles of administration" espoused by Gurlick and Ullick, was widely heralded as the key to effective program implementation and development. Progress required that various ministries, departments, and agencies responsible for development programs adopt the bureaucratic methods and techniques of the West.

All efforts to reform or modernize the administrative systems of developing countries were colored by the insistence of technical experts that Western models of bureaucracy that focused on hierarchy, unity of command, appropriate span control, impersonalized rules, and procedures were an absolute necessity. A lack of such administrative procedures and systems of authority and rationality was considered a key obstacle

to economic development. This barrier could be overcome only through the introduction of administrative
systems that emphasized the values of logic, efficiency, and formal authority. Institution building was
widely popularized as the most effective way to introduce Western systems of management and administration
into Third World political environments. Many institutes of public administration were established in
many Third World capitals as a way of training and
professionalizing a cadre of public officials competent
to "reform and rationalize" their own countries' respective central administrative systems. Wholesale
transference of U.S. college curricula in public administration, organization and methods, public personnel and budgeting, characterized their efforts to help
these nations to implement and achieve economic development.

The decade of the 1960s was the decade of the
planners. Much effort was expended in designing and
establishing central planning agencies. The planning
process was usually defined in macro-economic terms.
Economic models which sought to identify cause and
effect relationships among the crucial variables associated with development focused on the process of
planning with almost no serious consideration of how
and why such models would or could be implemented in
the "real world" of administrative agencies, local
government councils and village-level farmers. The
less developed countries'...

The less developed countries' (LDCs') capacity to
plan, develop strategies, and administrate reform
proposals expanded rather rapidly.... However, the
capacity to implement lagged far behind because
the need was more complex...Foreign experts,econo-
mists or public administrative specialists, often
did not know how the local administrative system
functioned. They had no knowledge of how the
people at the higher or lower levels would react
to their proposals. Consequently, the plans for
economic development and administrative reform remained largely academic and ivory tower products.[2]

Much of the emphasis of the pre-1970 period tends
to focus on the planning process as "an organized,
conscious and continual attempt to select the best
available alternatives to achieve specific goals."[3]
Planning too often was defined as a process which
culminated in the publication of a massive document
prepared by a staff of planners working in a national
institute of planning. One scholar in the early 1970s
sought to articulate a new definition of planning which
involved more than merely the preparation of some

impressive document. Planning, if it is to be useful, must consider both the goals to be achieved but also the practical steps and procedures needed to implement policy and achieve goals. Thus the process of implementation came to be seen as important if not more important than the creation of some plan document.[5]

Implementation was gradually acknowledged as a complex and continuous process of managing, monitoring, evaluating and restructuring the original plan in ways to bring about a wide range of social, economic, and political changes. Gradually development experts became sensitive to the need to: 1) obtain information and to become aware of the role that a culture plays in the lives of people, and 2) clarify the needs, the attitudes and the perceptions of the people to be impacted by the proposed plans. While lip service was paid to these types of information in earlier development programs of the 1950s and 1960s, it was only in the 1970s that special efforts were made to structure such information into the process of implementation. It was this new sensitivity to the importance of such social and cultural factors which generated a more profound attachment to the utility and appropriateness of farmer participation. That is, the people likely to be affected by the proposed development should be consulted, and policies and programs should be modified on the basis of the information thus obtained through their participation and involvement.

In an effort to clarify the pre-1970 approach to development, let us distinguish between "administrative development" of the 1950s and 1960s and "development administration" of the 1970s and 1980s.

...Administrative development refers to improvement, expansion and creation of administrative capacity. It refers to the ability of administrative structures, institutions and organizations to cope with the formulation and execution of development plans, objectives and programs. It also includes the capacity of administrative personnel to perform development tasks efficiently.... (through) administrative reform, designing of new organizations, improvement in personnel and budgeting procedures and training of personnel...[6]

Rural development was thus defined in terms of administrative capacity. The focus was on improving, redesigning and "westernizing" the bureaucracy. Reform the bureaucracy and development will take place. Issues about administrative system-village linkages, "reality" testing of rationally derived plans, and ongoing strategies of effective implementation were seldom raised.

Development administration has been defined and
redefined over the past decade in many ways, but
the essence of this process is reflected in the
sequencing of 'development' before 'administration.' Thus it is 'development' with an emphasis on programs, procedures, objectives, and
goals directly related to the immediate and long-
term needs of rural people, instead of the administrative system that needs development. It is
the process of development that needs to be effectively administered, not the structures of
administration that need to be developed.[7]

Introducing a new position classification scheme
into the personnel system of the ministry of agriculture is clearly the focus of administrative development, while seeking to facilitate the processes and
procedures by which farmer productivity and peasant
quality of life might be enhanced is more reflective of
what we mean by development administration.

...The net overall result of the gigantic effort
of international and foreign aid-giving agencies
in the area of administrative development was over
bureaucratization, excessive controls and regulation of economy, proliferation of bureaucratic
structures, an increase in the size of bureaucracies and excessive concentration of power in the
hands of the administrative elite.[8]

THE NEW MANDATE

In 1973 the United States Agency for International
Development (USAID) announced a new approach for providing financial and technical aid to developing
nations. The U.S. Congress, seeking to enhance the
positive impact of aid on the lives of the people supposedly being helped, articulated a "New Mandate" for
action which requested that all financial supports to
developing nations be prioritized in order to "directly
improve the lives of the poorest of their people and
their capacity to participate in the development of
their countries."[9]
The impetus for this shift in orientation rested
upon an awareness that while American aid had generally
been effective in expanding the GNP and the broader
agricultural and industrial sector outputs of many
participating Third World countries, the real dilemma
of the "development decade" of the sixties was that the
vast majority of the rural poor had generally not been
affected by this growth.[10]
This "New Mandate" announced a significant shift
away from the large-scale capital transfer approach for

physical infrastructure development in roads, water systems, and industrial growth so characteristic of the Marshall Plan era. USAID would now emphasize projects and programs which would have a direct and specific impact upon the poor majority in the Third World. The high priority areas included: small farm food production; human resource development; local small industry expansion; health and education; local government development; nutrition and family planning. It has also become increasingly recognized that rural development cannot be viewed as merely a technical problem which requires rural peasants to utilize Western technology. The problem is a much wider one, that of developing appropriate organizations and institutions to mobilize members of the rural society to greater productive effort, to help them overcome the constraints in the way of utilizing available resources, and to enable them to distribute the results of their effort equitably among themselves. The institutional implications of this concern were also articulated by World Bank President Robert McNamara when he argued that the key challenge of the 1970s was the need to develop "new forms of rural institutions and organizations that will give as much attention to promoting the inherent potential and productivity of the poor as is generally given to protecting the power of the privileged."[11]

During the past several years, USAID has sought to restructure its methods and procedures to accomplish the goals of this "New Mandate" more effectively. Two specific problems stand out. The first is the identification of the targeted groups of poor who are most in need of help. This problem includes both the development of criteria by which "the poorest of the poor" are distinguished from other rural and urban indigents and the need to ʼsensitize host country officials to the utility and appropriateness of such a distinction. The second problem is that of designing and developing programs and projects to promote rural development with social equity through a management and administrative system structured directly to assist the disadvantaged beneficiaries.

In response to the first problem, USAID suggested a set of criteria by which the poor could be identified:

1. Per capita income below $150 per year;
2. Daily diet of less than 2,160 to 2,670 calories; or
3. Those living in countries where life expectancy at birth was below fifty-five years, infant mortality was over thirty-three per thousand, birth

rates were over twenty-five per thousand population, and less than forty percent of the population had access to general health services.[12]

It was estimated that about three-fourths of the
total population in AID-assisted countries (roughly 800
million people) were living within the guidelines of
poverty in the mid-1970s. It was concluded that USAID
programs should focus on those living in rural areas,
primarily at the bottom third of the poverty sector
which generally included subsistence farm families,
landless laborers, and small-scale nonfarm entrepreneurs and craftsmen. Although there is a tendency to
rely on some minimum income standard as the basis for
identifying a targeted group, still officials in USAID
recognize that no widely acceptable framework for
defining poverty exists and that even where data are
available they suffer from "systematic underreporting
and undercoverage.."[13]

Equally important is the question of how best to
design projects and management support systems that
will channel assistance directly to designated groups
of beneficiaries. One study of this whole problem of
project design and management system development notes
that the new mandate

> ...is a reversal of previous approaches to devel-
> opment, in which projects were intended to be
> broad in scope and impact, with the benefits fil-
> tering or 'trickling down' to various groups of
> the poor. Now projects are to be 'targeted' on
> specific groups of the poor with the impact ex-
> pected to spread to a larger population.[14]

There is much evidence that the traditional bureaucratic approach to government program implementation may be not only inappropriate but even dysfunctional to the process needed to make operational a
program committed to "development with equity."[15] Our
understanding of how managerial practices affect this
type of "targeted" approach to poverty reduction is
still in its preliminary stages. USAID experience,
with its traditional emphasis on large-scale infrastructure projects of country-wide development projects, has tended to rely on project management techniques appropriate in ministerial-wide administrative
systems and a rationally oriented bureaucratic apparatus which is founded on foreign technology and
expertise. The "New Mandate" technique often finds
such management and administrative approaches inappropriate for the type of rural development "mini projects" which focus on small, long-term social-oriented
projects which are labor-intensive, require locally

available resources and technology, and are structured
to involve the participating beneficiaries in the design and implementation.[16]

THE BASIC VILLAGE SERVICE PROGRAM (BVS)

The Basic Village Service program provides an
extremely interesting case study which can enhance our
awareness of the theoretical and operational issues
related to the process of local government development,
decentralization and management and administrative
capacity building for rural development in a Third
World setting. A review of recent shifts in Egyptian
local government and the Egyptian government's commitment to decentralization dramatizes the significant
relationships that exist between the need for local
revenues and financial resources; the need for increased management and administrative skills in program
design, implementation and evaluation; and the need for
increased local participation initiatives through
locally established village level institutions. The
purpose of this paper is to review the role that a
decentralized local government system might plan in
stimulating and developing a self-sustaining process of
rural/local development and to identify the crucial
financial, managerial and training strategies deemed
prerequisites to the establishment of an effective
local government system.

On August 29, 1982 The Government of Egypt (GOE)
and the government of the United States signed the
Decentralization Sector Support Agreement which formalized an effort to consolidate five USAID-sponsored
projects designed to encourage and support Egypt's
commitment to local government decentralization. A
sense of the support USAID plans to provide can be
demonstrated by the total authorization of over $500
million to be dispersed through 1985: (1) $26.2 million
for the local development fund structured to help village councils design and implement income producing
projects whose profits will be used to finance locally
sponsored development projects and hopefully initiate a
self-sustaining local resource base; (2) $225 million
for the Basic Village Services (BVS), designed to provide funds to local village councils which will seek to
identify, design, and implement various infrastructure
activities, including mostly water, roads and drainage
projects; (3) $75 million for the Provincial Cities
Development (PCD) program, authorized to help finance
technical assistance, operating and maintenance costs,
and the design and construction of water and sewerage
projects in various cities in three governorates of
central Egypt (al-Fayum, Beni Suif, and al-Minya); (4)
$100 million for the Decentralization Support Fund

(DSF) which provides grants to governorates for the purchase of heavy equipment. The DSF envisions the establishment of a support and maintenance system at the governorate level to facilitate the planning and procurement process in heavy equipment usage; and (5) $89 million for the Neighborhood Urban Services (NUS), which finances neighborhood level infrastructure improvements (mostly sanitation and sewerage) in Cairo and Alexandria. As of December 1982 roughly $180 million has been dispersed and reflect in dollar terms USAID's desire to stimulate and reinforce Egypt's efforts to decentralize its local government system.[17]

The Basic Village Service Program in Egypt is an example of a rural development program designed and structured to reflect this concern for appropriate management interventions at various stages in the development of this program. In an attempt to document the role of management interventions in this type of rural development program, let us review the various factors which should be considered in designing and implementing a rural development management system.

In the "Request for Proposal" (RFP) issued by the USAID Cairo office on October 10, 1980, the specific purpose and strategy of the BVS program was outlined as follows:

Purpose: Improve and expand a continuing capacity in local units to plan, organize, finance, implement and maintain locally chosen infrastructure projects.

Strategy: This project will provide funds to nine rural governorates and their 449 village councils for the construction of over 1,000 locally chosen, locally directed rural infrastructure projects. The latter will encompass greatly needed rural water works, feeder roads, small scale drainage improvement, canal cleaning and repair, and pilot alternate energy projects. While the individual projects are essential as outcomes, efforts will also be focused on building a network of management processes and skills in the targeted governorates and villages. This will take place through the involvement of 1,300 local staff and, in particular, the elected village councils. The processes and procedures will be set out in a series of BVS project manuals which can be applied as well to all phases of local development activity. Skill transfer to the local staff will come through project-oriented training applied to the process by which individual projects are identified, completed and put into use.

BACKGROUND AND NATURE OF THE PROBLEM

Today about sixty percent of Egypt's total estimated population of forty-one million lives in rural
areas. Since the Egyptian revolution of 1952 the
national government has done much to improve the economic well-being of these rural people.[18] The government has redistributed land to landless cultivators,
and built schools, roads, canals and health clinics in
rural areas. From 1952 to the mid-1960s the flow of
capital and technical assistance into the Egyptian
countryside was impressive as the national government
used the expropriated wealth of the disposed king to
undertake a wide variety of rural infrastructure projects.[19] However, beginning in the mid-1960s, the
exigencies of wartime needs coupled with a questionable
diversion of resources towards abortive land recla-
mation efforts reduced the flow of developmental resources into the countryside to a mere trickle. As a
result canals, roads and potable water systems constructed earlier slowly deteriorated, while efforts to
extend the provisions of rural services were abandoned.
In Egyptian agricultural productivity stagnated as
waterlogging and salinity became an increasingly
serious problem. Similarly, the lack of appreciable
investment in rural road construction and local storage
facilities seriously undermined Egypt's bid to become a
major exporter of fruits and vegetables.

Thus, the rural areas of Egypt suffered widespread
deterioration of small scale infrastructure which had
provided a vital link in sustaining economic and social
livelihood. Not only did construction dwindle, but
maintenance and reconstruction fell off, adding to the
decline. Such infrastructure deficits have generated
serious obstacles in the provision of basic human needs
to the rural population. Feeder roads enable the small
farmer to market his crops without being at the mercy
of the middle man; roads also make it possible for the
government to deliver social services and to build
schools that people can get to easily. Better sanitary
facilities and the provision of dependable sources of
potable water add immeasurably to health and the quality of life of the rural peasant. The small secondary
and tertiary canals are absolutely vital to Egypt's
rural population whose agriculture is totally dependent
on irrigation. These canals form the crucial link
between the large irrigated systems constructed by the
central government and the farmer.[20] The construction
and maintenance component has been the primary responsibility of the governorates, the districts and
villages, and the lack of central government support
and aid has added to the general deterioration of the
rural areas.

The decline in national investment in the Egyptian countryside also affected the record and performance of local government units in the rural areas. Local village councils were established in the countryside after 1960 with the initiation of Law 124 but their growth was stunted by the historic pattern of national government dominance in center-periphery relations. However, in 1975 under the Public Law 52, the national government took an important step towards decentralizing decision-making powers by providing for: the election, rather than the appointment, of local council members; the creation of councils on the markaz (district) level as an intermediary between village and governorate councils; and the increase in local council revenues by designating that seventy-five percent of all taxes levied on agricultural land be returned to these councils. Before moving to the mechanics of the BVS project let us quickly review the local government system in Egypt in order to better understand the structural environment into which this program is being established.[21]

THE LOCAL GOVERNMENT SYSTEM IN RURAL EGYPT

The Arab Republic of Egypt is divided into twenty-six governorates, twenty-one in the Nile Valley and five in urban and desert areas. Each governorate is further divided into some 145 markaz, usually consisting of one major town and several (five to seven) village council areas which would include roughly forty to fifty smaller villages. A typical district has a population of between 150,000 and 200,000, and a typical village council area has roughly 30,000 people.[22]

Public Law 52, enacted in 1975, mandated that local councils be elected at each of the three levels of the governmental hierarchy--the governorate, the district, and the village council area. At the district level, eight individuals are to be elected by the citizens in the district capital and four by the citizens from each of the village council areas. For example, in one District, located in Giza near Cairo, there are fourteen village council areas. The district council includes eight members from the district town and sixty-four members from the fourteen village council areas for a total of seventy-two.

At the present time there are some 835 village council areas in all of Egypt. Each area is represented by a village local council elected by the people within the village council area. Below is a rudimentary chart depicting the formal local government presently functioning in rural Egypt.

Level of Government	Elected Local Council	Executive Branch
Governorate (Muhafasah)	Governorate Council (Maglis Al-Muhafazah)	Governor (Muhafaz)
District (Markaz)	District Council (Maglis Al-Markaz)	District Leader (Ra'is Al-Markaz) District Executive Council (Maglis Tanfizi)
Village (Qarya)	Village Local Council (Maglis Al-Mahali)	Village Unit Leader (Rais Al-Wahda) Village Executive Council (Maglis Tanfizi)[23]

Each village council area has a main village with at least four representatives, and a series of satellite villages, each with at least one representative. Each local village council must have at least seventeen members, including at least one woman.

Potentially, a local council can play an important role in developing a deep sense of legitimacy and commitment among the citizenry for a functioning local government system.[24] It can provide a sense of participation for the inhabitants of a governorate, a district, or a rural community. A council provides an institutional structure by which local requests, complaints, and proposals can be channeled to higher governmental authorities. The truly effective council may develop a series of projects or programs of such obvious local value as a strong inducement to the local citizenry to contribute a significant portion of the financing.

Yet for a council to function in this manner, there must be a literate citizenry, a group of experienced and capable leaders who understand the strengths and weaknesses of a local government system, who appreciate the need for the local community to shoulder a larger portion of the costs, and who are willing to participate with the central government in reforming and developing the social, economic, and political conditions in the rural areas. Unfortunately, many of these factors do not yet exist in rural Egypt.

One significant question of the short-run effectiveness of the new village councils elected in November 1979, deals with the amount of continuity that exists between them and the former councils originally

established under Nasser. Most village councils constituted prior to that election had a fair number of
experienced council members going back to at least mid-
1960s. All of these were members of the Arab Socialist
Union (ASU) and tended to be reelected several times.[25]
A careful analysis of the data collected from interviews on one local council in the Delta suggests that
in this most recent election, only five of the seventeen members were newly elected members with no previous experience in a village council. This tendency
for the past members to be reelected is consistent with
most past elections.[26]

This local council is expected to meet on the
first Thursday of each month at 11:00 a.m. According
to Law 43, each satellite village within the boundaries
of the local council is allowed at least one member
regardless of size, and more than one if the population
warrants additional members.

CHAIRMAN OF THE VILLAGE UNIT

Article 72 of Public Law 52 establishes an administrative officer with power and authority over the
financial and administrative activities of all local
government organizations functioning in each village
council area. The official title of this new local
government leader is chairman of the village unit (rais
wahdat al-garya). He is selected by the Ministry of
Local Government and is head of the executive committee
whose other members are the chief administrative officials working in the village council area (doctor,
social worker, school principal, agricultural engineer,
police officer, and building engineer) and the village
secretary.

The chairman of the village unit should be distinguished from the chairman of the village council,
who is elected by the council members. Thus, the
chairmen of the village units are executive officers
selected by the central government and responsible for
the implementation of all government programs and
policies within their area of jurisdiction. The chairman of the village council, on the other hand, is a
legislative officer who presides over the village
council meetings which are usually held once or twice
each month. Given the central government's predis-
position to control and direct most activities in the
village council areas primarily through financial and
budgetary regulations, the chairman of the village unit
tends to have more administrative and budgetary power
and authority at his disposal than does the chairman of
the village council.

Organization Chart of the Village Units

Village Unit

Village Council Chairman	Chairman of the
	Village Unit
(Rais al-Maglis al-Qarya)	(Rais al-Wahda)

Village Council	Executive Committee
(17 members)	(8 members)

A preliminary analysis of the data collected from specific interviews over the past five years with those officials who live and work in the Egyptian village provides the following kind of initial impressions of these village chairmen. They tend to be mature administrators, usually with a college education and generally with over ten years' experience in villages. All of them had more than five years' experience as village council chairmen before the establishment of Public Law 52 in 1975. There is no consistent pattern which characterizes their place of residency, although a slight majority of those interviewed did live in a nearby town, rather than in the village itself. It appears that most of these chairmen have a good sense of their responsibilities in the village, although many of them admitted that additional training in planning, budget preparation, and management (supervisory skills) would be helpful.[27]

Some specific problem areas mentioned in the interviews are:[28]

1. There is some confusion as to who is the chief authority in the village—the chairman of the village unit or the chairman of the village council. Those with the stronger personalities appear to dominate in their villages. Some of the chairmen of village units, who also happened to live in nearby towns, tended to let the council chairman take charge in the village.

2. Several chairmen of village units complained that village council members were inexperienced, untrained, and totally incapable of performing the duties assigned them under Public Law 52. The vast majority had no experience in village council work, often missed meetings, and did not take their position seriously. It is hoped that they will receive continual guidance and training, certainly during the next year or two as the BVS program is implemented.

3. Some chairmen of the village units felt that their ability to coordinate and follow through had been curtailed now that they are no longer voting members in

the village council. Most of them do attend the council meetings on a regular basis, but the village council chairman presides over these meetings in a fairly
authoritarian way, and the chairmen of the village
units have less influence in the council than they had
under the earlier system.

4. All of the chairmen of village units complained that they did not have adequate supervisory or
administrative authority over the members of the executive committee or even over ordinary employees and
workers in programs financially and administratively
under the control of a specific ministry. Officials
and employees under the direction of the Ministries of
Health, Education, Agriculture, Social Affairs, etc.,
still do not take directions or suggestions from these
chairmen of the village units. The long tradition of
strong centralized authority under fairly autonomous
ministerial service delivery systems will not easily be
removed. It is anticipated that executive control and
authority will eventually be decentralized down to the
district level and should allow the district chairman
to begin the process of integrating and unifying the
service programs being implemented in the villages.

5. These chairmen of the village units all have
had years of experience in a village environment which
was clearly not the case among council chairmen ten to
fifteen years ago. Most of their experience, however,
has been within the structures and formal restraints
that characterized local government under President
Nasser. Most of them still work through other government officials or leaders of the main families. There
is very little evidence that these chairmen clearly
communicate with a broad cross-section of the village
population. These professional village administrators
need training in the general areas of community development, supervision, communication techniques, and
popular participation and involvement.

The key governmental decision-making body in the
village is the executive council, which is made up of
the Rais al-Wahda, the village secretary, and representatives from the six major ministries that function
most directly with the rural population: Health,
Social Affairs, Agriculture, Housing, Interior, and
Education. This council meets twice each month on the
first and third Thursdays. Its members are the chief
administrative officers of the village unit area. They
are responsible for the supervision of local clinics,
various primary and preparatory schools, social units,
post offices, and youth clubs that exist within the
boundaries of their jurisdiction. The executive council
is required to prepare an annual budget which must be
approved by the local council.[29]

As one reflects on the local government system
that has existed and that is evolving in rural Egypt
and attempts to relate these developments to the
broader issues of development administration, it becomes evident that three crucial issues must be addressed if this is to be a self-sustaining process of
local government capacity building in the Nile Valley:
(A) How do you best initiate a process of project
implementation which builds local government capacity
to plan, design, implement and monitor needed infrastructure projects in the rural areas of Egypt? (B)
What is the relationship between the process of decentralization, the establishment of independent local
sources of revenue, and the eventual creation of self-
sustaining and viable units of local government which
may effectively meet the true needs of the rural people
of Egypt? (C) What specific types of training methodologies are most appropriate for reinforcing and oper-
ationalizing the management and administrative processes needed to stimulate effective implementation of
projects and long term self-sustaining local government
institutions in rural Egypt?

PROJECT IMPLEMENTATION AND LOCAL GOVERNMENT CAPACITY
BUILDING

In order to understand the challenges of implementing the BVS program, special efforts must be made
to chart the focus and orientation of the program.
Project orientation refers to the purposes and
goals of the rural development project. Such goals usually involve a set of policy alternatives and specific
management choices concerning program design, administrative policies and procedures, and implementation
strategies.
The orientation of the BVS program is influenced
by two factors. One is the objectives laid down by the
government for the BVS program and the resources to be
allocated to it. The other is the environment in which
the program has to be implemented.
The objectives of the BVS lay down the framework
within which operational goals have to be specified.
The complexity of the environment in rural Egypt is a
key factor that has influenced the choice of goals and
action plans of the BVS program. This greater complexity clearly makes the tasks of managing the BVS
program very difficult and challenging. Recognizing
that ministerial and even governorate level officials
will get overloaded as day-to-day operation decisions
are passed up through the system, the BVS program
specifically seeks to encourage a decentralized system
of decision-making.

A concerted effort to encourage a decentralized planning, designing, and implementing process at the village level will hopefully reinforce a single-focus approach to capacity building of local village institutions. While the focus is single in nature (increase project management skills), the long-term implications of the approach can be significant.

The commitment to limit the BVS to only nine governorates is as much a response to the limits of Egypt's local government management capability as it is to resource constraints in the conventional sense. Abundance of donor funds does not necessarily eliminate managerial problems and the need to cope with these constraints through an organizational learning process.

The BVS project has two critical outputs: 1) the construction of over 1,000 locally chosen and locally implemented rural infrastructure projects; and 2) the training of 1,300 officials from the governorate, the markaz, and in particular, the village levels of government in basic administrative and technical skills. These two outputs are equally vital and inextricably connected. If Egyptian rural development is to become a reality, basic improvements in the rural infrastructure must take place. Yet, if Egyptian rural development is to become an ongoing and self-sustaining reality, it must develop an organized cadre of trained administrators and technicians at the local level capable of carrying on the process with a minimum of dependence on outside expatriate assistance. The supply of expatriate financial and technical assistance was perceived to be essential at the outset to plant the seeds of development in the Egyptian countryside. But if those seeds are to grow and flourish, administrators and technicians at the village level must increasingly come to assume the responsibility of planning, devising and implementing projects for their own future.

Since the credibility of the BVS project and the morale of those involved in the project requires the achievement of certain concrete results at an early stage, it was proposed that as many rural infrastructure projects be undertaken in the first year as possible. The physical presence of ongoing projects of the Organization for the Development of the Egyptian Village (ORDEV)[30] in a number of Egyptian Villages will provide a ready local level institutional base with which to link this project. Furthermore, it seems likely that many districts and villages in the more developed and centrally located governorates, al-Faiyum, Giza and al-Minufia, already possess the organizational capability and technical expertise to plan and implement their own infrastructure projects.[31]

The rural infrastructure component of the project focuses on the village council. The elected and appointed members of the village council, acting in conjunction with the council mayor, decide what types of infrastructure projects are needed in their community. The council's administrative and technical staff then prepare the basic technical documents for the desired projects, with assistance as required from markaz and governorate staffs. Completed council proposals are set to the governorate where they are consolidated with those of other village councils and then forwarded on to the BVS Interagency Committee which approves or denies council project proposals on the basis of technical design, cost benefit analysis and environmental and social impact.

In order to ensure quality control and the speedy implementation of approved village council projects, financing of these projects must follow those already being used by BVS. Once the BVS Interagency Committee approves a project, funds are transferred to a governorate service account in the proper governorate. The governor then notifies the village council of interagency approval and upon the dual signature of the governor and the proper BVS official in the governorate, an increment of funds is released to the service account in the village bank that services that village council. With the release of these funds the technical staff of the village council with assistance from the markaz staff begins preparing engineering drawings, bills of quantities and tender specifications as required. Upon completion of the engineering documents, the village council then solicits bids from public and private contractors. These bids are evaluated by the village council with the assistance of the markaz and governorate technical staffs. After the contract is awarded a second increment of funding is released to the service account in the village bank and the contractor will begin work. Further releases of funds to the village bank are based on work progress displayed by the contractors, as evaluated by senior BVS officials in the governorate. In all instances funding of village projects occur only on an incremental basis with proper sign-off procedures by BVS officials. Such funding policies have been adopted to ensure a proper measure of project quality control and speedy work progress by the contractor.

Although most infrastructure projects tend to be designed and implemented by local village councils, whenever a project like a feeder road requires the cooperation of two or more village councils, the markaz council is designated as the appropriate local government unit for project implementation. Moreover since many village councils lack the requisite technical skills to carry out infrastructure projects alone, the bulk of projects do require close village-markaz and even village-governorate cooperation. Close interaction between councils on these three governmental levels, together with the training component of the BVS program, has done much to encourage local village councils to subject projects to more rigorous cost benefit and environmental analysis. One of the principal reasons for close governorate and BVS supervision over village council-implemented projects is the need to instill efficient management and technical practices into the decision-making structures of these bodies.

IMPLEMENTATION ISSUES AND STRATEGIES IN THE BVS PROGRAM

The Egyptian administrative system has an information and reporting system. Yet such information gathering activities tend to document the observance of procedures and rules governing the processes of decision-making, budgetary control, etc., rather than performance. The BVS program has sought to shift the focus of this information gathering process away from mere procedures to a much greater concern for program impact and performance. The BVS program has sought to develop a simple information system in which timely feedback will be given to local government staff. As this information gathering process is used for problem-solving and mid-course corrections at the governorate, district, and village level, monitoring tends to be a live process, perceived by staff as functional. Special effort has been made to monitor project progress and to emphasize such feedback as being directly relevant to program management by virtue of the information it provides during the process of implementation. Given the many administrative constraints existing in rural Egypt, an effective and timely monitoring process is a useful tool for raising the level of motivation and commitment of the local staff people charged with the responsibility of implementation.

Program implementation is the difficult process of translating general project goals into verifiable project results with hoped for impact. An effective implementation planning process can outline in some detail the critical activities which are needed if the project goals are to be achieved within the agreed upon constraints of time and resources.

The most common problems of effective implementation relate to:

(1) Lack of any effort to identify the activities, the resources, and the coordination needed to start the project.

(2)   Conflicting and often incompatible perceptions among various actors in the project as to what
are the key objectives and goals of the project.

(3)   Unwillingness of the various levels of the
project to develop some consensus on the reporting,
monitoring, allocating, supporting and directing responsibilities each level is to have, the crucial roles
of management and implementation the key actors in the
organization are to play, and some agreed upon problem-
solving mechanisms to facilitate the progress of the
project.

(4)   The common underestimation of time requirements to recruit and train employees, procure and prepare equipment, and orient and put in place the required technical assistance personnel.

(5)   No specific institutionalized process to review, modify, change and adapt original project designs
to the changing environment of the project over time.

In analyzing the process of implementation being
established by the BVS program the following specific
characteristics of implementation need to be considered:

(1)   Regardless of the care and sophistication of
the project planning process the actual implementation
functions of a project will need to be modified, re-
structured, and/or adapted to unanticipated changes
inevitably found in any project environment. Political,
social, economic, administrative, and even cultural
factors are subject to conflicting cross pressures,
unexpected personnel changes, and constantly shifting
demands upon the project environment. The key to effective implementation rests not on the project staff's
ability to consistently reflect the rationally described project plan but rather on the ability of the
project staff to accomplish the desired results and to
achieve the hoped-for purposes in spite of the changing
situations observed in the project environment. Although specific changes can seldom be predicted it is
clear that appropriate preparation of change in general
can be made.

(2)   Implementation requires the cooperation and
commitment of a wide variety of people within the project organization, between agencies involved in the
project and among various levels of government supporting the project. Such cooperation requires first
that all activities and tasks required for project
implementation have been identified, that each person
understands his/her specific duties and responsibilities within the broad framework of the tasks and
activities to be performed, and that specific management systems have been established to direct, motivate
and support the project staff.

(3) Most crucial in the establishment of an implementation process is the need to establish a program schedule which identifies the sequencing of activities, t he prerequisites for the commencing of key subobjectives, and the summarizing of various benchmarks of success which must be reached before later tasks can be started. There are a variety of management tools and information systems which can facilitate the monitoring of progress within the project schedule. Such tools include logical frameworks, performance networks, GANTT, bar, and organizational responsibility charts, and monitoring and reporting plans.[32]

(4) Implementation planning is often defined as a product with a specific set of outputs -- i.e., schedules of activities, definitions of responsibilities, lists of tasks, etc. Unfortunately implementation planning is perceived as a set of outputs (written documents), as if the writing up of such outputs will in fact lead to implementation. Far more significant than the use of certain management tools (GANTT and bar charts, logical frameworks, or performance networks) is the actual process that a project management team goes through to generate such outputs. Thus implementation planning is best conceptualized as a process of interaction by which the participating actors (key management staff) learn to work together.[33] Various team building strategies can be especially helpful as a means of clarifying different points of view, generating greater sensitivity and tolerance of individual differences, developing various interpersonal skills in communication, problem-solving, decision-making, conflict resolution and coordination of diverse activities and responsibilities. Implementation planning is not merely a process of creating a list of who is responsible for what but rather is a process by which the participants in the planning situation come to know each other, come to appreciate the contribution each can make, come to be open and candid in their comments and feelings, and come to take a personal interest in the project. When an outside management facilitator participates with the project staff in an implementation planning process, new kinds of interpersonal ideas can be introduced, new organizations norms which build upon trust, openness, and cooperation can be strengthened, and a variety of skills in giving nonevaluative feedback, conflict resolution, reflective inquiry and process consultation can be made a part of the decision-making and problem-solving procedures needed to initiate the whole process of implementation.

EGYPTIAN BUREAUCRACY - THE REAL CHALLENGE FOR AN EF-
FECTIVE RURAL DEVELOPMENT PROCESS

At this point it may be helpful to review in some
detail the basic characteristics of the Egyptian bureaucracy as a means of identifying the behavioral and
procedural constraints to the implementation of the BVS
program in Egypt.

The key officials in the Ministry of Local Government who have participated in bringing about organizational and procedural changes in the local system of
Egypt over the past two or three decades have learned
that it is not enough to draft a new law, write up new
executive regulations, and issue instructions putting
change into effect. Fundamental changes in the attitudes, behaviors, expectations and levels of motivation must be made at the ministerial, governorate,
district and village levels. Put succintly, effective
change in the local government system of Egypt will
require alterations in the behavior of individuals and
groups that function in the local government system of
Egypt.

Change always upsets the state of affairs in an
organization. Some may welcome the upset because they
found prior conditions restrictive or oppressive.
Others, who had no argument with the old, may also
welcome the new because they see enlarged opportunities
and potential gains. But change in the status quo is
likely to be viewed askance by many who do not want to
be disturbed in their ways and who are uncertain of
what the future may bring in its wake. This is especially true of older persons who no longer have the
energy or the desire to make the effort required to
adjust to the new.

As the Ministry of Local Government begins the
tough work of implementing the BVS program in ways
which will maximize political, economic and social
development in the rural areas of Egypt, it must consider both the factors encouraging change and those
factors that act as barriers to change in Egypt in
order to direct attention to the problems that the
Ministry of Local Government must consider in developing and carrying out its plan.

The first important factor operating in favor of
change in Egypt is the clear evidence that President
Mubarak and his key advisors and ministers strongly
support the new proposals for rural development and the
establishment of an effective system of local government. Second, Egypt has gradually, through successive
shifts and slow changes, provided an environment where
the local councils may begin to function as effective
instruments of representation, planning and evaluation.
Moving very slowly from a fairly centralized system to
a more decentralized one, the local councils have been

given adequate time to prepare for the arduous tasks of self-government. Finally, specific efforts are being made to provide these local councils with funds and resources necessary to eventually emerge as independent local government units capable of identifying needs, generating sufficient funding, developing and implementing programs, and then pursuing the tasks of evaluation and follow-up.

But how does Egypt in the next two or three years implement this new system in the most efficient and effective way? The success of the Ministry of Local Government in implementing rural development programs hinges on the extent to which the Ministry is able to help council members and executive committee members alter their behavior. They will no longer be allowed to do many things that they were accustomed to do and they must learn how to do many new things. Such a transformation of behavior in Egyptian government will not be easy to effect, and unless all of the resources of the ministry in conjunction with all ministries concerned with rural development work together, it is likely that the change expected will not be effectively implemented.

All human behavior is learned. Hence, the success of the implementation process will also depend on the opportunities afforded the members of the local government systems at the ministerial, governorate, district and village level to receive training in new skills. The Ministry of Local Government must provide a climate for learning and devote adequate resources to the task. The acquisition of new skills is the crux of the implementation process.

A whole series of new skills and behaviors is going to be needed if the local government laws are to be implemented effectively:

(1) How to motivate people who are under you, above you and with you.
(2) How to communicate in an effective way which utilizes a two-way system of interaction.
(3) How to monitor and check up on people without making them feel they are being overly supervised and controlled.
(4) How to plan and implement programs which will help people to solve their real problems.
(5) How to acquire technical skills in leadership, budgeting, preparing agendas, plans of action, and community development strategies.

Adults usually learn more informally, largely as a result of alterations in the environment. All the training in the world will introduce no change unless

behaviors are changed. A whole series of changes will
be required. The relationships between supervisors and
subordinates, the criteria used to assess good work,
the level of expectation and activity, and the incentive and reward system are all required if new behaviors are to emerge. The challenge that the Ministry
of Local Government faces is to alter the basic mechanism and controls available to it in such a manner that
they contribute individually and collectively to bringing about the changes in behaviors of elected members
in the councils and the appointed members of the executive committees required to make a success of the new
local government system. To this end the ministry must
introduce appropriate changes in its personnel policies
and in its control measures; it must also make provisions for a continual monitoring and feedback system
including periodic surveys of villagers' opinions, continual visits from district level supervisors, and opportunities for executive committees and council
members as a group to visit the district offices for
team-building training and encouragement. Only a continual interaction between district-level and village-
level officials will stimulate the effort required to
make the village council a viable institution of change
and development.

One of the key responsibilities the Ministry of
Local Government must face is the establishment of an
incentive and reward system that clearly and quickly
rewards the new behaviors desired. For example, any
individual who knows the villages of Egypt well re-
cognizes that the officials who work in the villages,
except for a few, tend to be one or more of the following: Apathetic: "There is nothing I can do."
Unconcerned: "They (fellahin) really don't want to
change any way." Critical and superior: "They
(fellahin) are really too stupid to understand what I
am trying to do." Isolated and lonely: "I am so far
from my friends and family, and no one here really
cares about me." Discouraged: "I really tried for the
first few months but nothing happened." Anxious to
leave: "I will soon be leaving--let the next person
try to do something." Helpless and unqualified: "I
have never lived in a village before, and there is so
much to do, and I don't know where to start." Fearful
and unsure: "Some of the key people in the village
told me to mind my business and do what they say, and I
will be all right." Indifferent: "I do what is required in paper work and no more--that is what I am
paid for." Easy-going: "Ma'alaysh, baada bukra,
inshallah; we may try something." These attitudes will
dominate in the villages until there is an incentive or
reason to change. The Ministry of Local Government and
most other ministries will continue to pour hundreds of

thousands of Egyptian pounds into wages for their officials and employees with very little effect until the behaviors needed are identified, practiced, encouraged, and rewarded. It is recommended that careful analysis of the pay scale and alternative programs be considered, especially at the village and district levels. At the present time there is little distinction between competent and incompetent village chairmen or between aggressive, highly motivated district leaders and the more passive officials in terms of pay or special bonuses. Obviously, criteria of effectiveness must be developed to reward and reinforce those behaviors needed to ensure the effectiveness of the new local government system.

The Ministry of Local Government must recognize and surmount another hurdle in its personnel actions if a plan for change is to have any chance of succeeding. It must be alert to the key officials in the ministry and governorates who cannot or will not support the new system. Opposition to the changes may arise from different sources and express itself in different forms, but in any case such behavior, unless checked and contained, can prove very disruptive. There is probably no greater threat to the implementation of the BVS program than if key officials, at whatever level of local government, through lack of capacity or lack of willingness do not uphold and support the new system. For the success of this new local government program depends upon the integrity and competency of those responsible for implementing this program.

CONCLUSION

One key factor related to the success of the BVS program is the identification and development of program staff and local council members. The routinized processes of the Egyptian government for the recruitment, development, and compensation of personnel run counter to the more flexible processes that might be available. The BVS program needs to identify, select and develop an effective administrative cadre. Thus it is recognized that the match between people and program tasks becomes crucial. The administrative and managerial requirements of the BVS program calls for significant departure from and flexibility with the normal rules and procedures of the Egyptian system. Part of the reason for granting some measure of autonomy to the BVS program is to facilitate modest departures from these norms and to enable them to evolve more suitable processes to recruit and train their staff. For the BVS program to be successful it must be sensitive to human skills and motivation, and this will require a significant commitment to careful recruitment, selection and training.

The Egyptian government officials identified four positive trends in the environment as they began their search for a rural development strategy.

(1) The basic needs for water and transportation were widely supported.

(2) The existence of an already established local council system which could identify projects, marshal local support, and oversee implementation.

(3) A support system in the local government hierarchy at the governorate, district and village level which could provide technical help in engineering, designing and quality control specifications.

(4) A local capability in the project implementation by local private sector contractors.

Based upon recent literature in rural development management, the BVS program appears to reflect some sound management approaches. Even though there was some pressure to pursue a wide variety of goals articulated by experts in health, education, agriculture, and welfare, both Egyptian and USAID officials involved in the design of the BVS program seem to have opted for the pursuit of a single or dominate goal: the transfer of adequate capital to local village councils in ways which will strengthen the capability to plan, implement and keep up various infrastructure projects. This single thrust approach, which focuses on strengthening the administrative and managerial capability of the local government system in Egypt, gives them an achievable goal to begin with.

NOTES

1. For a critical review of these institutes see: Francis Sutton "American Foundations and Public Management in Developing Countries" in Lawrence D. Stifel, et al., Education and Training for Public Sector Management in Developing Countries (New York: Rockefeller Foundation, 1977); Dwight W. Waldo "Reflections on Public Administration and National Development," International Social Science Journal, 26, 2, 1969.

2. Nasir Islam and Georges M. Herrault, "From GNP to Basic Needs: A Critical Review of Development and Development Administration," International Review of Administrative Science 45, 3 (1979) 257.

3. J. Waterston, Development Planning: Lessons of Experience (Baltimore, Johns Hopkins Press, 1965).

122

4. C. Leys, "A New Conception of Planning" in M. Faber and D. Seers, eds. The Crisis in Planning (London: Chatto and Windus, 1972).

5. Recent books which seek to articulate a development process that is more implementation oriented include: N. Caiden and A. Wildavsky, Planning and Budgeting in Poor Countries (New York: Wiley, 1974); M. Faber and D. Seers, eds. The Crisis in Planning (London: Chatto and Windus, 1972); and O. Mehmet, Economic Planning and Social Justice in the Developing Countries (London: Groom Helm, 1978).

6. Islam and Henault, 258.

7. Richard W. Gable, Development Administration: Background Terms, Concepts, Theories and a New Approach. (Washington: SICA-American Society for Public Administration, 1976).

8. Mahbub-ul-Haq, The Poverty Curtain: Choices for the Third World (New York: Columbia University Press, 1976) 33-34.

9. U.S. Public Law 93-189, Foreign Assistance Act of 1973, 87 Stat. 714, Section 2 (B) (5).

10. See: Charles Elliott, Patterns of Poverty in the Third World (New York: Praeger, 1975) and Raanan Weitz, From Peasant to Farmer (New York: Columbia University Press, 1971) James B. Mayfield, Local Institutions and Egyptian Rural Development (Ithaca, N.Y.: Rural Development Committee, Cornell University, 1974), and K. Griffin and Azizur Rahman Khan, Growth and Inequality in Pakistan (London: MacMillan, 1972).

11. Robert S. McNamara, President's Address to the Board of Governors, (1973), 16-17.

12. Marcus Ingle, Dennis Rondinelli, and Thyra Riley, "Managing Benefits for the Poor: Approaches, Experience, and Strategies for Improvement"(Washington, D.C.: Practical Concepts Incorporated, 1981), 1-3.

13. U.S. Agency for International Development, Country Development Strategy Statement, FY 1982, Philippines (Washington, D.C.: U.S. International Development Cooperation Agency, 1980), p. 1. For a critical review of how little we really know about the rural poor in the Third World see: Robert Chambers, "Rural Poverty Unperceived: Problems and Remedies" (Brighton, UK: University of Sussex, Unpublished Manuscript, 1980).

14. Ingle, et al., Managing Benefits 1-6.

15. See: G. Hunter and A. Bottrall, eds., Serving the Small Farmer: Policy Choices in Indian Agricultural Development (London: Groom Helm, 1974), p. 17, and David K. Leonard, Reaching the Small Farmers: Organization Theory and Practice in Kenya (Chicago:University of Chicago Press, 1977).

16. Robert Chambers, "Project Selection for Poverty-Focuses Rural Development: Simple is Optimal," World Development, 6, (1978) 389-416.

17. USAID, Country Development Strategy Statement (Egypt). Annex E. Decentralization: Status, Constraints and Strategy, (Washington, D.C.: Agency for International Development, February 1983), p. 6.

18. Samir Radwan. Agrarian Reform and Rural Poverty in Egypt 1952-1975 (Geneva: International Labor Office, 1977); J. Field and G. Ropes, "Development in the Egyptian Governorates: A Modified Physical Quality of Life Index." L'Egypte Contemporaine, 69, (April 1978) 149-161. Muhmoud A. Fadil, Development, Income Distribution and Social Change in Rural Egypt, 1952-1970 (Cambridge: Cambridge University Press, 1975).

19. Saad M. Gadalla, Land Reform in Relation to Social Development in Egypt (Columbia, MO: University of Missouri Press, 1967); Magdi M. El-Kammash, Economic Development and Planning in Egypt (New York: Frederick A. Praeger, 1968); Donald C. Mead, Growth and Structural Change in the Egyptian Economy (Homewood, Illinois: Richard D. Irwin Inc., 1967); and Gabriel S. Saab, The Egyptian Agrarian Reform, 1952-1962 (London: Oxford University Press, 1967)

20. John Waterbury, Hydropolitics of the Nile Valley (Syracuse: Syracuse University Press, 1979); James B. Mayfield and Muhammad Naguib, "The Challenge of Implementing an Irrigation Program in an Egyptian Village," (Cairo: Egypt Water Use and Management Project, 1980).

21. For a good analysis of rural institutions functioning in the villages of Egypt see: Iliya Harik, The Political Mobilization of Peasants: A Study of an Egyptian Community (Bloomington: Indiana University Press, 1974) and Richard H. Adams, Jr. "Growth Without Development in Rural Egypt: A Local-Level Study of Institutional and Social Change" (Berkeley: University of California, Unpublished Dissertation, 1981).

22. James B. Mayfield, Rural Politics of Nasser's Egypt, Chapter 8, (Austin: University of Texas Press, 1970), and Ali Fowzi Yunis, The Legal Basis of Egyptian Decentralization: A Historical Review: in Building Capacity for Decentralization in Egypt, edited by Tjip Walker (Washington, D.C.: Development Alternatives, Inc., RD Working Paper 10, 1981).

23. The Village Executive Council (Maglis al-Tanfizi) which is made up of key government officials representing the Ministries of Health, Education, Social Affairs, Agriculture, Housing and Local Government is mistakenly called the Village Council (Maglis al-Qarya) by many of the sources contacted in rural areas.

124

24. For a good description of the village councils' potential for rural development in Egypt, see: Abdolhossain Zahedani et al., The Basic Village Service Program: Technical and Financial Assessment (Washington, D.C.: Development Alternatives, Inc., 1980).

25. For an analysis of the local politics in Egypt and its impact on local government institutions see: James B. Mayfield, Rural Politics in Nasser's Egypt, Chapter 6 (Austin: University of Texas Press, 1971). Leonard Binder, In A Moment of Enthusiasm: Political Powers and the Second Stratum, (Chicago: University of Chicago, 1978); Fathy A. Fatah, The Contemporary Village Between Reform and Revolution, 1952-1970 (Cairo: Daral-Thaqata-al-Jadida, 1975, in Arabic).

26. While there has been a fair amount of continuity from one village council to the next since village councils were established by Law 124 in 1960, it appears that President Sadat did structure the 1975 elections to ensure that a new group of rural leaders were elected who would be more supportive of his government's new programs and polices. See: James B. Mayfield, Local Government in Egypt: Some New Change Strategies and Training Opportunities (Washington, D.C.: Agency for International Development, 1976) 16-34.

27. D. Mickelwait, D. Stanfield, I. Omar, and G. Cilerts, "Monitoring and Evaluating Decentralization: The Basic Village Service Program in Egypt"(Washington, D.C.: Development Alternatives Inc., 1980).

28. See: James B. Mayfield, Local Government in Egypt: Some New Change Strategies and Training Opportunities (Washington, D.C.: Agency for International Development, 1976), 11-15.

29. For a detailed analysis of the village executive council and its role in the administrative and budgetary process, see: James B. Mayfield, The Budgetary System in the Arab Republic of Egypt: Its Role in Local Government Development (Washington, D.C.: Agency for International Development, 1977).

30. The role of the ORDEV organization is significant enough in its role in Egyptian Rural Development to warrant a totally separate study. For a general summary as to how ORDEV functions as an institutional link between the Government of Egypt, USAID, and local government units in the governorates, districts, and villages see: James B. Mayfield, The Budgetary System in the Arab Republic of Egypt: Its Role in Local Government Development (Washington, D.C.: Agency for International Development, 1977).

31. Abdolhossain Zahedani, et. al. The Basic Village Service Program, Egypt: Technical and Financial

Assessment (Washington, D.C.: Development Alternatives, Inc., 1980).
32. For a detailed description of these management tools see Marcus Ingle, Procalfer Management and Implementation Manual (Washington, D.C.: Development Project Management Center, US Dept. of Agriculture, 1981), 10-32.
33. R. Chambers, Managing Rural Development: Ideas and Experiences From East Africa. (Appsala: Scandinavian Institute of Africa Studies, 1974).

Introduction to Part III

Jean-Claude Garcia-Zamor

The four chapters in this part provide case studies of public participation in Sri Lanka, the Philippines, Bangladesh, and the Yemen Arab Republic. In the first chapter, Norman Uphoff discusses popular participation in water management in Gal Oya, Sri Lanka. The experience of the Agrarian Research and Training Institute (ARTI) in Colombo and the Rural Development Committee of Cornell University offers an extended case study of participatory planning and management. This team created farmer organizations in the Gal Oya irrigation scheme in southeastern Sri Lanka to achieve more participatory water management.

The rehabilitation project for Gal Oya as initially designed gave little attention or resources for the "software" of irrigation improvement. No funds were provided for introducing farmer organization, though ARTI was requested to undertake collection of socioe-conomic baseline data, monitor and evaluate studies, and develop and test a "model" of such organization. The presumption of the project design was that farmers' behavior was the "problem" and tighter control and discipline by technicians was the "solution." Most inefficiency in the system was thought to exist at the field channel (tertiary) level.

Such presumptions were found incorrect once research and observations had been done. For achieving the ultimate project objective of better water use, the development of farmer participation in water management, operation and maintenance, planning, conflict resolution, resource mobilization, etc. was as important as the physical rehabilitation of the system. The system could deteriorate to its previous state fairly quickly without such cooperation.

According to Uphoff, it became quickly evident that the greatest problems were at the main system, not tertiary level, as water allocation within the system overall was more unequal than farmers' allocation of water among themselves. Engineers' performance was in

127

many ways the "problem," to be improved through what came to be known from this and other project experience as "bureaucratic reorientation." The initial presumption that farmers would not change their behavior and activities unless and until engineers changed theirs proved to be incorrect. One of the main "lessons" from this experience was that performance change is more iterative and interactive. Farmers' initial participatory management efforts helped to change engineers' stereotypes and attitudes, and engineers' more respectful orientation in turn encouraged farmers to demonstrate still more responsibility.

Uphoff found that many things had to be learned and unlearned in the course of implementation. ARTI and Cornell explicitly adopted a "learning process" approach in this project, coming to describe their strategy as one of "inductive planning," with hypotheses formulated in advance of action, but continually reassessed and modified in light of unfolding experience. The role of a "knowledge-building institution" played by ARTI, and supported by Cornell, was crucial for thinking through an effective on-the-ground program to promote farmer participation. The Irrigation Department, which was not initially very supportive of such participation, came to accept and collaborate in this experiment as positive results accumulated.

The second chapter, written by Frances F. Korten, analyzes a participative approach to irrigation development in the Philippines. In 1976 the National Irrigation Administration (NIA) of the Philippines began experimenting with a participatory approach to irrigation development. By 1982, the participatory approach had grown to a full scale national program involving a total of over 140 irrigation systems. The NIA experience holds lessons regarding both the importance of people's participation and the nature of the bureaucratic reorientation needed to support it. Under the participatory approach, the NIA community provided assistance to small scale gravity irrigation systems for many years. Minimal attention was given to the local farmers who were expected to manage and maintain the irrigation system once construction was completed.

Experience with the participatory approach indicated it improved the economic and social impact of the projects in a variety of ways. The use of the knowledge of both the farmers and the NIA technical staff appeared to result in system layouts and designs that were better than those done by technical staff alone. While the approach brought numerous advantages, it also imposed demands on the agency. It called for hiring a community organizer to work with each association and required "lead time" before construction so that the association could be developed and involved in preconstruction activities. In general, the participatory approach generated a context in which farmers demanded greater accountability on the part of the agency, and the agency demanded greater contributions on the part of the farmers. Engineers at the NIA were sufficiently convinced about the superior nature of the approach that was adopted in all of NIA's small scale irrigation work and was being adapted to large scale irrigation systems development as well. To maximize the learning that accrued from these projects, process documentation research was done on several of the pilot sites. For this research full-time social scientists were assigned to several pilot sites to provide monthly reports on the activities and concerns of farmers, community organizers, and engineers. This process documentation provided detailed knowledge of the field level action, so that the implications for agency change could be discovered even by those not directly involved in the field.

The third chapter, by Mohammad Mohabbat Khan, discusses experiences of rural development programs in Bangladesh. People's participation in the sense of active involvement in policy planning and decisions pertaining to implementation of rural development programs (RDPs) have not taken place in Bangladesh. All government-sponsored RDP's have intended to mobilize rural masses to increase agricultural production. The reasons for nonparticipation of the rural poor, who form the majority of the population, in RDP's are: (a) the highly stratified nature (in class terms) of Bangladesh society in which a microscopic minority of rich and middle-income farmers in the rural areas have links to urban politicians, bureaucrats and intellectuals allowing them to exploit the rural masses by strictly owning and controlling the means of production and (b) a bureaucratic-technocratic bias in rural development. To ensure meaningful participation of the rural poor and disadvantaged, Khan suggests that the following should be done: (a) rethinking about rural people and rural institutions, (b) undertaking drastic land reform measures, (c) redistribution of surplus land to landless peasants, (d) formation of production-oriented cooperatives where small farmers will have their say, (e) encouraging agricultural laborers to form trade unions to strengthen their bargaining power, and (f) elimination of any kind of bureaucratic management and control in RDP's.

The fourth chapter, by Sheila Carapico, discusses self-help and development planning in the Yemen Arab Republic (YAR). Under rather unique circumstances, local development associations in the Yemen Arab Republic have been notably successful in bringing basic services to rural and urbanized areas. They have extended rough vehicular tracks to virtually every village and hamlet, built thousands of primary schools, improved water collection and storage facilities, and contributed to health, electricity, and other public services. In the absence of alternative institutions to mobilize development resources, informal and semiformal efforts to raise capital for social and economic infrastructure have been significant.

Indirectly, local and regional associations have drawn on the remitted earnings of emigrant labor which provided discretionary cash income to many families during the 1970s' oil boom in the Arab Gulf. The dispersion of cash among large numbers of households, outside banks and beyond the state's taxation capacity, made it possible to raise money in the form of voluntary contributions and locally administered taxes. Initially local and regional efforts were able to provide a very rudimentary level of services with only a minimum of planning, and an ad hoc organizational framework. Gradually, however, active associations have come to appreciate the necessity of some centralization and rationalization of planning processes. To meet the imperatives of the 1980s -- a more sophisticated level of services and increased capital investment in productive activities -- new and more carefully planned financial and organizational procedures are being fostered by the YAR government. It is hoped that in the coming decade local associations and cooperatives will continue to provide development services in coordination with ministries and central credit facilities.

7. People's Participation in Water Management: Gal Oya, Sri Lanka

Norman Uphoff

The desirability of having more participation by the beneficiaries of development projects is not much disputed. There remain, however, many questions and reservations about the practicality of and the procedures for such participation. Empirical considerations are the most pressing ones: What kinds of participation are required, by whom, and under what circumstances? What factors inherent in public participation are most likely to contribute the success or failure of development efforts? Work done under the auspices of the Rural Development Committee (RDC) at Cornell University has shed light on these factors both in terms of conceptualization and field experience.[1]

Probably the most instructive experience in which the RDC has been involved concerns introducing people's participation in an irrigation water management project in Sri Lanka. This has been undertaken by the Agrarian Research and Training Institute (ARTI) in Colombo with RDC collaboration under the AID-financed Gal Oya Water Management Project started in 1979. The RDC was supported by the Rural Development Participation project (1977-82) and funded under a cooperative agreement with AID's Office of Rural Development and Development Administration (now Office of Multi-Sectorial Development). It is being continued with direct funding from the AID mission in Sri Lanka.

THE GAL OYA PROJECT

Sri Lanka has relied on irrigated rice (paddy) production for at least 2,500 years, having developed sophisticated tank irrigation systems before the Christian era. In this century, efforts were made to improve irrigation performance by the rehabilitation of ancient tanks and the construction of several new ones. The largest project to date, the Gal Oya irrigation system, was created by construction of a major new reservoir, completed in 1952, with a storage capacity

131

of 770,000 acre-feet. It was planned to irrigate 120,000 acres, 42,000 of which would be served by the Left Bank main canal. Since then, between 15,000 and 25,000 acres have been added to the Left Bank command area, most without authorization. The largest concentration of low-income farmers are to be found on the Left Bank. Because the area to be served has expanded, the system of canals and control structures to deliver and distribute the water has deteriorated badly.

The Government of Sri Lanka, acting through its Irrigation Department (ID), and USAID began to improve water management capacity in Sri Lanka by rehabilitating the Left Bank of Gal Oya and to introduce improved organization and training for water management.[2] It was recognized that improving water management in Sri Lanka would take one or two decades and would not be accomplished through this single project. But the Gal Oya project was a first step, intended to develop institutional capabilities, personnel, and operating principles for extension to other areas through subsequent projects. Such a long-range plan is an important, but often overlooked aspect of donor-assisted projects.

In retrospect, it may have been unwise to embark on a process as complicated and ambitious as making institutional and behavioral changes among officials, engineers, and farmers with an irrigation system that was not only the largest in the country, but also the most problem ridden. The canal system was extremely long and complex; many of the areas did not have good soils for irrigation; the water supply was usually inadequate for the command area (the tank had filled in only two of thirty years). There were significant ethnic differences and tensions between the Sinhalese settlers (at the head of the system) and the Tamils (located at the tail), increasing the divergence of interests between those served first and last by water deliveries. Indeed, the lower third of the system was not getting water for irrigation and barely enough for domestic purposes during the dry (yala) season. To compound the problems, Gal Oya being relatively remote from Colombo, was regarded as an undesirable posting for government staff and was characterized by low morale and rapid personnel turnover.

The project staff presumed that most of the inefficiencies in water use were at the tertiary (field channel) level rather than a result of shortcomings in main system management.[3] Farmers were seen as the "problem" and the Irrigation Department's planning and enforcement of water delivery schedules were seen as the "solution." Farmer regimentation and law enforcement rather than farmer organization and participation as the strategy for improving water management at the field channel level was the practice. In fact, subsequent monitoring of the amount and reliability of water deliveries and of yield variations showed that any improvement in water management was to be achieved at the primary rather than the tertiary level. Cursory field studies quickly showed that the ID's operation of the system was a significant part of the problem. So in a fundamental sense, the project design was ill conceived. The AID mission recognized the deficiencies of this approach and added provisions for farmer organization as well as systematic socio-economic research on the project area to the project design. With ID approval, ARTI was subcontracted to take responsibility for both the farmer organization and socioeconomic research activities.

Apart from a generalized endorsement of farmer water user organization (the project paper called for all 19,000 farmers in the project area to be "organized" at the end of the project's fourth year), the only participation explicitly provided for was for farmers to contribute free labor to reshape and improve all field channels, as funding was budgeted only for primary and secondary level rehabilitation work. There was no consultation with any farmers about this. It was simply assumed that this would be done and that it would constitute farmer "participation." While this provision may be objected to on normative grounds, as will be seen, in retrospect, it was turned to the farmers' advantage, in the curious way that many beneficial [4] project outcomes are unintended and unanticipated. The strength of the project's design was that it allocated funding from the start for systematic research on the area (though ARTI's socioeconomic work amounted to 4.5 percent of total project cost) and engaged two knowledge-building institutions (ARTI and Cornell) of the sort that Korten describes and prescribes for a "learning process" approach to development. This meant that there was capacity within the project for redefining problems and redirecting efforts as experience and data warranted. [5]

INITIAL ACTIVITIES

A Water Management Research Group was constituted within ARTI to carry out its responsibilities under the project, with just three research and training officers (R&TO). A fourth R&TO, not assigned to the group, was at this time beginning graduate studies at Cornell and became part of the water management group at Cornell supporting the project. ARTI prepared a draft plan for socioeconomic monitoring, evaluation and research, while the Cornell group tackled questions of farmer organization strategy, building on its knowledge of

similar efforts elsewhere. Two members of the Cornell
faculty visited Sri Lanka briefly during the fall of
1979 to assist in training field investigators and
refining the data gathering instruments.[6]
The initial conclusion was that the mandate given
ARTI and Cornell in the project paper to develop, test
and extend a model for farmer organization was not
appropriate. No single "model" (blueprint) was likely
to be optimal for the whole project area given its
hydrological and sociological diversity, and moreover,
no systematic testing would be possible under the constraints of working within a government-run project.
Instead it was decided to seek development of a "process" for introducing farmer organization, not speci-
fying in advance much about the nature or structure of
such organization. Such specificity would be introduced on an experimental basis as more became known
about the situation and needs in Gal Oya and would be
modified as experience was gained.
By January 1980, ARTI had formulated a program of
socio-economic research approved by AID and ID. Also
during that month, the author, Walt Coward (a rural
sociologist from Cornell) and David Korten (an administration specialist with the Ford Foundation in Manila,
assisting the National Irrigation Administration with
introduction of farmer organization in the Philippines)
visited Gal Oya for the first time with members of the
ARTI Water Management Research Group (C.M. Wijayaratne,
M.L. Wickramasinghe, and H.A. Rambanda) to assess the
situation.
It quickly became clear that the situation was
much more complicated than the project design team had
appreciated. For example, there were large areas cultivated with drainage water which were not officially
recognized; it was not clear how they would be related
to the recognized water users, since gains in water use
efficiency by the latter would cut the supply of water
to the former and create a serious conflict situation;
also since the former were not legal cultivators, their
status was ambiguous. The appropriateness of what
Korten had proposed as a "learning process" approach to
rural development became very much apparent. The most
important new appreciation we gained was that given the
tense, even conflictual relations between farmers and
technical staff of the ID, our task could not focus
narrowly on "organizing farmers." Much of the so-
called water "waste" by farmers reflected the un-
certainty of water deliveries and the poor management
of the main system. We formulated as a group the proposition (subsequently modified as discussed later)
that unless and until the staff of the Irrigation
Department changed their behavior and attitudes, one
could and should not expect farmers to change their

behavior and attitudes. Although we had no recognized mandate to work with the Irrigation Department in this regard, we were convinced that we had to expand our focus of activity and interaction to include the ID staff.

Also, we needed to gain a better understanding of how the main system was operated, and it was arranged that a Ph.D. candidate in agricultural engineering from Cornell would spend sixteen months doing research on the Gal Oya system, feeding technical knowledge into the organizational efforts which ARTI was about to undertake. His liaison with the Irrigation Department proved to be an added contribution to the farmer organization effort. Also with AID funding, Cornell was able to second to ARTI for a year beginning in June 1980 a geographer (Edward Vander Velde) with experience on irrigation and water management in India, to strengthen the interdisciplinary team work there.

From problems identified in this initial exploration and from subsequent experience and discussion, two concepts emerged which had guided the work, explicitly or implicitly. For capacity to be created among rural people for participatory development, there needed to be more favorable attitudes and more supportive performance of functions from the relevant officials and technicians working with them. The need to consider the operation of the bureaucracy working with rural clienteles, and not to focus just on the clienteles by themselves, led to the concept of "bureaucratic reorientation" as an objective and as a strategy. Second, while the concept of "learning process" is both valid and valuable, it implies less structure than may be desirable. The idea of "inductive planning" has been suggested as the converse of conventional "deductive planning."[9] The latter presumes to know all ends and means in advance of action and leads to the "blueprint" approach which Korten has correctly criticized. An inductive approach points practitioners and researchers toward the specification of hypotheses according to which initial planning is formulated, but planning is an ongoing process, and specific plans are modified as experience warrants revision and presents new problems for resolution. One begins with some specification of ends and means; both are subject to reassessment throughout the project. This is antithetical to a "blueprint" approach, and might be viewed as a methodology or application of "learning" process.[10]

I will first review the basic "hypotheses" on which the farmer organization effort was based. Then I will discuss the strategy for introducing farmer organization and getting it established in the field. Third, I will review our learning to date, how the initial hypotheses have stood up, or not. Finally, I

will highlight what have been the most significant or
unexpected things learned so far. We have tried to
avoid using the word success to characterize the program, preferring to think and speak in terms of progress. To be sure, this has been much greater and more
rapid than any of us involved with the program expected
three years ago. We have encountered and continue to
have many problems; and we can anticipate some major
difficulties that could arise in the short- or long-run
for the program. So we are clear about reserving judgment on it even as others are less hesitant to brand it
a success. The program has passed some critical tests,
including several unintended ones which threatened the
program's standing. The main indicators of progress
are the momentum and reputation it has built up, among
officials and farmers, and the widespread acceptance it
has earned.

PROGRAM DESIGN

The initial premises or assumptions on which the
program was based were spelled out in the various documents and memos drafted by ARTI and Cornell personnel
between January and July 1980. In formal terms they
can be treated as hypotheses, though this is not necessary. The main thing is that they were explicit in the
planning of the program, as follows:

Farmer organizations for water management would be
more likely to succeed in this situation if introduced
by specially recruited and trained "catalysts" rather
than by the regular government staff. Our first visit
in 1980, reinforced by the feedback which ARTI was
getting through its field investigators doing socio-
economic research, persuaded us that some kind of new
start was needed. Our team was indelibly impressed by
the plea from one tail-end farmer with whom we had just
spent several hours in a group discussion, tugging on
the sleeve of an ARTI colleague, asking that the rehabilitation project be implemented by some other, any
other, agency than the ID. Conversely, engineers expressed no willingness to have farmers undertake responsibilities for water management. Such was the
level of mutual confidence and regard. At the seasonal
irrigation planning meeting between officials and
farmers on Gonagolla branch channel in the project area
(March 1980), farmers berated the ID staff for poor
performance, nonfunctioning gates, poor attendance at
the office, etc., a situation the more tense because it
was Sinhalese farmers criticizing Tamil officers. (As
seen below, this situation was turned around completely
within a few months once farmer organization was introduced.)

We know of the positive experience in the Philippines where the National Irrigation Administration engaged "community organizers" to help farmers set up Irrigators' Service Associations, to plan improvement of their dams and canals with NIA engineers, to help in construction, and to assume responsibility for their management and repayment upon completion.[11] We also knew of the FAO-supported Small Farmer Development Program (SFDP) in Nepal and other Asian countries which had introduced "group organizers" into communities with great success.[12] One of our Rural Development Committee studies had also concluded that "catalyst agents" were likely to be needed in programs aimed at reaching and assisting the rural poor.[13] So under the circumstances, we proceeded on the assumption that some such role would have to be designed and that appropriate persons would need to be recruited and trained and deployed. (This turned out to be much more difficult and protracted than initially indicated to us by government officials, but that is a long story.)

It would be better to begin with "informal" organization and to proceed toward more "formal" organization as members gain experience and confidence. Sri Lanka has had a rich history of rural local organizations, local governments, cooperatives, Rural Development Societies, etc., but the majority have not sustained their effectiveness over time.[14] They often start quite energetically but decline after the initial impetus and become pro forma. As the director of ARTI said, it is not difficult to set up organizations in rural Sri Lankan communities--the difficult thing is to keep them going. Trying to profit from previous experience, we conceived of starting to work informally, with farmers organizing their own water rotation and channel maintenance activities in whatever way they preferred. They would elect a representative when they were ready to work through someone, but not a slate of officers as is usually done, with a government charter and a bank account, etc. Conventional organizations are usually led (and dominated) by a set of leaders who are politically motivated and possibly biased toward more privileged interests. It was thought that by starting with practical work, rather than formal organization, those leaders who were less self-serving and who were capable of handling technical and organizational matters involved in water management would distinguish themselves. Such a new cadre at the local level would likely remain unmobilized if we started with formal election of officers as the first step in the organizing process. When there was reason to elect a number of officers and get official recognition of the organization, this could be done to meet the needs of the members.

Rather than start by organizing water users at the
secondary (D-channel) level, involving fifty to two
hundred farmers, it would be better to initiate organizations at the tertiary (field channel) level, involving ten to twenty farmers; the structure of organization that would emerge would build from the bottom
up, based on cohesive primary groups. A consultant on
irrigation law provided to the Government of Sri Lanka
by USAID had proposed enactment of a new irrigation
ordinance which provided for a comprehensive system of
water user associations. These would be initiated by
irrigation engineers (in contrast to our first hypothesis), would be conventional formal-legal entities (in
contrast to our second), and would focus at the distributary level, with field channel representatives or
committees as subsidiaries of the D-channel organization. Sociological theory and experience elsewhere
in Asia suggest the importance of small groups as the
"building blocks" of any larger-scale organization.[15]
The organizational effort might take somewhat longer
when following this (and the second) hypothesis, but it
was expected the results would be more effective and
lasting.

The boundaries of water user organizations should
match areas defined hydrologically rather than administratively. Settlers in Gal Oya had been assigned to
colony units and fell under the jurisdiction of different gram sewakas (village-level officers), agrarian
service centers, subdistricts (AGA areas), and districts (presided over administratively by a government
agent, and politically by a district minister). Unfortunately, these areas differed from the various
command areas served by field channels, distributaries,
branch canals and main canals in an ascending order.
Where administrative boundaries are numerous, putting
head- and tail-enders under different jurisdictions
complicates the normal problems of getting communication and cooperation between these cultivators. So
the organizational effort was planned to proceed along
hydrological lines, trying to unite water users within
the respective command areas below field channel turnouts, distributary offtakes, and main or branch canals.
(The proposed revisions of the irrigation ordinance
referred to above had made the assumption.) It was
assumed that there were probably at least some informal
communication and cooperation already, at least along
field channels, though there was often also a legacy of
conflict and distrust to be overcome. Head- and tail-
enders in any command area would have conflicting
interests when water was scarce, but a common interest
vis-a-vis other water users is getting more total water

for their area. Farmers along a D-channel would similarly have a common interest as would those aggregated at higher levels within the system.

The promotion of improved water management would proceed better and produce better results if not focused exclusively on water management, but rather if associated agricultural and social activities were undertaken by the organizations when and as members desired them. This could be stated as a paraphrase of the Chinese development motto, take water management as the base but encourage all-round production. It was difficult because the organizational effort was taking place under the aegis of the Irrigation Department, which had water management but not agriculture as its mandate. The Department of Agriculture handling extension, and the Department of Agrarian Services handling inputs both came under a different ministry. In the past, each department had sought to have its own organizational base at the local level, creating competition and confusion.[16] Avoiding this was our initial and sufficient rationale, but other reasons emerged as well. First, at the head where water supply was not a major problem, but where organization was needed to encourage and enforce more efficient use of water thereby saving it for the tail, water management would probably not be a sufficient boon to give farmers incentive to join and participate actively. Thus improved extension services or better access to credit and inputs could be the side payments that held the organizations together.[17] Second, the productive returns to better water management would be greater to the extent that the complementary inputs were available and used in a timely, correct manner. Thus, all members should have more incentive to participate if they were able to put together a more complete agricultural package through the organization. Third, as we appreciated more clearly later, while farmers at the head, who were overusing water, could economize on its use without reducing their yield, they would get no benefit from their labors unless yields went up. Bringing in other activities to boost production could change a zero-sum situation to a positive-sum one, in effect compensating head-enders for their cooperation in saving water for the tail.

The organizational effort, despite the difficulties entailed, should be linked to the process of physical rehabilitation of the system rather than proceed as a separate and parallel activity as conceived in the project design. The project paper had delegated responsibility for farmer organization to ARTI, expecting this to be done by the end of four years, by which time responsibility for operation and maintenance of the irrigation system at the lower levels would be

handed over to the water user associations, resembling
a "turkey" project. It will be recalled that the project paper also called for farmers to do the tertiary
rehabilitation work themselves, but this was not stipulated as part of the organization process. If this
created antagonism, the organizational effort would be
futile, so in a sense we had no choice but to get engaged in integrating the rehabilitation and organizational planning. Sociological theory clearly suggested it was unlikely that (a) organizations could be
created without some immediate task to form around and
to sustain commitment (starting organizations that
would not be given responsibility for several years
seemed futile), and (b) farmers would feel responsibility for maintaining a system that had been fixed up
for them rather than with them (engagement in the
rehabilitation process if effective should create a
feeling that it was also "their" system). An additional reason was that farmers knew the system and
its problems after thirty years better than any technical staff and could be helpful in identifying these
(and even in suggesting solutions, as engineers found
out once they began entering into consultations with
farmers).[18]

This hypothesis caused the most difficulty of any,
requiring ARTI to tie its schedule of activities and
its deployment of organizers to the reconnaissance and
construction efforts of the ID. Still, it turned out
to be, as discussed later, one of the key decisions,
because it led to closer collaboration with the ID, at
first resisted but eventually accepted. It was essential not only for improving linkages between the
farmers and ID, the main objective of the organizational effort, but also for facilitating BRO. Thus
painful as it often was to carry through, linking
organizational work to rehabilitation activities proved
important to the whole effort.

If farmers were approached in a well-conceived
manner, with their interests clearly to be served, they
would respond with resources, responsibility and initiative. In a sense, this was the overarching hypothesis, and the whole effort ultimately depended on what
talents and efforts could be mobilized from below.
Although Sri Lanka has had an open, democratic system
since independence, it has languished under the legacy
of a colonial-bureaucratic state. Self-restraint
development from the grassroots has been seen from time
to time, enough so that there was reason to expect the
capacity for productive participation existed.[19] But
communities seemed to be oriented to dependent relations with the bureaucracy and parties, alternating
between periods of partisanship and passivity. The
organizational effort had to be an honest one, seeking

mutuality of farmer interests among themselves and with officials, not imposing a manipulative or extractive mechanism upon them. Farmers had to be approached in a respectful, flexible manner, seeking to understand their problems (and their capabilities and sense of responsibility).

The leadership role of ARTI in this effort, the talent and commitment of its core Water Management Group, was certainly necessary. But they will be the first to give credit to the Institutional-Organizers (IOs), discussed next, who brought great energy and intelligence, sensitivity and innovation to the effort in its grassroots application. There were mistakes, most of inexperience and zeal, but the IOs carried the program beyond what ARTI or Cornell could plan and manage. Even more crucial to program progress was mobilization of conscientiousness and creativity within the farming community. This is not to say there have not been disappointments or missed opportunities. But the driving force behind the program, and what has contributed most to the changed attitudes of officials, has been the farmer response. We have seen some slacking off in some areas, but gains in others. We have had to learn to have more realistic expectations of[20] what is possible and what is necessary. But the main lesson has been a confirmation of our macrohypothesis on the potential for productive participation.

PROGRAM STRATEGY

The farmer organization effort revolved around the fielding of Institutional-Organizers (IOs as they came to be called).[21] A number of first-round decisions were made, which can be stated also as hypotheses, subject to continuous review.

At least to begin with, university graduates would be used. Sri Lanka has one of the highest educational levels of any LDC, well above its GNP level.[22] So graduates are available, several thousand being unemployed. We assumed that graduates would grasp the concepts of the program more quickly and would have more status when dealing with officials. On the other side, they might have more difficulty working with farmers given status differences and their cost would be more. By recruiting only graduates with farm backgrounds, preferably from Gal Oya or similar areas, we thought we could minimize the first problem, and we reckoned that if yields could be increased by only five bushels per acre, about fifteen to twenty percent of the potential for improvement, the program would pay for itself, so the second was not a deterrent.[23] We

were prepared to consider secondary graduates at some
later stage once the strategy and roles had been
refined.

The training should combine some presentation of
concepts with some field experience, and also some
social and institutional knowledge with agricultural
and irrigation knowledge. The first batch of IO re-
cruits got two weeks of training in Colombo and then
four weeks in Gal Oya. One innovation was that the
training program was itself made participatory, with
the trainees organized in different committees to take
responsibility for hosting and introducing speakers,
overseeing the canteen and meals, arranging recreation
in free time, etc. In the field visits, IOs were given
responsibility for meeting with farmers and preparing
reports on what they learned to share with others.
Because we gave less technical training to the first
batch, and this was seen as a deficiency, we gave much
more to the second batch, and probably overdid this.
We found that much of the learning for the job occurred
on the job. After six to nine months, from their discussions with farmers and technicians, augmented by
some (but probably less than optimal) in-service training, IOs were quite knowledgeable in most needed areas.
Preservice training was needed certainly for confi-
dence-building.

The main element of organizing strategy was for
IOs to live in the communities and to move closely with
farmers and their families. There was some initial
reservation and even suspicion on the part of farmers.
There had been various other programs where government
staff were sent to the village, though not to stay.
(Also there had been an insurrection in 1971 led by
unemployed radicalized students, and the memories of
such organizing efforts lingered.) In one incident
during the first month of contact, some farmers chid-
ingly described the program as a scheme for unemployed
youth, but were dissuaded of this when an IO who over-
heard the remark asked a nearby farmer planting rice,
whether he could assist. The sureness with which he
broadcast the seed satisfied the skeptics that the IO
was no novice in agriculture and no city snob. IOs
were issued bicycles not motorcycles (unfortunately
often with some delay), and their humble mode of transport (often going on foot) reduced whatever social
distance their education and dress implied. The positive attitudes of IOs toward farmers and their problems
rather quickly broke down social barriers, and one of
the most gratifying things for ARTI and Cornell staff
was to hear the laudatory statements farmers made about
IOs.

The initial strategy was for IOs to get acquainted
with the persons and the area to which they had been

assigned, by compiling profiles to serve as a knowledge base for subsequent work. This gave the IOs something to do when getting started, otherwise it might have been awkward. It turned out to have the danger that farmers would think this was just one more study which would not change or improve their situation. In fact, this initial phase of activity, expected to last up to three months, was cut short and never completed because it seemed more important to respond to the near-drought conditions by getting involved directly in water management efforts. This kind of initiation has been useful in the Philippines NIA and Nepal SFDP experience, but for various reasons it did not figure as prominently in our program's development.

The approach was for IOs to start by dealing with farmers individually, then in small groups, and to organize meetings of all the farmers along a particular field channel only after all had been acquainted with the purposes of the new program. This approach, which amounted to a kind of "nonformal education," differed fundamentally from the usual approach to organization, which consisted of calling all the farmers together for a meeting, having an official explain what was expected of them, and asking them to elect officers and start work as planned by the government. The discussions in this approach centered on the farmers' problems, what they had tried to do about them, what worked or did not work, and what could be done now by group action to deal with these problems.

The IOs would be deployed in teams with group responsibility for larger areas, rather than assigned individual areas of exclusive responsibility. This turned out to be one of the most important elements of the program's strategy, though we arrived at the right thing for the wrong reason, one might say. One of the corollary hypotheses to be tested in Sri Lanka rural conditions was whether women could be effective as IOs. In the Philippine experience, women were at least as effective as men in organizing roles (and some would say more effective). Sri Lanka has more taboos about what unmarried women can do and where they can go, and when, though it is a much more liberated society than the rest of South Asia. Recognizing that it might be difficult for women IOs to operate as isolated individuals, we thought of composing IO teams, with at least two women so they could travel together when necessary. This meant assigning the team a whole D-channel common area, letting it apportion field channel assignments to individual IOs. But the IOs would help each other, attending each other's meetings when feasible and knowing the farmers in each other's areas. This meant that one IO could fill in for another when the other was sick or had to take leave.[24]

It turned out that the team concept facilitated communication and problem-solving. Supervisors, rather than contacting each IO individually, could work through the IO designated as team coordinator. (This role was more facilitative than supervisory, and a smaller organizing area was given the person acting as coordinator since these responsibilities required some time for travel and reporting.) The teams met regularly to discuss their progress and problems, and group problem-solving became the first line of strategic innovation and modification. This approach developed into a mechanism for making the program more "bottom up" than originally conceived (though not more than intended--our conception had not evolved far enough to see at the outset how to make the program itself more "participatory.")

The sequence of activity was to be "bottom up" in conception. The first focus of discussion and effort was to identify what farmers by their own group action could do to alleviate their problems, by water sharing, by repairing structures, by putting in new drainage channels, etc. The foundation of the program was self-help activity, though it was to exist in isolation. There were invariably some problems that farmers needed technical or financial assistance with. Their representatives could and did take these to the appropriate government staff. Indeed, what evolved at farmers' and IOs' initiative were monthly meetings between farmer representatives and the field officials assigned to that area. The fact that farmers were undertaking self-help strengthened their claim for getting officials' cooperation and assistance, but it also challenged some of the negative stereotypes the latter had about farmers, as being uncooperative, selfish, always simply demanding things from the government. There were things which could not be done without authorization or resources from the district level, and approaching officials at this level constituted a third tier of activity. The fact that the farmers and staff had already done what they could within their own authority and resources prompted more positive response at this level, and again served to affect attitudes. This strategy was roughly formulated in the initial training session but was probably first articulated in such a succinct and systematic manner by one of the IO team coordinators in June 1981.[25]

The process of organization would be documented throughout. One of the key elements of the NIA organizing strategy in the Philippines was process documentation, to get in writing a continuous record of how the organizers made contact, how meetings with farmers and between farmers and officials went, what farmers

thought of the activity, etc. Special process documenters (PDs) were engaged to monitor and give independent feedback on the process of organization. For a
similar purpose but with a different role design, the
SFDP in Nepal designated its group organizers also as
action research fellows (GO/ARFs). It turned out in
practice that in fact the first function crowded out
the second, and SFDP process documentation took a
backseat. We introduced several modifications to the
Philippine approach. First, because there was pressure
to deploy as many IOs in direct organizing as quickly
as possible, to get ahead of the redesign activities
and facilitate farmer input to them, we could assign
only four persons initially to PD responsibilities.
This meant that not all teams had process documentation. We felt that a sampling of experience would
suffice under the circumstances. (All IOs were required to keep daily diaries to help fill in the gap of
not having PDs for all teams.) Second, we combined the
roles in that process documenters were also given some,
though fewer, field channels to organize. This meant
that the process documenter would not be sitting in
judgment on the other IOs, since he had similar responsibilities. What we gave up in objectivity in this
regard we hoped to gain in more thorough familiarity.
Third, jeopardizing objectivity even more, we asked the
PDs to discuss their fort-nightly reports with the
whole team before sending them in, so that the other
IOs would know what was being said. Initially this was
proposed so as to avoid interpersonal suspicions and
tensions. But it meant that problems observed and
reported were called to the IOs' attention immediately,
not when an ARTI staff member read the report and gave
feedback. The team could undertake its own problem-
solving discussions and experimentation directly. Given
the problems of maintaining active supervision (discussed next), this turned out to be very advantageous,
reinforcing the "bottom up" management of the program
noted earlier.

In the training we had stressed with the IOs that
we expected there would be problems and mistakes (we
accepted the philosophical approach which Akhter Hameed
Khan pioneered at Comilla). We said that if no problems
and mistakes were reported, we would become sus-
picious, and that we would not criticize or penalize
mistakes in dealing with problems. Everyone made
mistakes. The real error would be in not learning from
them. So we would be unhappy only if problems were not
reported and shared with the whole program. This attitude of humility and self-criticism has been reasonably
well maintained so far as can be seen from the process
documentation and from group and individual discussions

with IOs. ARTI and Cornell staff have had to share in
the attitude to give it credence and effect.
    In practice, less attention has been given to the
process documentation than would be ideal. Feedback
from ARTI has been slower and less regular than intended, and eventually written feedback gave way to
oral discussions during ARTI staff visits to the field,
discussed next. While we have not made good use of PD
outputs as in the Philippines for central management
and evaluation purposes, the PD work has been important
as an instrument for self-management. Also the materials have been used for subsequent training of new IOs.
So the device developed in the Philippines has been
turned to different purposes. That the program has
progressed as well as it has suggests that the same
level of resource investment in PD as in the Philippines was not needed, at least under the conditions
encountered, though we do believe we could have improved the program's performance (certainly its even-
ness) if we had had more time and resources to do and
utilize process documentation.
    The work in the field would be monitored and re-
vised by ARTI staff with Cornell assistance. We conceived of a management team based at ARTI, with the
geographer and agricultural engineer from Cornell
participating, which would visit Gal Oya on a regular
basis to assess progress and problems and give gui-
dance.²⁶ At the same time recognizing that the IOs
were only temporarily under ARTI's auspices and were to
be transferred into positions in the government service
once the period of experimentation was completed (sic),
it was thought best that they be operationally supervised in the field by a ministry officer. This way
they would work more or less within the regular framework of appointments, leave, salary, etc. The Ministry of Lands permitted ARTI to interview senior colonization officers recently screened to be eligible for
appointment as project managers. The person selected
by ARTI had worked as a colonization officer in the Gal
Oya scheme nearly twenty years earlier so he knew the
area and had worked with a youth settlement scheme (and
liked working with younger people).²⁷
    In practice, it turned out to be very difficult
for ARTI staff, even augmented by a Sri Lankan sociologist to arrange as much time and transport as would
have permitted direct field observation and supervision
on a regular basis. Consequently, the supervisor in
Gal Oya played a more active problem-solving, not just
administrative role, and the IO teams had to be more
self-reliant. As with the shortcomings in process
documentation, since the program has done reasonably
well, it appears that we did not absolutely need as
much supervision as planned for. There were possibly

even some positive outcomes from our being thinner on
the ground than we were comfortable with as it encouraged more self-reliance on the IOs' part. On the
other hand, there could have been more learning on our
part if we had had closer and regular contact with
field operations during the first several years. Also,
we were gambling more than probably desirable, though
given our staff and resource constraints we had no
choice. We lacked redundant capacity[28] to deal with
unanticipated problems and were fortunate that none of
the problems became so severe or clustered that they
overwhelmed the program.

After the organizations had been launched, the
number of IOs in an area would be thinned out, as a
majority of the IOs would begin organizing work in new
areas; the rate at which this would be done and the
ratios would have to be determined experimentally.
Initially we thought in terms of a two-phase strategy
with fairly drastic reduction in numbers. The organizing phase, lasting one or two years, would be followed
by a long-term support phase, with eighty or ninety
percent of the IOs being redeployed. We asked farmer
representatives about how long they thought it would
take before the organizations were essentially self-
sufficient, and they said one to two years, but they
themselves said it would be good if some IOs could
remain behind. The concept of ombudsman is not easily
translated into Sinhala, but that function is understood. When explaining the thinning out concept, we
found it useful to draw an analogy with the construction and maintenance phases for an irrigation
system. There needs to be a fairly large up-front
investment in creating physical structures, then there
needs to be some continuing maintenance investment,
albeit at a lower level, to maintain the physical
system's performance. As new farmer-representatives
are elected, there will need to be more informal
training. While farmers should be their own spokesmen,
an IO presence can guarantee that farmers are listened
to by officials and treated respectfully. Problems of
financial mismanagement or personal aggrandizement
might be more easily handled within the family if a
supportive IO could be involved in groups' sorting them
out. We are thinking in terms of three phases --
organization, consolidation, and maintenance, with a
less rapid redeployment (at the suggestion of IOs and
farmer-representatives).

LEARNING FROM THIS EXPERIENCE SO FAR

Although the project is ongoing, at least through
the end of 1985, it is appropriate so far. These are
my interpretations and not necessarily those of my

colleagues at ARTI and Cornell. I will review the hypotheses and rationale stated above to indicate in what ways we have found them supported or not, and in what ways we might now correct or drop them.

Catalyst Role. The rapid change in attitudes and performance of farmers and engineers toward the IOs. Farmers are the first to credit the IOs with the progress, but engineers now also speak highly of them. The deputy director of irrigation in Gal Oya suggested that IOs be deployed in projects two or more years before rehabilitation is to begin.

IOs found that they had to modify our initial concept of how a catalyst worked in the field. The first months they often had to take more initiative than prescribed in our training, as a pump priming exercise -- setting up meetings with officials, or even chairing meetings of farmers at first -- to get things going. They kept in mind our admonition that they must not allow themselves to become the leaders of the farmers, or their spokesmen, because this would create a dependency relationship and discourage the emergence of farmers' own leadership.

Getting the role institutionalized within the bureaucracy has proved to be less easy than planned. There was an agreement at the outset that if the IO role proved useful (everyone agrees it has), it would be incorporated within the Irrigation Department at the end of two years. This has not happened, though there is agreement now that there should be a permanent home for the IO cadre. Whether that will be in the ministry or the ID remains to be worked out, since the ID has been reluctant to absorb a larger number of nontechnical staff. The IOs, working on year-to-year contracts, request some regularization of their status, to make careers in institutional development for water management. Because of delays in creating such career prospects, as of July 1, 1983, over half the IO cadre left to take permanent teaching positions offered by the Ministry of Education. This was a real blow to the program, but it did not collapse, as recruitment and training of new IOs went ahead, including a Tamil-speaking batch.

There is some fear, prompted by experience with the U.S. Peace Corps overseas, that there can be burnout after a while when persons are engaged in such intense, face-to-face activities under difficult physical circumstances. The organizational model that is now proposed, and accepted in principle by the government, is that about twenty percent of the cadre, those most committed to the program's aims and best able to provide leadership, would be appointed as permanent staff, to manage the recruitment, training, supervision and evaluation of IOs, while a continuous flow of new IOs

would be trained and deployed on two or three-year
contracts. The best of these would be made permanent,
and any others who were judged effective organizers and
who wanted to continue would be given new contracts.
In this way, the number could be expanded as needed
(there is a lot of demand to start the program in other
projects) and eventually contracted; also persons could
be posted to new areas more easily if there is a turnover. It is hoped that this structure can permit institutionalization of the IO cadre without bureaucrat-
izing it. Those IOs appointed to the staff would serve
as coordinators for administration, for training, or
for monitoring and evaluation, as well as team and area
coordinators. They would constitute the core for
starting up the program elsewhere, as there are proposals to extend it to new AID and World Bank projects
for irrigation and rehabilitation and on an experimental basis to the Mahaweli project.

We need to remain open to the exact definition of
the role, since in different settings and with different organizations (like the Mahaweli Board contrasted with the ID) the responsibilities should probably be reshaped, and even the level of appointment
might vary. We need to avoid being wedded to the
precise role introduced and validated in Gal Oya. We
feel few qualms about this since there is a demand for
those IOs who have proven themselves capable and committed. They could be employed now several times over.
Indeed, we had been losing a number to more permanent
employment in other organizations even before the
teaching posts were offered, though the best of those
we have lost say they would return if there were some
career prospects in farmer organizing. Job satisfaction, despite the difficult conditions and demanding
hours, has been quite high.

Informal Organization. Starting with work and
proceeding subsequently to more formal organization has
proved possible and more effective than organizing
people first and then proceeding to undertake work. We
may have been moving too slowly toward formalization.
There have been requests from farmers for some model
bylaws or constitutions, and if they want to be officially recognized, so they can be given contracts to
perform paid rehabilitation work, for example, these
are needed. Officials from the government agent
(district administrative head) on down have been willing to work with the organizations as if they had some
formal status. Simply electing farmer representatives
at the field channel level has sufficed, though some
groups have chosen secretaries (if the representative
is not functionally literate), or even some assistants
on longer field channels.[29]

D-channel-level organizations have also started
informally, for consultation among field-channel representatives and to allocate water among field channels and do needed maintenance. It is proposed that
the D-channel organization be formally constituted and
recognized but that field channel groups remain essentially informal. This permits some ambiguity as to
who is a member at the lowest level, since legally only
the permit holder for the original four-acre allotment
or his successor can be recognized. Any de facto
cultivators can participate in the group by common
consent, whereas the higher-level organization is made
up of recognized representatives, with their own
elected officers, accounts, etc.

As noted previously, farmer representatives have
begun holding fairly regular meetings with relevant
officials at the next higher level (roughly the command
area of a branch channel). Initiative in convening
these meetings, inviting officials, and chairing them
rests with farmers. These are not authoritative,
decision-making meetings but rather consultative ones.
All of the organizations tend to work toward consensus,
which is more culturally acceptable than majority
voting anyway. While we know that water problems can
be quite conflictual, we have been impressed with the
leadership efforts to resolve problems amicably.

One of the biggest and most welcome surprises to
date was the decision by the government agent, with the
district minister's blessing, to allow the farmer representatives to select four of their number to attend
District Agricultural Committee (DAC) meetings. The
DAC is otherwise made up of district-level department
heads and MPs. For farmers to be able to have a direct
voice at this level, rather than have to work through
politicians or beg administrative intercession has been
greatly welcomed by farmers in Gal Oya (especially when
in the 1982 dry season with drought threatening, the
allocation of water to the left bank was increased con-
comitantly with seating farmer representatives on the
DAC). What has evolved is a four-tier organization:
field-channel, distributary-channel, branch canal (or
area) and district (or scheme) level. The Ministry of
Lands is preparing a new draft of the irrigation
ordinance which would give legal sanction to such a
structure in the not-too-distant future. In contrast
to the earlier proposed revisions in the ordinance,
what is now suggested is based on experience and we
presume much more workable.

Although we did not set out to implement prescriptions from earlier analyses by the Rural Development
Committee, that rural local organizations were likely
to be more effective if composed of multiple tiers
vertically linked,[30] we have seen practical evidence

for this in the evolution of this system. Also the finding we made from analysis of 150 case studies of rural local organization throughout the Third World, that a degree of informal organization rather than strictly formal structuring is fruitful, has been supported in this operational situation.[31] One should not have to choose between the two modes of organization but would rather aim to have the best of both.

Field Channel Organizational Base. The decision to begin at the field channel level was a correct one. The caliber of leadership has been good. Any farmer having political motivations and connections who wants to be part of the water management organizational structure must start at the lowest level and perform effectively on behalf of his neighbors. Even in the head-end areas where water supply itself is not a problem, there are many improvements that can be made by group action, including quality of life through amenities like bathing places if other needs are not more urgent. The capacity for self-management at this level is readily apparent so farmers can start with more confidence in an organization they control. If some field channel groups are not performing well, because of social conflicts or inactive leadership, their members are the main ones who suffer. They are the ones with incentive to change the situation when their losses are sufficient. We do not have firm data on the number of farmer representatives replaced by members to date, but about ten percent have turned over, most of them because members expected better performance, a good indicator of interest in the organization.

Just having organization meetings creates a structural situation where head-enders and tail-enders can discuss water and other problems (whether this is along a field channel or between field channels). Those not getting water can voice complaints legitimately and expect cooperation from other members of improving water supply. If a similar complaint were made simply individual-to-individual it could be ignored. But in a public forum it needs to be addressed, and in Sri Lanka it is almost impossible to defend selfishness or unfairness when it comes to water distribution, because people's livelihoods are at stake.

One small but significant indicator of the validity of the approach is that two of the most prominent and influential farmers in the first organizing area, who opposed the IOs' efforts at the outset (persons with strong political ties and reputation, having held important local offices in the coop and village council) within several months came around to

support the program, and even to articulate its participatory and egalitarian ideals with evident sin-
cerity. Perhaps the calculation was simply that if the
new farmer organization program could not be beaten, it
should be joined. But these farmers (subsequently
elected as representatives, and chosen to represent
farmers at DAC meetings) have spoken out against the
interjection of politics in water management organization and have praised the IOs, even extravagantly, in
public. If the base-level organization is taking shape
cohesively, such leaders, who could readily dominate
higher-level meetings given their experience and connections, seem to have to adopt different leadership
strategies.

Hydrological Organization Base. When a field
channel or D-channel is crossed by colony or other administrative boundaries (which often coincide with differences in settlers' place of origin), it is usually
more difficult to get hydrologically defined organizations started. But water management problems would
be harder to resolve if head-enders are in one organization and tail-enders in another. We have been encouraged by the extent of cooperation on channels where
administrative or social boundaries crossing hydrological areas have separated farmers in the past. As
one farmer said, during irrigation periods they used to
have to stay up all night to be sure their water was
not stolen. Now that representatives of the field
channels involved have worked out fair schedules,
everyone can get their sleep. One problem which arises
is that the Department of Agrarian Services has farmer-
officials already in the field. They are called col-
loquially vel vidanes (the name for traditional irrigation headmen), though their Sinhala designation (yaya
palakas) translates as tract manager, connoting the
top-down philosophy animating their establishment. They
are responsible for coordinating agricultural inputs
from the agricultural service centers and are elected
(or selected) for administrative rather than hydrological areas. They are responsible for large areas,
between 250 and 500 acres, five to ten times more area
than a field channel farmer representative in our program deals with. The fact that jurisdictions of DAS
farmer representatives cross-cut irrigation channels
has contributed to confusion in water management in Gal
Oya. The DAS has agreed that in the area where farmer
organizations have been established in the future the
two roles will be merged in effect by electing yaya
palakas according to field channel areas. There can be
problems with this. Agricultural service as well as
water management responsibilities might overburden
farmer representatives, though the law provides that
such persons are to receive one-quarter bushel of rice

per acre per season for services rendered to farmers.
It is not clear whether this would now go to the individual or to the group, which could compensate his
expenses but also support its other activities with
these resources. We want to leave this option open to
the groups, and the government agent agrees.

Activities Beyond Water Management. Officials in
the Ministry of Agriculture and Department of Agrarian
Services have been very cooperative in trying to work
out multifunctional base-level organizations, not wor-
rying that these will belong to another department or
ministry. Since ARTI is not a line department, it has
probably been regarded as neutral and thus an honest
broker. At the field level, multifunctional evolution
has proceeded fairly readily, and it has been IOs, not
sure of program policy, who were holding it back.

With yaya palakas elected, YPs on a field channel
basis, linkage to agrarian services will be built into
the farmer organization. Beyond this, agricultural
extension agents trying to make their T&V (training and
visit) system work with little success, once they came
to know about the farmer groups, asked representatives
in many instances to serve as the contact farmers. One
payoff of this is that during the dry season of 1983,
for the first time, farmers on channels where their
representative was serving as the contact farmer for
extension work planted crops which required less water
than does rice. The DAC has encouraged the representative in this role, to serve as the channel for pas-
sing information downwards and upwards. Our position
has been that it is up to the farmers to decide what
and how many activities to get involved in apart from
water management. The Irrigation Department has presented no obstacles to linkages with other departments.

Involvement in Rehabilitation. As indicated already, this has been the most frustrating and difficult
aspect of the effort, though an important and even
necessary one. The IOs' efforts in the first year had
to be concentrated at the head of the Left Bank system,
where redesign and reconstruction was to start, instead
of in the middle of the system where we postulated it
would be easier to begin organizing. Farmers in the
middle would have more serious water problems than at
the head, giving them more reason to organize, but not
such serious shortages that there would be no point in
it, as at the tail.[32] As it turned out, farmers at the
head were quite responsive, more so than we anticipated
--though the IOs now working in the second organizing
area, in the middle, report that farmers there are even
more quick to respond, perhaps confirming our initial
supposition.

The IOs at the very head of the Uhana subsystem
had to work inordinately hard and quickly to get field

154

channel groups mobilized in the first few months, to contribute ideas and criticisms for the channel re-design. Because the ID was itself often uncertain of the design criteria it would follow, IOs were put in a difficult position when they could not explain what farmers could or should expect from the rehabilitation. And when the ID changed its mind about how many facili-ties it would improve or provide, after involving the IO in the consultations, this reflected badly on the IO in farmers' eyes. At times the IOs were behind the ID in working on redesign, and then far ahead.

When the fielding of a second batch of IOs took longer than expected, an accelerated ID survey effort carried technical staff through the Weeragoda area in advance of any farmer organization, missing out on the kind of consultation that occurred in the Uhana area. Initially engineers had resisted going out to talk with farmers about the problems on specific channels, to en-sure that remedies were built into the redesign. But once the consultation process was started, the ideas fed into it, and the good will it generated for the ID among farmers, encouraged all to continue it. Pressure from the donor to catch up on construction schedules unfortunately led to the acceleration mentioned above which overthrew the consultation process that had been rather painfully but rewardingly built up in the first year. At least now the ID is willing to listen to sug-gestions or complaints at any time and to try to make modifications that are possible and feasible. This is a change from before.[33]

One of the factors which contributed to this change appears to have been, ironically, the provision in the project design that farmers would participate by providing free labor to rebuild field channels. ARTI was able to persuade the ID that it needed to consult farmers on the redesign in order to build up confidence from the farmer side that the changes would benefit them, and that problems the farmers recognized would be remedied. ID engineers were at first reluctant to en-gage in such dialogue, partly because they were unsure themselves of what could and would be done under reha-bilitation. As noted already, after some awkward be-ginnings, the consultations became more routinized and fruitful.

This was due partly to the IOs' diligent efforts to brief farmers before the meetings, even to engage in role playing, to ensure that problems and ideas would be well presented to the ID, and also due to several of the engineers' personal support for cooperation with farmers, at a time when their superior officer was quite unsupportive. ARTI agreed that the project would not accomplish its objective -- primary and secondary rehabilitation would be of little value if there was no tertiary improvement -- unless farmer cooperation was achieved and institutionalized. And IOs were obvious facilitators of this goal. Unexpectedly, the project design made farmers' giving or withholding their labor for field channel work an instrument of some power, and this contributed to changed behavior and attitudes.[34]

Farmer Response. The extent and variety of farmer initiatives in response to the IOs' efforts confounded the prevailing stereotype of Gal Oya farmers and even surpassed what ARTI and Cornell personnel thought possible. Settlers had been brought in over the decade of the 1950s from upland and lowland Sinhalese communities. They were often the cast-offs or cast-outs who could be sent to what was judged an undesirable location. In a meeting with IOs during their first months in Gal Oya, a very high official referred to the settlers in a term that might be translated as riff-raff, and another in my hearing referred to them as donkeys. Yet during the yala season of 1981, when the IOs dropped their work on profiles to encourage farmers to institute water management practices (channel cleaning, rotation among fields to ensure that tail-enders on a channel got a share of the water, and if possible, saving of water to send to tail-enders farther down the system) ninety percent of the field channels in the pilot area (over 4,000 acres) agreed to one or more of these measures. Despite water shortage, a substantial number of tail-enders who had not gotten crops previously during yala seasons did so this time.

The most dramatic instance of this was when farmers along one fairly short and well-watered distributary proposed sending one of each five days' water issue down the Gonagolla branch canal for tail-enders. When one farmer objected that this inconvenience or risk was unnecessary, a young farmer who emerged as an active leader offered to take the person resisting the suggestion down the canal to see for himself. He took that farmer on his bicycle several miles along the bumpy bund road and when they returned, the farmer had been so moved by the deprivation he saw--people there did not have enough water for drinking and bathing let alone growing a crop--he proposed saving two days' water, and this was started.[35] That Sinhalese head-enders would try to save water for the sake of Tamil tail-enders was very impressive, especially to an Irrigation Department having mostly Tamil engineers.

The indications of ethnic solidarity continued. When communal riots broke out in the Gonagolla area, as elsewhere in the district, in August 1981, Sinhalese farmer representatives took it upon themselves to guard the houses of several Tamil ID officers, whom farmers had publicly criticized for dereliction of duty only a few months earlier. In January 1982, when there was a

threat of island-wide communal disturbances, these
farmer representatives went to Tamil fishermen at the
Navakiri Tank and suggested they remain home the next
day, offering to guard their boats and nets to ensure
no damage would be done. When I visited the Weeragoda
area in January 1983, I observed a group of twenty-
seven farmers (fifteen Tamil and twelve Sinhala)
cleaning their field channel, a major job requiring
three days since no proper maintenance had been done on
it for about twenty years.

This was an area where only eighteen months before
there had been violence between the two communities.
When Sinhalese farmers have been asked about the possibilities of cooperation with Tamil counterparts, the
response has been "there are no[36] Sinhala farmers, no
Tamil farmers, only farmers," brave words in a
country still troubled by ethnic differences, but encouraging and impressive ones.

At a January 1982 meeting between fifteen farmer
representatives and the director of the Irrigation
Department, one farmer recounted how he had lived in
the area for twenty-seven years, and had previously
made no effort to save water, being the second farmer
on a head-end distributary. But "since June..." (when
the IOs began their field activity, a date I often
heard farmers refer to), when he had been chosen as the
farmer representative for his channel, he had been
limiting the water flow to his field and so did all
other farmers. He even made some night patrols to be
certain, he added. At the end of the meeting, one of
the farmer reps got up and asked the director if this
program could be extended to other schemes in Sri Lanka
because they knew that other farmers had similar problems, and this should help them too. This almost
sounded as if it were prompted by the IOs, so we asked[37]
but were vigorously assured that this was their idea.
This much enthusiasm is perhaps more than average, but
new and commendable farmer initiatives continue to be
observed throughout the program area. It has in turn
helped to motivate the IOs to sustained effort.

IO Cadre. We have been pleased that university
graduates have been able to build very strong and effective rapport[38] with farmers, and also with officials
at all levels. Whether secondary school graduates
could do as well (or better) cannot be known until we
experiment. The pool of talent to draw on seems great.
The second batch seems as good on average as the first,
and a special batch recruited and trained to fill in
vacancies in the first two batches showed more[39] rather
than less enthusiasm than its predecessors.

The biggest challenge is to balance demands for
expansion of the program in the next year or two, into

perhaps half a dozen new schemes, with our own perceived requirements for cautious growth. We do not
believe that enough learning has been accumulated (in
many ways, it never will) to offer a model which can be
replicated. An approach, a strategy, a philosophy have
been developing, though their test is not how well they
can be articulated by ARTI or Cornell but how well they
are understood by IOs and applied by farmers and officials in the field. We have been pleased with the
cadres so far, but not all have the leadership skills
to train and supervise other IOs, even if they are good
in working with farmers (only about ten percent are not
very good at this, a reasonably high effectiveness
rate). Between twenty and thirty percent have the kind
of talents which we think can spur the program on in
new areas, though most of the rest can carry on the
work elsewhere.

We have learned that it is hard to predict field
effectiveness from application or interview scores or
from performance in training sessions. We have kept
rankings at various stages of the program to see what
if anything can predict subsequent effectiveness, but
nothing stands out very clearly so far. About half
have done about as expected, but a few sleepers have
blossomed, to mix metaphors, and a few who evoked great
expectations have disappointed us. We are trying to
determine reasonable predictive criteria for recruitment and final selection.

Training. Now that we have more field experience
and some role models, we are shifting from more formal
training methods to more applied presentations. An
approach of apprenticing new IOs can cut training costs
and speed up the process if it is effective. It might
well be more effective than the initial, more formal
training, if only because the techniques and philosophy
are clearer now than they were two years ago.

Living in Communities. The close identification
which IOs are able to establish with farmers and their
families comes in large part from their living with
them. This approach has not only been used by NIA in
the Philippines and SFDP in Nepal, Bangladesh and the
Philippines, but also with some success by other programs in Bangladesh and Thailand.[40] The valuable role
of promoters who approach and live in communities to
get local self-help organizations started, has been
highlighted in the work on participatory organizations
by Benno Galjart and his colleagues at the University
of Leiden,[41] and also in our own comparative analysis
of case studies, though this is not to say that purely
locally initiated organizations are not more likely to
be effective.[42] If no organizations exist and some
agency desires to promote them, a role and strategy
such as introduced in Gal Oya is likely to be needed.

This reflects the paradox which Stiller and Yadav have
commented on, that some top-down initiatives may be
needed to get bottom-up processes started.[43]
Community Profiles. As noted already, this part
of the methodology of community organization has not
figured prominently in the IO effort, though we know it[44]
has served important purposes in other situations.
In some ways, the single most important decision in the
program to date was to stop working on the profiles and
to begin water management efforts on an emergency
basis. I have already commented on how the success of
these activities legitimated the program in the eyes of
the farmers and the Irrigation Department. The decision was important also because the tactical sense and
the risk-taking involved made the program belong to
ARTI, the IOs and the farmers as it could not, when
much of the impetus had come from AID and Cornell. It
also emphasized to us that it was their program, as
they had taken responsibility for its redirection, an
important move whether or not it paid off substan-
tively. Probably none of us fully appreciated at the
time how much of a gamble was involved. Working on the
profiles was the safe thing to do, and we may have to
return to making this part of the strategy more routinized and effective as the program is expanded. But
departing from the game plan was of critical importance.
Nonformal Education. We did not characterize the
approach of talking first to farmers individually and
then in small groups, before holding meetings on the
entire field channel area, as nonformal education in
our initial formulations. The theory to explain our
progress so far, stated earlier, stresses the importance of creating new structures for public discussion of problems. But when I have asked IOs and
farmers how they explain the changes in behavior, they
give considerable weight to the informational normative
effect of IOs' educational efforts about the virtues of
group action and the vices of water management. We
have probably not prepared IOs as systematically for
this non-formal training role as we might, though they
have apparently improvised it, probably assisted by
team discussions, with significant effect.
Also, as suggested already, this bottom-up educational approach has created a situation in which even
local leaders previously more domineering are induced
to operate with more public-serving orientation. We
went into the situation expecting to have to do battle
with local elites, and we are not yet comfortable with
all those with whom we must deal. But we have seen
such elites play very supportive roles for participatory development. One of the factors in this turn-
around seems to be bypassing them in the first

instance, going directly to individual farmers to explain what is expected and desirable. From that point,
some new accommodations appear to become possible.
When it comes to giving more formal training to farmer
representatives, we have been leery of focusing all
training on present representatives. This can create
status and power differentials that become frozen and
ultimately have adverse effects. Interestingly, farmer
representatives have themselves asked, through the IOs,
that training be given to more than one person from
each group.

Team Concept. Of the various elements of program
design, the one we have most often congratulated ourselves on improvising is this one. It has affected,
positively, the shape and operation of the program in
many respects. It is an accepted proposition that organization theory that organizations tend to replicate in
their external relations the attitudes and interactions
dominant internally.⁴⁵ The extent to which the teams
are themselves participatory and self-managed has been
projected in some way into the farmer organizations.
Highly regimented and closely supervised IOs with individual rather than group programs of work would have
given different signals to the farmer organizations and
the camaraderie within teams presented an example for
farmers accustomed to the opposite in their social
dealings.

The issue which prompted us to deploy IOs in
teams, inclusion of women in the IO cadre, has been
fairly well resolved. Women IOs have proved to be at
least as effective as men. Perhaps they have been
selected more carefully; perhaps they felt they were
more on trial than were the men. At the end of one
year we felt that the women IOs were probably better,
but after two years we judged them essentially on par
with the men. The attrition rate has been similar for
both sexes. One difference is that five of the nine
women have gotten married, most to fellow IOs, and we
have had the problem of maternity leaves, which complicates the organizing task. Fortunately, the team concept has compensated for this, as other IOs have been
able (and willing) to fill in for those on leave. (The
same applies for medical leaves). But there is un-
avoidably some interruption, and there have been discussions in ARTI and among IOs about this. The consensus is that we should continue taking in women as
IOs. The proposal suggests that the permanent cadre,
recruited from and managing and supervising a contract
cadre, might operate with the expectation that women on
contract, liable to assignment anywhere in the field,
would not be married or at least would not have children. If appointed to the permanent cadre, they should
be able to accommodate family responsibilities with

those of training, monitoring or other supervisory
tasks. From a program point of view, it would be pre-
ferable to have only unmarried IOs (male as well as
female). If there are distractions or interruptions,
presumably it is the farmers who lose some of the assistance intended for them. But some accommodation can
and should be made with regard to women IOs since they
have proven such assets to the program. They have been
well received by farmers (about ninety percent male),
and male IOs say that the women get better cooperation
than they do.

Self-Reliant Emphasis and Relations with Officials. The three-phase sequence of activity, beginning with what the farmer groups can do on their own to
improve their situation, has been apparently an important factor in winning more respect and cooperation
from officials. It has also given farmers more pride
in their organizations, and more leverage. This approach has set in motion, we think, a pattern of collaborative activity with officials at field and district levels which has modified if not reversed our
earlier thinking. Like most others, we had tended to
view field-level officials as inhospitable to farmer
participation, as part of the problem rather than as
part of the solution. Fairly quickly, once IOs and
farmer representatives arranged the first meetings with
officials, we found the latter taking a positive attitude (with one significant exception) toward working
with farmers. This in turn encouraged farmers, who
felt they were getting a respectful hearing for the
first time to bolster their organizations, which gave
them access to officials. Repairs of channel structures, field inspections, adjustments in schedules,
etc. followed from these consultations, as officials
also felt they could better do their jobs now being
able to deal with organized farmers. Requests could be
treated as representative of or sanctioned by a group
rather than simply self-interested petitions. Having
meetings between officials and farmer representatives
seemed to change behavior just as did having meetings[46]
among farmers along or between field channels. Part
of our learning experience was to come to recognize
that these lower officials could become part of the
solution[47] rather than being obstacles to participation. So far we have not encountered more than
short-run resistance from officials who have been cor-
ruptly profiting from their positions, something which
farmer organizations would want to end. We do not
think that corruption is as[48] pervasive as in some irrigation systems in India. But we recognize that we
may still run into opposition from officials who stand
to lose financially from having effective associations
around.

A second way in which our thinking has changed is to revise the view, stated earlier, that changing attitudes and performance of officials, summarily described as bureaucratic reorientation, was a requirement for getting farmer participation and organization. What we have seen is that it is necessary, to borrow a Chinese motto, to walk on both legs. The fact that we proceeded with farmer organization and the fact that the organizations showed capability and responsibility, as already described, reduced officials' negative orientation, and their ventures into cooperative activity with farmers produced positive reinforcement. These modified (not yet changed) a basis for BRO to the extent that the ID now formally endorses farmer participation in decision-making up to the entire project area. If we had formulated our strategy to make the BRO a prerequisite for participatory initiatives, we might still be waiting for bureaucratic change, with no farmer organization. We could not wait for ideal conditions emanating from the bureaucracy, and that proved to be fortunate. Our thinking has progressed dialectically to recognize that our thesis, work with farmers, and our antithesis, work first with officials,[49] were both inferior to the synthesis working with both.

Process Documentation and Supervision. We have already seen that resource and time constraints kept ARTI or Cornell from playing as active a role in these functions as planned and thought necessary. We hope to be able to improve upon our performance in this regard if and when we start organizing efforts in new schemes, but to avoid postures and expectations that would smother the initiative and sense of responsibility demonstrated by IOs in Gal Oya to date. Many factors have made it possible to get progress without as much investment of time and resources as most reasonable analyses would prescribe. Some of the organizational techniques like the team concept helped greatly. Our inductive planning and learning process approach surely helped. Also the quality of the people involved at all levels, seldom fully apprehended in advance, certainly figured in the progress. The program, perhaps because of the first two considerations just mentioned, seemed to bring out the best in persons involved in it.

A contributing factor, hard to factor into formal institutional analysis but definitely important in this whole process, was the friendship among practically all of the participants, from the ministry to field channel level. People tended to give each other the benefit of the doubt and to be supportive of each other personally in the ways their formal roles, either as peers or as superior-subordinate, did not prescribe. A further supportive element which I mention without wanting to give the Cornell involvement undue credit (and which I

mention because USAID deserves credit for making our
involvement possible on as flexible terms as it did),
is that we were able to play a free-lance role, trying
to anticipate problems, to get actors together who
would not normally meet, to step outside normal proto-
col when urgency or delicacy justified this. Our
bringing such flexible resources to the mix, which ARTI
managed together with the Irrigation Department and
Ministry of Lands, helped to compensate for what were
unavoidable gaps in planning, monitoring and supervision. We tried to be sensitive to the pluses and
minuses of our role as outsiders, working as much as
possible through the channels and at the tempo already
established for Sri Lankan conditions, taking cues from
our Sri Lankan colleagues and being used tactically by
them when the system might otherwise impose inordinate
burdens on the program. We were aware that any pilot
effort must beware of hothouse successes due to redundant resources (which were limited in our case). At
the same time, we followed Korten's dictum that the
first task, within reasonable constraints, is to learn
to be effective, then to try to become more efficient,
and then to enter into extending the program.[50] We
sought to discover what would work within a structure
and budget that was justifiable if the program produced
the desired results.

The Ford Foundation staff in Manila (particularly
David and Frances Korten), working with the National
Irrigation Administration in the Philippines, filled a
similar function. They were working with and through a
government agency, but had some flexibility in terms of
resources which NIA did not and could not have. If
funds were needed quickly for unbudgeted items, there
was the possibility of getting them. If specific kinds
of training needed to be added, means could be found
for this, perhaps even out-of-country. When the status
or expertise of nationals did not suffice when dealing
with certain agencies, the consultants could be mobilized to buttress the case being made. Sometimes it
was just a matter of being able to draw on some additional hands and heads to deal with the crises, large
and small, that lie in wait for any innovative program,
understaffed and underbudgeted in part because it is
new and not yet accepted. These issues are raised as
appropriately under the heading of process documentation and supervision as anywhere else, because they
pertain to how the program is made to work, when it is
not yet well understood and when indeed it is still
being created.

Thinning Out. We can say the least about this
because it is a process which has just begun. Instead
of cutting teams back so that about one IO remained in
an area previously served by six, the IOs themselves

felt as many as two or three out of six were needed for a transition phase of consolidation which had not been spelled out before. In the first stage area, physical rehabilitation work was being completed, and it was anticipated that a new system of (reduced) water deliveries to be instituted in the coming dry season, two years after IOs started, created unknown demands on farmer management and cooperation. The IOs were probably right that it was too soon to cut back drastically. Eventually when the groups are more experienced, we would expect a remaining IO to work with groups established by six to ten IOs, but such ratios, as well as the timing involved, remain to be determined in light of experience. We have a need to redeploy as many experienced IOs as we can spare from the first area, but we have to be careful not to disengage too much too rapidly, because this could undercut the progress achieved so far. In economic terms, this would amount to disinvestment. We will have to see how to increase the economic efficiency of the program without throwing away the investment that has been made.

The Last Shall Be First, or the Worst Shall Be Best. I would conclude with some reflection on how one of our very first judgments may have been wrong. Earlier I reported the view that it was probably unwise to begin such a complicated and chancy undertaking as this, introducing participatory water management, in as difficult an environment as Gal Oya's. The physical system was very large and complex; the hydrological and agronomic problems were overlaid with ethnic divisions and tensions; the staffing by government was thin since the posting was generally judged undesirable; the settlers had a history of little cooperation. When returning from Gal Oya the first time, the ID's deputy director for water management said that if we could make progress on water management in Gal Oya, we could make progress anywhere else in the country. For some time at least the Cornell group felt some regrets that we had to be working in Gal Oya where the deck seemed stacked against progress. We considered with some envy the UNICEF experiment working in H Block of the new Mahaweli Scheme where the irrigation system had been deliberately designed to have turnout areas with each field channel serving about thirty acres and twelve farmers. Gay Oya field channels had command areas up to 200 acres and fifty or more farmers, larger than the theoretically desirable small, solidary primary groups one would like to base cooperation on. We thought it would be nice to have a more favorable physical setting for social experimentation, rather than one as adverse as Gal Oya.

In January 1982, ARTI organized a national seminar on water management, to which several Cornell faculty were invited as resource persons. Among other things, we learned about the problems experienced in H Block. Damage to irrigation structures was now widespread (in large part because of faulty design and construction of turnouts, cross-checks, etc., coupled with a rigidly planned system of water rotation that was unrealistic).[51] Shortly thereafter the groups were disbanded and water management activities put under an official without accountability to the farmers. Perhaps familiarity breeds fondness, but those of us from Cornell independently arrived at the conclusion we were glad we were working in Gal Oya with our colleagues from ARTI and the ID. The conditions were unfavorable, but the farmer response had been much more energetic and constructive than we now thought would be possible in H Block. The new settlers had many legitimate grievances against the situation they had been put in, but they also showed something of a dependency complex. They expected the government to put things right because it owed them such assistance, having made many promises to get them to settle in the new scheme.

Perhaps Gal Oya settlers had such expectations many years ago when they first arrived. But after thirty years of difficulty and neglect, they must have concluded that if they do not help themselves, others are unlikely to do so. The communities which have not been cohesive have at least become settled and permanent enough to constitute a social reality. Being more remote from Colombo there is also more basis for de facto decentralization of authority, permitting some innovations without central approval that might not be ventured closer to the national office. We cannot know how well the strategy and structure evolved in Gal Oya would work in other schemes in Sri Lanka, let alone elsewhere. We are about to get an opportunity to try it out, with whatever modifications seem appropriate, in other locations in Sri Lanka. We are surprised that the progress in Gal Oya has been so substantial thus far.

Perhaps having had modest expectations and some anxiety was a good psychological mindset. We have been aware that anything done there must be tailored as much as possible to the needs and peculiarities of Gal Oya. At the same time, we have been drawing on experience and lessons from experiments with participatory development elsewhere. And we have tried to formulate our experimentation and conclusions in universalistic rather than particularistic terms. We cannot know how applicable our learning is to other situations, but we suspect that the approach and philosophy have some relevance for work in other countries, not just LDCs but also the United States and Europe. That, of course, like all the propositions here, is an empirical one.

FORESEEABLE PROBLEMS OR DANGERS

Fortunately most of the problems are those of progress as the program moves to new challenges, rather than lingering unresolved ones or ones born of failure. Still, we keep reminding ourselves that there are many perils which the effort faces. We pinch ourselves periodically to see whether things are not too good to be true, expecting that sooner or later the other shoe -- of woes -- will drop. We remain mindful of the truest axiom of applied social science: every solution creates its own problems. We can catalogue current items of concern.

Permanency of the IO Cadre. As indicated already, the initial understanding was that the project would have two years for experimentation, to work out the strategy for using IOs to establish farmer organizations, incorporated into the Irrigation Department or ministry to continue working with and sustaining the organizational infrastructure that had been created (and to extend the structures to other irrigation schemes). We advised the ID and ministry after one year that the program looked successful enough that it warranted incorporation, and at least the ministry agreed at that point. We also stated that unless there were some prospects for permanent employment, we would lose all or most of the cadre.

As noted already, we have, as we warned, lost a majority of IOs due to the delays in creating a permanent cadre, though the recruitment, training and fielding of new batches has gone ahead. The ID's deputy director in Gal Oya, who has seen the fruits of IOs' efforts, now recommends that any rehabilitation effort be preceded by the fielding of IOs into the system at least two years in advance to get farmer organization started.[52] Both the World Bank and USAID are presuming that the IO approach, with appropriate modifications, will be employed in the large irrigation rehabilitation and water management projects currently being planned for the other systems in Sri Lanka. But the status of the IO program administratively remains unresolved. ARTI is continuing in an interim administrative capacity for the program.

Transfer of IO Program. When the program is moved from its ARTI base to the ID or ministry, there may be problems in keeping its form and focus. There is some strong support for the program at highest levels but also some resistance (even though resistance at the field and district level has disappeared). The challenge to ARTI and Cornell has been to think through how the program can be institutionalized without becoming bureaucratized. As much as possible, without compromising the strategy and philosophy which have made the

program effective in our view, we have tried to operate
in harmony with government departments, staffs and
rules. To coin a new term, the IOs are like parabu-
reaucrats. It is clearly in the interest of the ID and
the rest of the government to have such roles in operation, bridging between farmers and officials. The
climate of cooperation between 1980 and 1983 has changed dramatically for the better as anyone familiar with
the earlier situation can see. But that is no guarantee that the adjustments needed to maintain the program's thrust and innovation will be made.
Expansion to New Areas. Our initial assumption
was that it would be difficult to start effective
organization in the head-end areas, and we were wrong
about that. We then had some anxiety about the middle
areas where we were getting into water-short situations
and where Sinhala-Tamil differences existed. Still,
the work has proceeded, possibly somewhat better than
before. Now we look to the tail-end areas, many of
which simply have never gotten water from the irrigation system, and where ethnic differences are most
pronounced. We do not know how, if at all, the strategy and organization will need to be changed, or whether
we might encounter firm resistance. We have had to
deploy the second batch of IOs much more thinly to keep
up with construction plans of the ID, and that presents
possible problems in itself. Even more problematic, of
course, will be extrapolation of the program into new
schemes.
Possible Ethnic Problems. There have twice been
serious communal clashes in the Gal Oya area since our
program began. As we get farther down the system and
work with Tamil groups, the question of sharing water
between Sinhala head-enders and Tamil tail-enders will
become pointed. Our objective is to have a three- or
four-tier organization which brings them together at
higher levels for consultation and even negotiations on
allocation and scheduling. Whether this will be possible, let alone successful, remains to be seen. Mean-
while, the program has confronted its own ethnic problems. It has been difficult to recruit and keep Tamil-
speakers as IOs. ARTI has continued to make special
efforts to build up such capability, but this problem
has not been resolved.
Possible Backlash from Officials. As reported,
after some initial reluctance, cooperation from most
local-level officials has been good. The few lingering
efforts to protect the old way doing business with
farmers have been rebuffed by farmers themselves as far
as we can tell. But there are some pecuniary interests
at stake, and perhaps we have had a honeymoon. Efforts
to sabotage effective farmer organizations will probably be unsuccessful, but we cannot be sure all will be

so effective. If officials have a strong interest in undermining the groups, they have ways of doing so. We have to orient IOs to developing strong and good personal links with officials, though not at the expense of their links with farmers, so that suspicion and jealousy are minimized. Any resistance which turns on self-interest can be attacked as illegitimate. Top officials in the Irrigation Department have welcomed farmer organizations' involvement in oversight of rehabilitation as a means of curbing corrupt or negligent practices by contractors and staff, so we do not anticipate such backlash from above.

Politicization. That government in Sri Lanka is as responsive to farmer needs and interests as it is (and it is substantial compared to many other LDCs) is due in large part to the vigor and competitiveness of the party and electoral systems. But this also means that almost everything has political aspects and pitfalls. It has been interesting to see some of the most politically prominent farmers, from both major parties, decry politicization of farmer organizations. One who had been village council president and multipurpose cooperative society president, as well as campaign organizer for a previous M.P., described politics to me as cancer for water management. Another politically connected farmer representative told farmers at an irrigation scheme thirty miles from Gal Oya at a meeting with them, that they must keep politics out of their organizations at all costs.

When it looked like the IO program might be made an object of political controversy during the 1982 presidential campaign, after the issue was raised, both sides backed off and left the program out of the charges and countercharges. Still, we know that any effective aggregation of power is a promising target for political interests. IOs have been very good at forswearing their own party sympathies in all contact with farmers, something I had been uncertain they could and would do. Some of the credit for keeping the program nonpartisan goes to the district minister who has shown unusual circumspection and sympathy toward it, wishing to keep a good thing from becoming used and spoiled by any political side, including its own. But politicization can sweep through an area and a program like wildfire, so we and the IOs know this remains a hazard.

Support Capacity. We think the program has had good support thus far, but more in qualitative than in quantitative terms. We are sill devising a field supervision structure in Gal Oya which involves the more respected and energetic IOs in coordinator roles for administration, training and monitoring. The first IO supervisor has worked his own kind of modest wonders in that role, though the role itself has not been without problems. We have gotten cooperation from the Irrigation Department at the district level, and a young engineer has been assigned to work with the IO program in a liaison and support role. We have still to develop an arrangement we are confident in that will institutionalize support for the program in the field.

With regard to ARTI's capacity, it has accomplished in my view more than anyone had a right to expect given the limited staff for this task and its imperfect logistical support, both due to quite understandable institutional constraints within ARTI. The leadership of ARTI has been strategically very supportive throughout this enterprise, though this mode of action research verging into major operational responsibilities has been a new and difficult kind of responsibility to managed within the institute. The ARTI staff working on water management have brought to the enterprise impressive talent and commitment which were indispensable for the progress to date. The new coordinator though only recently assigned to the group is a very experienced and strong ARTI staff member. Three new research and training officers who have been added to the group are very capable and energetic. Though trained more in agriculture than social science, they have a good sense for and commitment to the kind of participatory water management ARTI has been supporting. Other group members include a rural sociologist, an economist who worked six months as an IO before being hired as a research and training officer, and one of the original three ARTI staff members who left the group when he went to England for graduate training (and who comes from Gal Oya himself).[53]

There are plans to establish a water management research and training center within ARTI, drawing at least initially on USAID funding. This can expand staff and functions beyond the present situation, where the group has to work within the same constraints as all other working groups in ARTI, having no specially assigned facilities. Given the importance of improved water management to the country as a whole, some increased investment and institutional capacity is well justified, and ARTI has made enough of a contribution already that it is the logical base for an expanded program. Still, even though ARTI has considerable experience in this area, it will be easier said than done to put together (and sustain) an expanded capacity to support the IO program (really the farmer organization program) as well as other initiatives to come in the field of water management. Expectations and demands can easily increase more rapidly than institutional capacity, so relative progress can appear to lag even while absolute progress is substantial. The latter may

become unappreciated or simply inadequate. Our appre-
hensions are less in this area than the other six
because there is much good will and the promise of
significant resources to build on. But even in this
area, complicated problems of insufficient support
capacity can develop that undercut the progress and
momentum for participatory water management created
thus far.

NOTES

1. John M. Cohen and Norman Uphoff, Rural Development Participation: Concepts and Measures for Project
Design, Implementation and Evaluation, Ithaca: Rural
Development Committee, Cornell University, 1977; and
Cohen and Uphoff, "Participation's Place in Rural Development: Seeking Clarity Through Specificity," World
Development, 8:3, March 1980, 213-236.
2. The Irrigation Department views this as a rehabilitation project, taking water management for granted, whereas AID was more concerned with water management improvements. Since the bulk of funds were directed into physical rehabilitation, it loomed large in
AID's project implementation perspective and, as so
readily happens, concrete activities and goals tended
to take precedence over less tangible organizational
activities and goals.
3. See Robert Wade and Robert Chambers, "Managing
the Main System: Canal Irrigation's Blind Spot," Economic and Political Weekly, September 24, 1980.
4. Albert O. Hirschman, Development Projects Observed, (Washington: Brookings Institution, 1967).
5. David C. Korten, "Community Organization and
Rural Development: A Learning Process Approach,"
Public Administration Review, September-October, 1980,
480- 511.
6. ARTI and the Cornell RDC had had informal cooperative relations since 1973, and the author had
spent his sabbatical at ARTI as a visiting research
fellow during 1978-79 when (coincidentally) the project
was being designed. Professor Gil Levine, an agricultural engineer and chairman of the RDC at the time,
visited Sri Lanka in June 1979 when cooperation on the
project was being discussed, and again in September
when field investigators had been recruited to start
monitoring studies. Professor Randy Barker, an agricultural economist, spent two weeks with ARTI in November 1979 when the baseline study was being planned.
7. This research is contained in the thesis by D.
Hammond Murray-Rust, Irrigation and Water Management in
Sri Lanka: An Evaluation of Technical and Policy
Factors Affecting Operation of the Main Channel System,

Department of Agricultural Engineering, Cornell University, 1982. A master's thesis was done on the situation of the new generation of Gal Oya residents by the ARTI staff member mentioned above, available now in monograph form: Shyamala Abeyratne, The Impact of Second Generation Settlers on Land and Water Resource Use in Gal Oya, Sri Lanka, (Ithaca: Rural Development Committee, Cornell University, 1982). Another Cornell Ph.D. candidate in agricultural engineering (Mark Svendsen) served as a part-time consultant with an ARTI group between July 1981 and March 1982 while writing his thesis research on participatory water management in the Philippines.

8. See David C. Korten and Norman Uphoff, Bureaucratic Reorientation and Participatory Rural Development, NASPAA Working Paper No. 1, Washington: National Association of Schools of Public Affairs and Administration, December 1981.

9. See Norman Uphoff, "Contrasting Approaches to Water Management Development in Sri Lanka," Third World Legal Studies 1982, (New York: International Center for Law and Development 1982, 202-247).

10. See the author's previous paper prepared for a NASPAA workshop, February 4-5, 1982: "A Case Study of 'Learning Process' Applied to Farmer Organization and Participation in Water Management - The Institutional-Organizer Program in Gal Oya, Sri Lanka," Social Development Management Workshop Proceedings, Washington: NASPAA, September 1982, Appendix C, 1-22.

11. See Carlos Isles and M. Collado, "Farmer Participation in Communal Irrigation Development: Lesson for Laur," Philippines Agricultural Engineering Journal, X:2, 1979; and Frances F. Korten, Building National Capacity to Develop Water Users' Associations: Experience From The Philippines, Staff Working Paper 528, 1982, Washington: The World Bank; also Korten, "Community Organization."

12. See Dharam Ghai and Anisur Rahman, Rural Poverty and the Small Farmers' Development Program in Nepal, Geneva: Rural Employment Policies Branch, ILO, 1979, and "The Small Farmers' Groups in Nepal," Development, 1981: 1,23-28.

13. See Cheryl A. Lassen, Reaching the Assetless Poor: Projects and Strategies for Their Self-Reliant Development, (Ithaca: Rural Development Committee, Cornell University, 1980). This concept is also proposed by Eugene J. Meehan, In Partnership with People: An Alternative Development Strategy, (Washington: Inter-American Foundation, 1978). Our view of experience in 150 cases studies cross-nationally subsequently has attested to the value of this approach. See Milton J. Esman and Norman Uphoff, Local Organization and Rural Development: The State-Of-The-Art,

(Ithaca: Rural Development Committee, Cornell University, 1982).

14. Sri Lankan experience is reviewed in Norman Uphoff and R.D. Wanigaratne, "Local Organization and Rural Development in Sri Lanka," Rural Development and Local Organization in Asia, Volume I: Introduction and South Asia, (New Delhi: Macmillan, 375-579). This analysis suggests that whereas any individual set of organizations may have been ineffective at a particular point in time, the total complex of rural local organizations, including party branches, linked rural Sri Lankans to central institutions and gave them some bargaining power, providing them economic and social advantages over other South Asians.

15. See E. Walter Coward, Jr., "Principles of Social Organization in an Indigenous Irrigation System," Human Organization, 38: 1,29-36; also case studies in his edited volume, Irrigation and Agricultural Development in Asia: Perspectives From the Social Sciences, (Ithaca: Cornell University Press, 1980).

16. This is shown in Uphoff and Wanigaratne, "Local Organization."

17. This issue is generic to organization and is best analyzed by Mancur Olson, The Logic of Collective Action, (Cambridge: Harvard University Press, 1977).

18. This was also learned in the Philippine experience, as seen in Isles and Collado, "Farmer Participation." Farmers at Laur advised the NIA engineers that the proposed construction method and materials would not be sufficient to contain the force of the river at floodtide. These fears were disputed by technical arguments and construction of the dam proceeded. But it was washed out in the next monsoon season, confirming that farmers could make correct contributions even on technical matters by bringing to the planning process intimate knowledge of the circumstances in which scientific knowledge was to be applied. B.K. Shrestha reports a similar experience in Nepal, "Nuwakot District, Nepal," The Practice of Local Level Planning: Case Studies in Selected Rural Areas in India, Nepal and Malaysia. (Bangkok: U.N. Economic and Social Commission for Asia and the Pacific, 1980); as does World Bank Staff Working Paper 1983, by Michael Cernea, In Mexico, Community Participation In Local Investment Programming.

19. The best-known efforts in this respect have been initiated by the Sarvodaya Shramadana movement; see Nandasena Ratanpala, "The Sarvodaya Movement: Self-Help Rural Development in Sri Lanka," Philip Coombs, Meeting the Basic Needs of the Rural Poor, (London: Pergamon Press, 1980); Cynthia Moore, Para-professionals in Village-Level Development in Sri Lanka: The

172

Sarvodaya Shramadana Movement, Ithaca: Rural Development Committee, Cornell University, 1981); and Joanna Macy, Dharmaand Development: Religion as a Resource in the Sarvodaya Self-Help Movement, (West Hartford, CT: Kumarian Press, 1983). A remarkable case of participatory irrigation management instigated by a senior engineer is reported in N.G.R. de Silva, "Farmer Participation in Water Management: The Minipe Project in Sri Lanka, Rural Development Participation Review, III: 1, 1981, 16-19. A program using "change agents" as catalysts to assist the rural poor is going on concurrently under the auspices of the Rural Development Department, with positive results. A.B. Talagune, "Change Agents' to Promote Participatory Village Development in Sri Lanka," Rural Development Participation Review, III: 3, 1982, 21-24; and S. Tilakartna, Grassroots Self-Reliance in Sri Lanka: Organization of Bethel and Coir Yarn Producers. Working Paper No. 24, World Employment Program, (Geneva: ILO, 1982).

20. Our rural development participation project's work in Botswana, with farmer groups supposed to manage small catchment dams in semi-arid areas, underscored the importance of appreciating the net benefits (gross benefits costs) from different kinds of organizational effort, especially when effects of "seasonality" are seen. Agricultural activities usually have peaks and troughs of demand for labor, and seasonally varying returns to different activities. See Emery Roe and Louise Fortmann, Season Strategy: The Changing Organization of the Rural Water Sector in Botswana, (Ithaca: Rural Development Committee, Cornell University, 1982).

21. We did not want to call them community organizers as in the Philippines because this implied too broad a mandate, or to call them irrigation organizers as that would be too narrow, and might overly identify them in farmers' eyes with the Irrigation Department. (That is now less of a liability, but at the start it was a concern.) Institutional organizers translates rather loftily into Sinhala, so a term meaning farmer organizer was appropriately used in that language. The concept of "IOs" is now quite well understood and used by farmers and officials.

22. Literacy in Sri Lanka (78% in 1975) was more than twice as great as predicted from its per capita income level, as calculated by Paul Isenman, "Basic Needs: The Case of Sri Lanka," World Development, 8: 3, March 1980, 237-258.

23. A further consideration was that if graduates were required, the pressure for filling the positions through political patronage channels would be reduced. We felt it important to be able to select IOs on the basis of attitude, motivation, skills and experience

(to be sure, from among those graduates who were unemployed, so we were not going for the so-called cream
of the crop. As it turned out, many of these were
extremely capable and had been passed over partly
because they lacked political sponsorship; one even
qualified subsequently for appointment as an ARTI
research and training officer in competition with other
applicants, so we had a staff member helping with the
program who had himself done organizing work in the
field.

24. One of the consequences of recruiting women IOs
was that eventually some of them married and became
pregnant. However, with the team approach, it was
possible for other IOs to cover their area during
maternity leave. As discussed further, the positive
contributions of women IOs outweighed any problems
associated with their gender.

25. This is recorded in my trip report, "The Institutional Organizer (IO) Programme in the Field After
Three Months: A Report on Trip of Ampare/Gal Oya, June
17-20, 1981," - the first of five such narrative trip
reports to date, describing the program as it has
evolved in the field according to IOs, farmers and
officials. One of my roles in this project has been as
an intermittent collaborator with ARTI's Water Management Research Group, tracking the progress of the program and engaging in discussions of how to assist its
evolution. The other reports are for January 1982,
July 1982, January 1983 and June 1983.

26. Also there was an anthropologist, Douglas
Merrey, working with the ID as part of the team of
American consultantsassisting the ID in its tasks of
project implementation. He had previous experience
with farmer water user groups in Pakistan, and was
based in Gal Oya for part of the initial organizing
period. It was intended that he also be part of this
team, but for a variety of reasons, his inputs were not
utilized systematically in this supervision effort.

27. After being transferred to Gal Oya to work as
IO supervisor (a process which proved to be longer and
more protracted than initially predicted by the ministry), the government agent pre-empted half of his time
to serve in the district headquarters as a district
land officer (DLO). This was initially seen as a
potential source of trouble for the program since DLOs
got involved in land disputes and were often quite
unpopular, commonly being regarded as corrupt. The
person in this instance, however, quickly established
himself as very helpful and quite incorruptible, and
the good reputation he won in his DLO role at least
marginally helped the program. His contacts from
working in the district headquarters were of more than

marginal value to the program. As happened often, what could have been a liability turned into an asset.

28. Naomi Caiden and Aaron Wildavsky, Planning and Budgeting in Poor Countries, (New York: John Wiley and Sons, 1974).

29. One memorable example is the field channel where one farmer, unfortunately crippled, has been an informal spokesman for his neighbors for many years on irrigation matters (he cultivates at the tail-end and has had many problems getting water). He was elected representative by consensus, but because he could not ride a bicycle, it proved difficult for him to attend the various meetings or to contact all farmers on the channel quickly if necessary. So they chose an assistant for him. Subsequently that assistant was chosen as the representative, and the first farmer has been designated as his advisor. At this level, prescribing formal roles could hardly have produced better results.

30. See Norman Uphoff and Milton Esman, Local Organization for Rural Development: Analysis of Asian Experience. (Ithaca: Rural Development Committee, Cornell University, 1974); revised with data analysis extended through 1979 in Volume III of N. Uphoff, ed., Rural Development and Local Organization in Asia, (New Delhi: Macmillan, 1983).

31. The degree of formality and informality is one of many structural variables analyzed for the set of case studies with reference to local organization performance in Milton Esman and Norman Uphoff, Local Organizations: Intermediaries in Rural Development, (Ithaca: Cornell University Press, 1984, forthcoming).

32. One surprising but dramatic evidence of current ID responsiveness seen on a visit in January 1983 was the ID breaking down a freshly built measuring weir off the Uhana branch canal to reduce its impediment to flow into a particular distributary. In the redesign meetings, farmers had insisted the size of the offtake for this D-channel was too small, but the ID insisted its calculations supported no change. When it became clear to the ID's deputy director himself that not enough water was reaching the tail-end of that distributary command area, he agreed to enlarge the offtake as soon as flow in the branch canal ceased and in the meantime to increase flow into the D-channel as much as possible, even if it cost the ID some funds and embarrassment. Actually, the respect it would gain from such an act of good faith should well outweigh those costs. We were pleased and surprised to find the chief irrigation engineer for the district himself out checking the flow to the tail of the channel at 9:30 on a Sunday morning when we were making our own inspection (which he did

not know about). This is an example of changed orientation of the ID toward meeting farmers' legitimate needs.

34. We cannot prove it, but "cognitive dissonance" theory seems to have had some vindication in this situation. In the Philippines, the fact that NIA engineers are ultimately dependent on getting farmers' agreement to sign a contract for the dam's construction, to pay back the capital costs incurred by NIA (to the extent farmers contribute their own labor and materials, they can reduce this cost up-front), has created a similar kind of power, even though some have seen it as exploitative or extractive vis-a-vis farmers.

35. When the farmers closed their gate off the branch canal (they had to do this with their own boards since the gate was broken and inoperable), other farmers illegally cultivating in the drainage areas, deprived of excess water if the flow was stopped, broke open the gate at night, preventing continuation of this act of generosity. When the gate was repaired, the ID technical assistant turned the key over to the farmer representative of this group to operate it, trusting them not to overuse water and to close it when possible, quite a step forward in ID-farmer cooperation.

36. Discussion reported in January, 1982 trip report. This response was repeated in a meeting with farmer representatives, June 1983.

37. Ibid.

38. The government agent for Batticaloa, the adjoining district in which some tail-end areas of the Gal Oya Left Bank system are located, wrote to me in Ithaca to tell me farmers at a meeting he had attended had spontaneously praised the IOs work and said if all officials worked like these persons, their problems would be solved (letter, September 16, 1981).

39. At the end of their two-week training, before leaving for assignments in Gal Oya, they organized a departure party, with the following invitation (roughly translated from Sinhala):

We'll disperse tomorrow; we are going to a zone where people "sweat blood" to build the nation, and we will live with them. The friendship that has grown among us over the past few days causes our hearts sorrow (as we are dispersing tomorrow). But we will suffer it to build up friendship in the future. Comrades we invite you to join us." (February 25, 1983).

40. On the Bangladesh Rural Advancement Center's Experience, see Korten, and Ahmed Manzoor, "BRAC: Building Human Infrastructure to Serve the Rural Poor," in Philip Coombs, ed., Meeting the Basic Needs of the Rural Poor, (London: Pergamon Press, 1980); on the Thai Khadi Research Institute Experience, see Akin Rabibhadana, The Transformation of Tambon Yokkrabat,

Changwat Samut Sakorn, (Bangkok: TKRI, Thammasat University, 1980); and A Self-Help Organization in Rural Thailand: The Question of Appropriate Policy Inputs, (Bangkok: TKRI, Thammasat University, 1980).

41. See Dieke Buijs, "Participation Process: When It Starts," in Benno Glajart and Dieke Buijs, eds., Participation of the Poor in Development: Contributions to a Seminar, (Leiden: Institute of Cultural and Social Studies, University of Leiden, 1982); also Bouwe Grijpstra, "Approaches to Initiating and Supervising Groups for Rural Development," Rural Development Participation Review, III: 2. Winter, 1982, 1-7.

42. See Esman and Uphoff, Local Organization. Summary scores of overall performance calculated for local organizations according to how they were initiated were:

Local Residents	(N=14)	125
Local Leaders	(N=26)	138
Catalysts	(N=33)	114
Local & Govt.	(N=24)	50
Govt. Only	(N=53)	16
Total/Average	(N=150)	77

43. Ludwig Stiller and Ram P. Yadav, Planning For People: A Study of Nepal's Planning Experience. (Kathmandu: Research Center for Nepal and Asian Studies, Trubhuvan University, 1979).

44. See for example, K.K. Misra, "Safe Water in Rural Areas: An Experiment in Promoting Community Participation in India, "International Journal of Health Education, XVIII, 1975, 53-59; also Raymond B. Isley and Craig R. Hafner, "Facilitation of Community Organization, "Water Supply and Management, 6: 5, 1982, 431-442.

45. See discussion of this with regard to USAID by Coralie Bryant, "Organizational Impediments to Making Participation a Reality: 'Swimming Upstream'", AID Rural Development Participation Review, I: 3, Spring 1980, 8-10.

46. The organizational experiment with farmer-official committees at project and subproject levels at Minipe had the same effect. Without paying supervising lower-level officials more, their performance and output improved once meeting (having to meet) regularly with farmer representatives. See de Silva, 5.

47. Anecdotal but moving evidence of this came from a discussion with one of the most active farmer representatives, poorly clad and barely literate but commanding the respect of his fellow farmers, and able to organize voluntary labor to improve channels, roads, paths, drainage, etc. in an impressive way. When asked why they had not made these improvements before, during the previous thirty years (no government rewards or

incentives had now been provided, only the encouragement of the IOs), his answer was oblique but graphic.
He said that whenever previously they had visited and
spoken with any officials, the latter treated them with
such disrespect, they wanted to throw themselves in the
canal and drown themselves. But since June (when the
IOs started working with them), they were much better
treated and this encouraged them to take on responsibilities. I cannot prove this is true, but that was
how he explained the forty people working with heavy
hoes in the hot sun on a Sunday morning before my eyes.

48. On the Indian situation, see Robert Wade, "The
System of Political and Administrative Corruption:
Canal Irrigation in South India," Journal of Develop-
ment Studies, 18:3, April 1982, 287-328.

49. The most enjoyable, but also somewhat risky,
aspect of our working with engineers and administrators
was designing a game called "Rehabilitation," with
multidisciplinary group problem solving for a hypothetical distributary command area we concocted from
out knowledge of the area. We cannot know or demonstrate how important that day (in June 1981) and the
week spent preparing for it were in the evolution of
better attitudes and working relations. But we suspect
it was significant.

50. See Korten, "Community Organization."

51. These problems are discussed in World Water,
June 1983, 34-35.

52. Of course, we don't know how effective or quick
the organization effort would be if there were not the
immediacy of impending rehabilitation to focus communication and activity around. We might need some modifications in strategy if the IOs were much in advance of
the rehabilitation work. The DD reported that this
past January, when the first issue for maha season was
made and the distributary gates off the branch canal
were closed so that the remaining water issue would
reach the tail-end area, this was the first time the
gates have been left closed by farmers, a sign of
progress he attributes in large part to the IOs' work.

53. Cornell at present has an anthropologist (Jeff
Brewer) as a resident consultant with the water management group as well as the sociologist (Piyasena Gane-
watte), mentioned before, who has been a major contributor to program success, plus the part-time services
of an engineer (Cyril Kariyawasam) who previously
helped supervise the Gal Oya project when working for
AID. A lecturer in geography (Nalini Somasundaram),
from the University of Peradeniya has been engaged
part-time as a consultant for training the Tamil-
speaking group as well. This group augments the
capacity of the ARTI group operationally but is charged
particularly with informal, in-service training of

staff and IOs on the varied aspects of farmer organization and water management.

8. A Participatory Approach to Irrigation Development in the Philippines

Frances F. Korten

In 1976 the National Irrigation Administration (NIA) of the Philippines began experimenting with a participatory approach to irrigation development. On two small-scale irrigation projects in one municipality, the agency tried involving the farmers from the very beginning in planning and implementing the improvements to their irrigation systems. By 1982 the participatory approach had grown to a full-scale national program involving over 140 irrigation systems. The NIA experience holds lessons regarding both the importance of people's participation and the nature of the bureaucratic reorientation needed to support it.

THE PARTICIPATORY APPROACH

While NIA had provided assistance to small scale gravity irrigation systems for many years, it had previously approached the task primarily in terms of constructing physical structures either to improve and expand an existing system or to create a new one. Minimal attention was given to the local farmers who were expected to manage and maintain the irrigation system once construction was completed. Irrigators' associations were hastily created by calling a meeting and electing officers. Unless a strong association already existed in the area, this approach generally resulted in "paper" organizations, lacking the vitality needed for good water management and maintenance activities. The participatory approach radically changed NIA's style of intervention.

Under the participatory approach, once initial feasibility work determined that the site was suitable and farmers desired construction assistance, an NIA community organizer was sent to an area. The organizer's job was to help the farmers develop their irrigation association or strengthen their current one if one already existed. The organizer helped the association work with the engineers in developing the

179

physical irrigation system. The early pilot projects
revealed an array of issues on which farmers and engineers needed to work. Some of the key ones included:
  1. Initial topographic survey. Farmers accompa-
nied the survey team, discussing their knowledge of the
area, helping clear the way, and insuring the survey
team the right to enter the various properties.
  2. Location of structures and canals. Sessions
to discuss possible canal and diversion site locations
were held to blend the technical knowledge of the engineers with the local knowledge of the farmers. Alternative routes proposed by the farmers and engineers
were surveyed and discussed until agreement was
reached. Important to this process were "walk throughs"
in which farmers and engineers walked the proposed
canal lines, discussing advantages and disadvantages of
proposed locations and the precise structures to be
built in each location.
  3. Right of way waivers. Landowners were expected to donate right of way. Once canal lines were
agreed on, association members worked to obtain right
of way waivers from landowners. If a right of way was
impossible to obtain, farmers reopened discussions with
the engineers on alternative canal routes.
  4. Construction schedule. Sessions were held between engineers and farmers to determine the specifics
of the construction schedule in the various parts of
the system. This allowed coordination of construction
activities with farming activities, to help insure that
manpower would be available for construction and that
farmers would not plant in areas where construction
activities would destroy the crop.
  5. Labor recruitment and hiring. Farmers and
engineers held sessions regarding the labor and con-
tracting needs. When possible, work was broken into
small contracts so the farmers themselves could contract for the work. If outside contractors were used,
arrangements were made for the local farmers to have
priority working as laborers.
  6. Cost control. Since NIA's construction assistance was done on a loan basis to the irrigators'
association, farmers were concerned about curtailing
costs. They observed the bidding process for materials
and work contracts, they canvassed for the lowest
prices of locally available materials, they checked on
the quantity and quality of materials delivered to the
site, and during construction, held monthly cost re-
conciliation meetings with NIA personnel to verify that
the materials, labor and equipment charged to the
project were actually used.
     At the same time that they were involved in creat-
ing the physical system, the farmers also developed the
internal structures of their irrigators' association,

including its bylaws, procedures, organizational structure, leadership and membership. The community organizer's role was not only to link the farmers to the NIA technical staff, but to stimulate active participation in the association from as many of the farmers to be served by the irrigation system as possible. The organizer's goal was to develop a genuinely grassroots organization, whose members held their leaders accountable rather than an organization dominated by only a few people.

DEVELOPMENTAL IMPACT OF THE PARTICIPATORY APPROACH

Experience with the participatory approach indicated it improved the economic and social impact of the projects in a variety of ways.

More functional physical systems. Making use of the knowledge of both the farmers and the NIA technical staff appeared to result in system layouts and designs that were better than those done by technical staff alone. One engineer commented on a system that had originally been developed without farmer participation and was being rehabilitated with farmer participation. He noted, "Using the participatory approach we have no nonfunctional facilities, while when the technical staff worked alone, we had many." Examples of nonfunctional facilities were canals that ran just slightly uphill in some areas (gradients not observable in the interval on a topographic map), making them unable to carry water; canal crossings located where there was no trail, rendering them useless; and turnouts located at canal points that could not serve the area intended. The farmers' intimate knowledge of the land they cultivated for years and the farming habits of the people helped prevent such errors when farmers worked with engineers on system layout.

Farmers' local knowledge also helped prevent canals from being located in areas where it was impossible to obtain a right of way, and their local pressure tactics helped insure that rights of way for agreed upon routes were obtained. Their knowledge of water flows in the rainy season contributed to correct sizing of culverts, helping prevent rainy season flooding and canal destruction. Their self-interest in having a functional system often meant that construction quality improved when they built the canals to serve their own farms. Adequate supervision and instruction was of course important, and experience indicated that sometimes farmers overestimated their own capability to carry out complex construction tasks.

Stronger irrigators' associations. The planning and construction of a small-scale irrigation system (under 1,000 hectares) involved fifteen to thirty

months of intense effort. Farmers' active participation in the array of preconstruction and construction
tasks developed the irrigators' association in a
variety of ways.

First it provided a setting in which task-oriented
leadership could develop. With so many tasks to be
done farmers were generally not satisfied with leaders
who were simply in it for the prestige. In associations where initial elections led to prestige-oriented
leaders, in subsequent elections those leaders were
often replaced with individuals who demonstrated their
dedication to the system by their leadership in carrying out the many tasks to be accomplished. The organizers specifically encouraged the development of a
variety of committees that provided many positions of
leadership, allowing farmers to see who among them got
things accomplished.

The intense level of activity also provided for
membership growth. When an organizer first entered an
area, sometimes only a few farmers committed themselves
to the association while others hung back waiting to
see if anything would come of it. Gradually as activity levels rose, more and more joined the association. This involved considerable commitment as the
association placed numerous demands on its members.
Not only were there numerous committee assignments to
be carried out, but also members had to provide a
certain amount of free labor and materials, since the
association was expected to contribute ten percent of
the cost of the system during construction. All of
this set a useful precedent for the longer term operation of the system, when members would regularly need
to donate their labor for maintenance activities and
exercise leadership on systems operations and financial
management.

The demands of the preconstruction and construction period also forced the association to develop a
functional organizational structure. For communals
covering more than fifty to seventy hectares, associations generally found that for many activities, it was
not practical to work on the basis of the association
as a whole. Rather they developed sectors covering
smaller areas where it was easier for the members to
contact one another, hold meetings, and make decisions.
This development of the substructure of the association
with its intensive leadership style is crucial for
later operations and maintenance functions which also
needed to be carried out in a largely decentralized
manner.

The intense activity of the preconstruction and
construction stage developed organizational skills
among the farmers. The time pressures and tangible

nature of the work, plus the assistance of the organizer, helped them learn to set agendas for meetings, keep accurate records, make decisions, carry out promises, and interact with government officials on an egalitarian basis.

Minimum waste and corruption. Among the farmers, tendencies for individuals to take undue personal advantage of the irrigation system development were curbed by a combination of several factors. Each organizer worked to develop broad awareness and participation in the development activities from all the farmers in the area. The nature of NIA's assistance and its intent was made clear from the beginning and open discussion and careful record keeping was encouraged making it difficult for individuals to exercise undue personal influence. Similarly the farmers' full participation in the preconstruction and construction process provided a grassroots check on any agency level misuse of funds. Because it was the farmer association that repaid the construction costs, farmers tended to be concerned about any unnecessary costs and kept their own records of project expenses which were checked against NIA records. Some associations went so far as to impound government vehicles at night to make sure they were not used for personal purposes since the fuel would be charged to the association.

Healthier relationship between the farmers and the agency. One engineer based at a provincial head-quarters noted that he preferred to visit participatory projects rather than other projects. In the participatory projects he found that he was well greeted, and it was easy to talk with the farmers. In the other projects he commented that often what the farmers had to say was "hard on the ears." Those farmers, apparently having no basis for a genuine working relationship with the NIA, vented their complaints on any official that came around.

Farmers expressed feelings similar to the engineer's. Rather than being passive observers while others developed the system, they were glad to be treated with respect and to enter into a mutual process of system development. As one farmer commented, "Even though I have a low educational background, the NIA has trusted me and I have responded with my whole heart." Once a good working relationship was established, it appeared to lead to the association's openness to additional agency help, such as regarding the development of their water management plan and financial systems.

While the approach brought numerous advantages, it also imposed demands on the agency. It called for hiring a community organizer to work with each association and required lead time before construction so that the

184

association could be developed and involved in preconstruction activities. Engineers had to take more care in making accurate estimates of the area that would actually be irrigated once construction was completed. If farmers invested their time and energy in the association, and the water did not reach their fields, they would be angry. Similarly the agency had to keep more careful records of its disbursements and deliveries on a project by project basis since farmers wanted to check the records regularly. Engineers had to spend more time in discussions with farmers. Systems could not be designed in offices "on paper" and then constructed, but had to be discussed in the fields and various alternatives investigated. However, engineers generally commented that while the process took more of their time in the preconstruction stage, it took less during construction. Many of the issues addressed during the preconstruction stage were ones that would otherwise come up during the construction, but due to intense time pressures, would be difficult to resolve.

In general, the participatory approach generated a context in which farmers demanded greater accountability on the part of the agency, and the agency demanded greater contributions on the part of the farmers. Engineers at the NIA were sufficiently convinced about the superior nature of the approach that was adopted in all of NIA's small-scale irrigation work and was being adapted to large-scale irrigation systems development as well.

BUREAUCRATIC REORIENTATION FOR IMPLEMENTING A PARTICIPATORY APPROACH

Bringing about this significant shift in the approach taken to irrigation development was a major task. It meant changes in planning and budgeting systems, job descriptions, organizational structure, evaluation criteria, and operational procedures. Most importantly it meant developing a whole new set of attitudes and perceptions about the nature of the agency's job. No longer was the agency's task just to construct an irrigation system, but rather it was to enable local people to develop both the social and physical systems which could irrigate their crops. The reorientation process was self-consciously undertaken, utilizing specific approaches and concepts. Key among these were the following:

Agency-Based Learning Process. Learning a participatory approach began within the agency that would eventually implement it on a large scale. Leadership for the change process came from a highly placed NIA official, Assistant Administrator Benjamin Bagadion,

and pilot projects were carried out by agency personnel. This contrasts with a common pattern for pilot
projects in which a university, research organization
or private voluntary group implements the pilot in the
hopes that once an appropriate model is developed, some
large agency can implement it on a broad scale. This
approach often fails because the skills, attitudes and
procedures of the implementing agency are inappropriate
to the new approach.[1]

Pilot Projects as Learning Laboratories. Because
it was recognized that implementing a participatory
approach would require many changes in the approach of
agency personnel, the pilot projects were viewed explicitly as areas in which the agency could learn
through action what changes were needed. To maximize
the learning that accrued from these projects, process
documentation research was done on several of the pilot
sites. For this research full-time social scientists
were assigned to several pilot sites to provide monthly
reports on the activities and concerns of the farmers,
the community organizers and the engineers. This process documentation provided detailed knowledge of the
field level action, so that the implications for agency
change could be discerned even by those not directly
involved in the field.

Working Assistance from Research and Training
Institutions. Interested individuals from a variety of
academic institutions examined the pilot projects.
These individuals along with NIA personnel noted the
problems experienced and implications of these problems
for the capacities that the agency needed to develop in
order to avoid or alleviate those problems in the
future. When possible these same individuals conducted
some of the research, training and consulting needed to
help develop those capacities. Management specialists,
anthropologists and agricultural engineers all joined
with the NIA engineers and community organizers to
assist in the change process. While these individuals
initially worked with NIA on an informal basis, eventually a communal irrigation committee headed by NIA
Assistant Administrator Bagadion, was formed composed
of both key NIA officials and the academically based
individuals. The role of the academically based
individuals in this work was different from the usual
roles of applied academicians. The output of their
research was not the policy recommendations so common
to applied academic research, but rather tools that NIA
personnel and farmers could use to make better decisions. The training offered was not a predesigned
course, but rather a series of short workshops and
training modules developed to fit the needs of the ongoing action and based on the experiences of the pilot

projects. It required unusually action-oriented academic people with a systems perspective to carry out these roles.

Phased Expansion of the Pilot Project. The learning process took more than seven years to fully institutionalize the participatory approach within the agency. The time span can be viewed as containing three major phases as conceptualized by David Korten. The first period involves learning to be effective. This was from 1976-78 when those involved in the pilot project were developing an approach that made sense to the villagers and fit the needs of irrigation development. In 1979 two more pilot projects were started, moving the process to its second phase, learning to be efficient. While there was still substantial attention to learning to be effective, it was during these projects that many of the problems encountered in the first project were anticipated and avoided. In 1980, the program entered its third phase, learning to expand. One pilot project was established in each of the nation's twelve administrative regions, thus providing some experience with the new approach throughout the agency. In 1981, each of the twelve regions added two more participatory projects. In 1982, 108 new participatory projects were added covering all of the nation's provinces. And in 1983, NIA began carrying out all of its communal irrigation work using the new approach. The careful phasing of the expansion of the program was important in insuring that the attitudes, skills and knowledge of personnel, as well as appropriate agency policies and procedures, were developed to allow implementation of the new approach.

The NIA's experience is a promising demonstration of how a bureaucracy can reorient its approach to support rather than supplant local people's own development capacities. The program shows that social and economic development should not be viewed as separate activities, but rather as an integrated process in which local people participate in activities which simultaneously advance their social and economic condition.

NOTES

1. David C. Korten, "Community Organization and Rural Development: A Learning Process Approach," Public Administration Review, Vol. 40, pp. 480-511.
2. Ibid.

9. Rural Development Programs in Bangladesh

Mohammad Mohabbat Khan

INTRODUCTION

Bangladesh is a relatively small country with an area of 55,598 square miles. It is also one of the most densely populated countries in the world, with 1,675 people per square mile according to the 1981 population census. The total population is now estimated to be ninety million. The economy is predominantly agricultural with eighty percent of the population employed in farming and livestock raising and ninety percent of the population living in rural areas. A recent AID-commissioned study reveals that less than ten percent of rural households own more than half of the country's cultivable land, while more than sixty percent of rural families own less than ten percent of the land. One-third of all rural families own no cultivable land at all. Forty-eight percent of rural families own less than half an acre and hence are functionally landless. Though abundant rainfall and warm year-round temperatures make Bangladesh ideal for agriculture, the present rice yield is only 1.2 metric tons per year, low by any standards and far below the country's potential. Added to this, only twelve percent of cultivated land is presently irrigated.[2] Rural economic inequities increase every year. Per capita rural income and output have fallen in recent decades,[3] most noticeably during the last five years. Today rural Bangladesh is confronted by overwhelming problems of poverty, unemployment, illiteracy, malnutrition, and high fertility, mortality and population growth rates.

Keeping in mind the situation in rural Bangladesh, we shall attempt to present a framework of participation to facilitate critical analysis. Popular participation, as is generally used in development circles, has four dimensions: 1) the involvement of all those affected in decision-making about what should be done and how; 2) mass contribution to the development effort, i.e., to the implementation of the decisions;

187

188

3) sharing in the benefits of the programs,[4] and 4) local participation in evaluation.[5] Popular participation as a term connotes democracy, full employment or access to the means of production, and an equitable distribution of income.

Popular participation is defined here as the active involvement of the local population in the planning and management of development programs as well as in their implementation. This chapter attempts to analyze the successes and failures in achieving popular participation at the grassroots level of a few selected rural development programs in Bangladesh.

PAST EFFORTS IN RURAL DEVELOPMENT PROGRAMS

Rural development programs have been undertaken in one form or another for many years in areas which now constitute the state of Bangladesh.[6] Near the end of British rule of the Indian subcontinent, a few individuals, specifically civil servants belonging to the Indian Civil Service, took keen interest in promoting the idea of rural development. They encouraged rural masses to solve their problems unitedly through their own efforts, i.e., self-help and voluntary labor.[7]

Village Agricultural Industrial Development. After the creation of Pakistan in 1947, it took seven years before an organized rural development program, known as Village Agricultural Industrial Development (V-AID), was instituted. It advocated four basic principles: 1) experts at development centers, or thana headquarters; 2) trained workers at the village level; 3) village councils as the base agency for carrying out actual work, and 4) issuance of grants, for "aided self-help."[8] The V-AID through its programs intended to modernize agriculture, improve health facilities, spread educational opportunities, disburse credit, promote cottage industries, improve sanitation and housing and supply drinking water. Though the programs brought the concept of government in development work to the limelight, they failed primarily because of the absence of people's participation and the overdependence on foreign trained experts and aid.[9] The program was abolished in 1961.

Basic Democracies. In 1959 General Mohammad Ayub Khan introduced reforms that directly affected the process of rural development in Pakistan. Ayub Khan said one of the two major missions of his new local government system, i.e., Basic Democracies (BD), was to "organize the people to take care of the problems of their areas and to inculcate in them the spirit of self-help."[10] Unfortunately, the four-tier BD system (the lowest being the union council for rural areas, followed hierarchically by the thana council, the district council and the divisional council), failed miserably to find local solutions to local problems as envisaged by the founder of the system. Instead of becoming the nerve center of their areas, where all local problems of development and civic responsibility could be studied at close range and their solutions[11] discovered and applied with concentrated attention, the BDs[12] were monopolized by wealthy and influential people. Hence the poor, rural people were deprived of active participation in local affairs.

Comilla Rural Development Program. The Comilla Academy of Rural Development in mid-1960s provided a strategy, on the basis of experimental pilot activities in rural development, conducted by the academy in the Comilla Kotwali thana. The strategy was built on the participation of small farmers into specialized organized cooperative groups. Within those cooperatives, the cultivators elected managers and model farmers who would receive and[13] retransmit weekly lessons on improved farm practices. Participation in the form of self-criticism was encouraged at all levels. The whole project was frequently modified in response to this self-examination. Participation on the policy output side[14] was a very strong component of the Comilla approach.

The Comilla strategy, under the very able and inspiring leadership of Akthar Hamil Khan, the director of the academy, received enthusiastic and generous support both from the then government and aid-giving agencies.

The basic components of the Comilla program were:[15] 1) devising a system to coordinate activities of various government departments in a local development center, termed the Thana Training and Development Center (TTDC); 2) forming the two-tier system of village cooperative societies for small farmers (Krishak Samabay Samity -- KSS), linked at the thana level with a central cooperative association, Thana Central Cooperative Association (TCCA); 3) launching of a rural works program (RWP) to build up communication and other infrastructural facilities. The responsibility to identify a project and implement it was given at the thana level; and 4) introduction of the thana irrigation program (TIP), using the thana as the unit for the drawing up and implementation of irrigation schemes, digging canals, sinking tubewells for agricultural production, and for organizing the supply and service of irrigation equipment to village irrigation groups.

Initially, the Comilla experiment received wide acclaim both at home and abroad. But with the dawning of the 1970s many observers began to question the success of the experiment.[16] By the end of the 1960s many village cooperatives in Comilla came under the effective control of big farmers.. Kulak farmers, owning three to seven acres of land, generally defaulted on their loan repayments and perpetuated various types of corrupt practices in the cooperatives. Blair's assessment of the situation painted a pathetic picture of the state of participation in the cooperatives:

> "... everywhere it seems, there has been some combination of takeover and subversion at the local level by village elites, sabotage at the national level by landlord interests; over extension of very limited bureaucratic capacities for supervision and funding, governmental apathy and inattention or conversely administrative control and strangulation of any meaningful participation from the bottom."[17]

The Comilla system failed to ensure the desired extent and quality of participation of the majority of rural population. Mass mobilization was no part of the policies at Comilla. As a result, the loose structure and wider membership of TIP groups provided opportunities[18] for participation only to a limited group. The TIP and RWP projects, though locally planned, had to wait in many cases, for approval from the higher levels of local government, and the people in general had little to do with the execution process. Not surprisingly, the beneficiaries of the projects were largely a privileged group which neither worked in the projects nor paid for their execution.

RURAL DEVELOPMENT PROGRAMS IN BANGLADESH

Integrated Rural Development Program (IRDP)/Bangladesh Rural Development Board (BRDB). In 1971 the Integrated Rural Development Program (IRDP) was launched by the government to promote and organize a Comilla model two-tier cooperative system throughout the country. The two-tier cooperative system pioneered by the Comilla model was experimented with in only twenty-three thanas in then East Pakistan. The other three innovations, i.e., the Rural Works Program, the Thana Irrigation Program and the Thana Training and Development Center were replicated nationwide in the late 1960s.
     The main thrust of IRDP was to provide administrative support and other physical facilities to cooperatives to enable them to become self-managed, self-financed and autonomous organizations. The major programs of IRDP were the two-tier cooperative system, area development programs, and programs for the disadvantaged. The aim of the two-tier cooperative system

was to organize small farmers for group action to facilitate institutionalized input distribution, credit supervision, rural capital formation, technology dissemination, etc. The two objectives were to free them from exploitation by the rich farmers and money lenders and to enhance production. In each village a multipurpose agricultural cooperative society (KSS) was to be formed, with forty to sixty land-holding farmers participating. The primary societies were federated at the thana level into a thana central cooperative association (TCCA). The main functions of cooperatives were to collect thrift deposits, introduce group management for irrigation equipment, provide institutional credit, impart training in modern methods of cultivation and market the output of the members.

The three area development programs of IRDP were financed by international donor agencies and foreign countries concentrated their efforts in fifteen thanas of four districts. This comprehensive type of program with a multitude of components was formulated with two-tier cooperatives as the main vehicle for rural development. (The programs will be replicated in the near future in other districts, under a new board, discussed below.)

The programs for the disadvantaged include cooperatives for women, youth, and the landless.

In early 1983, the government dissolved the IRDP and constituted in its place the Bangladesh Rural Development Board (BRDB). The dissolution of IRDP came in the wake of its failure to make a significant contribution to the enhancement of agricultural production despite disbursement of huge credit over the last decade. Significantly, the richer section of the rural population was able to dominate all the cooperative programs of the IRDP, including the landless cooperatives, and to enjoy the benefits.[19] Unfortunately even with dominance of rural elite in the IRDP cooperatives, the desired participation of local leaders in the decision-making process became a fading possibility because of bureaucratic dominance, disruption in the administrative structure and neglect of local institutions.[20] Several case studies have repeatedly demonstrated that IRDP cooperatives were controlled by big landowners who used the credit facilities and other agricultural inputs for their own benefit.[21] Blair observes that "despite the rhetoric ... there is little evidence that rural development is promoting equity in the distribution of either income or political power. In fact the agricultural programs would appear to have lessened rural equity in no small measure, in the sense that the inputs have gone to the surplus farmers as have the benefits of increased production"[22]

The dominance of rich farmers resulted in 1) comparatively less representation of marginal farmers; 2) uneven distribution of credit and other agricultural inputs among members; 3) enhanced control over and influence of local touts (middlemen); and 4) no meaningful role in organizational decision-making for marginal farmers in most of the IRDP cooperatives.[23]

The successes of IRDP cooperatives can be gauged from the fact that after little over a decade's existence it has brought 430 thanas under its program. The number of KSSs and TCCAs have increased to 49,000 and 317 respectively, with a total paid up membership of 1.93 million and accumulated capital of Taka 1339.87 million. The cooperative societies now own 840 deep tubewells (DT), 11,391 shallow tubewells (ST) and 1,220 low lift pumps (LLP). Second, programs in many areas helped in increasing agricultural production. Third, programs have been marginally successful in mobilizing rural savings. Fourth, farmers have been exposed to improved methods of agriculture, i.e., use of tractors, shallow, deep and low lift tubewells and also supplied with superior varieties of seeds, fertilizers, etc.

Swanirvar Movement. "Swanirvar" in Bengali means self-reliant or dependent on one's own self and resources. The Swanirvar movement was based essentially on the principle that rural development programs should be planned, initiated and implemented by the voluntary participation of the local people. The main thrust of the movement was to utilize and to mobilize local resources to the maximum extent possible to obtain greater production with three known forces: people, people's representatives, and government officials.

The Swanirvar movement progressed from isolated locally organized programs in 1972-1973, to district development programs in 1974-1975, to the consolidation of the district development program into a national program in the later part of 1975.[24]

Swanirvar, excepting in the first phase, when it was directed by students, villagers and social welfare oriented organizations, came to be dominated by civil servants, especially the district officer, a generalist-career bureaucrat. The civil servants felt that "localized and isolated programs under phase I failed to generate popular consciousness on a massive scale with regard to the need for a voluntary labor utilization strategy. The involvement of the collectors in phase II ... proved beyond doubt the efficacy of the collectoral (district level officer) pattern in influencing and mobilizing rural public opinion for the application of the principle of self-reliance."[25] The leadership of the movement in the second stage quickly passed into the hands of the district officers as the Swanirvar movement spread in all the districts of

Bangladesh. The district officers' only concern centered on mobilizing the local population for attaining self-sufficiency in food. During this stage, the political leadership had neither the ability nor the willingness to even implement the programs of the movement, allowing the district officers to monopolize it all the way.

During the third phase, a six-tier organizational structure was formed to coordinate and accelerate the pace of the movement. But in reality, civil servants at the field became more powerful as they were vested with chairmanships of all the Swanirvar committees, from district to thana levels. The task of forming Swanirvar committees at still lower administrative levels was given to subdivisional officers (SDO) and circle officers (CO).

Rural development efforts under Swanirvar became heavily dependent on the traditional administrative apparatus and resulted in the steady bureaucratization of its operations, allowing little opportunity for people's participation in its activities.

The Swanirvar movement, after initial hesitation and confusion, paved the way for the establishment of a so-called "people-oriented representative institution," Swanirvar Gram Sarkar, and the initiation of "participatory development projects" like Ulashi - Jadunathpur (U-J) in Jessore district, both of which are discussed below.

Swanirvar Gram Sarkar. The Swanirvar movement aimed at achieving a breakthrough in agricultural production, together with reducing population growth. On the other hand, Swanirvar Gram Sarkar (SGS) emanating from this movement for self-reliance, was an administrative arrangement to organize better mobilization of existing indigenous resources.[26] Thus SGS was one instrument of the Swanirvar movement.[27]

In a typical SGS village, a gram shava (village assembly) was formed and consisted of all adult members of the village. The members of SGS were chosen through consensus. Each SGS had one gram pradhan (village chief) and eleven members, representing landowners, landless, artisans, women and youth, who came to be known as gram montris (village ministers). The SGS had been assigned by the national government with the responsibility of doubling food production, eradicating illiteracy, reducing population growth, invigorating rural cooperatives and maintaining law and order within the village.[28]

Each village montri was given charge of one of the departments (i.e., cottage industries, agriculture, forestry, fisheries, livestock, youth, women's affairs, education, health and family planning). The responsibilities of ministers were: 1) to assist in the conduct of village surveys and in the preparation of correct statistics; 2) to identify sectorial problems on the basis of available information; 3) to prepare pragmatic plans to remove constraints; 4) to effectively organize and manage projects for the implementation of plans; and 5) to generate funds, secure men and materials, select the place, and determine the time limit of development projects.

So far quite a few studies have evaluated the extent of participation of different economic and functional groups in SGS's developmental activities. Hossain, Mahmood and Ahmad, in a study of three areas in the districts of Jessore, Kushtia and Rangpur, found that "the participation was lowest among the landless, and in general, higher landownership was associated with wider participation".[29] They also found that most of the ministerial positions were occupied by larger landowners, and representatives of youth, women and cultivators also came from rich landowning households.[30] Another study[31] noted that common people showed little enthusiasm in forming SGS, as they believed it was an extension of the then ruling party (Bangladesh Nationalist Party) in the villages. The researchers observed that government officials, chairmen and most of the members of the union parishad (elective local government bodies at the union level) were disinterested in SGS. Still, at the behest of the national political leadership, SGSs were formed in all three villages. Khuda[32] carried out his investigation in twenty-six villages in the Comilla district to examine among other things some of the broader leadership characteristics of those in SGSs. He found that SGSs are controlled and managed by a handful of persons of relatively affluent households who belong to dominant social groups in the village.

SGS failed to become the forum in which rural poor could participate as active members in its locally sponsored development programs.

The Ulashi-Jadunathpur (U-J) Development Project. The Ulashi-Jadunathpur (U-J) development project, located in the Sarsa thana of Jessore district, involved an earthwork of 16.5 million cft. It was completed within the stipulated time of six months through people's participation, under the direct guidance of district level officers, especially the deputy commissioner. The leadership in the implementation phase of the program was provided by the deputy commissioner himself. But as the deputy commissioner described the process in other ways. "In the day-to-day decision-making process pertaining to the implementation of the project, the villagers participated with the sponsors -- the concerned government officials. In this the role of the latter was largely one of catalysts in

decision-making, through consensus. For the participants, it was their own project, from the point of view
of both formulation and implementation".[33]

The timely completion of the U-J development project was the result of the following:[34] 1) the personality of the deputy commissioner, who created enthusiasm among and engaged in persuasive conversation with
the villagers, and sometimes imposed his decisions on
them; 2) the strong support and encouragement from the
government leadership through all the phases of the
project; 3) equitable distribution of the projects'
responsibilities among potential beneficiaries; and 4)
such factors as payment of compensation, appropriate
propagation of potential gains, physical works undertaken by local leaders, close supervision, adequate
motivation and effective monitoring and reporting
systems.

But as one observer[35] pointed out, the U-J was
primarily a mass mobilization experiment which could
not be replicated in other parts of the country and
hence could not be considered a model. To buttress his
statement, he mentioned quite justifiably that the project was undertaken as per instruction and approval of
the president of the country. Also the officials played a dominant role in almost all aspects of the U-J
project. In fact, they designed, planned and managed
the whole work, and local leaders were not involved in
the process of planning, policy-making and management.
Another observer, after undertaking a survey in U-J
area, reached the conclusion that "absence of genuine
local participation and of local sharing of costs have
been a major weakness of U-J project."[36]

Rural Development through Decentralization. The
present military government of Bangladesh, since
seizing power through a bloodless coup in March 1982,
has vowed to take administration to the doorsteps of
the rural masses. So far the regime has backed its
promises with determined action. On April 28, 1982,
Chief Martial Law Administrator Lt. General H.M. Ershad
constituted a high-powered Committee for Administrative
Reorganization. The committee's terms of reference
include among other things to recommend "an appropriate, sound and effective administrative system based on
the spirit of devolution and the objective of taking
the administration nearer to the people".[37] The committee recommended[38] that:

1) Thana should be made the basic unit of administration.
2) Subdivisions should be upgraded into districts.
3) Elected local councils should operate at
   union, thana and district levels.

4) Chairmen should be directly elected for union parishad (UP), thana parishad (TP) and zilla, or district, parishad (ZP).
5) All UP and TP members will form electoral colleges for the election of ZP chairmen.
6) Chairmen of UP will be members of TP.
7) Chairmen of TP will be members of ZP.
8) Officials (government) at union, thana and zilla levels will attend and participate in parishad meetings.
9) ZP/TP will be provided with (by the national government) senior staff support.
10) UP/TP/ZP chairmen will act as coordinators of governmental activities at their levels, except on judicial matters.
11) Adequate powers will be elected chairmen to ensure accountability of local officers.
12) All existing thana level committees are to be abolished, and TP's may form committees.
13) Development of infrastructure at thana level is to make development of adequate authority possible.

It appears that the thrust of the present reform/reorganization efforts is to associate rural people with the developmental activities. Administrative decentralization as well as devolution of powers are under way from the national level to the thana level. Elections to the parishads have not yet taken place. But once elections are over, it is expected that elected representatives of people will plan, direct, coordinate and implement all developmental projects at their respective levels. Interestingly, direct participation of people is not envisaged. But it is too early to undertake any evaluation of the recent efforts, as the process of reorganizing the local government system is far from complete.

It is obvious that the recommendations of the committee for decentralizing developmental activities suffer from one obvious flaw. The committee, in its recommendations, looked at the problem of decentralization from a purely administrative angle. It ignored the political dimension of the concept of decentralization which is so vital to understanding the development process in a country like Bangladesh.

Proshika - NGO's Approach to Rural Development. In Bangladesh, since independence, a number of nongovernmental organizations (NGOs) have been involved in experimenting with innovative approaches and strategies to better the lot of the poorer sections of the rural population. NGO's like Proshika and Bangladesh Rural Advancement Committee (BRAC) have had successes in organizing and motivating marginal peasants, landless laborers and rural women to identify and implement

income-generating activities to enable them to become
self-reliant.[39]
This section discusses Proshika's approach to
rural development. The word "Proshika" in Bengali sig-
nifies development of education, training and action.
These three elements are at the core of Proshika's
approach to rural development.
Proshika's objectives include:[40]
1)   The creation of a process of development
through which the rural disadvantaged and the under-
privileged groups can get involved in their own socio-
economic uplift effort.
2)   The provision of training to community
leaders, animators (Kormy), and target group leaders,
in both human skills and practical skills, to upgrade
their ability to identify problems and mobilize as far
as possible their own resources in solving problems.
3)   The support of income-generating activities
initiated by these groups, in an effort to reduce their
socioeconomic dependency.

Participative decision-making forms the core on
which Proshika's rural development programs stand.   A
study[41] on Proshika concludes that the utilization of
the participatory decision-making approach played the
crucial role in developing the organization into one
where poor people felt that it is theirs. As a result,
Proshika, starting from scratch in 1976, expanded its
activities by 1980, in around 1,000 villages serving
4,000 groups of which ninety-five percent are the landless.[42]   The participatory decision-making approach
counteracted the growth of a vast bureaucratic apparatus which is so common in many rural development
programs.[43]
Proshika still faces a number of problems.
First, Proshika Kormis (workers) are on the payroll of
the organization. It is doubtful how long, with
further expansion of its activities, the dedication and
commitment of its locally recruited personnel will
last. This is very important as the future success of
Proshika will depend on workers who are hardworking,
committed and dedicated. Second, as a foreign funded
organization, however commendable its role may be,
Proshika will be looked at suspiciously, especially by
the vested interests.
In the end it must be recognized that of all the
rural development programs in Bangladesh discussed so
far, Proshika's approach comes closer to providing
opportunities for the rural poor to initiate and participate in developmental projects.

CONCLUSION

Rural development, in the sense of liberating the rural poor from oppression, injustice and subjugation, has not occurred in Bangladesh. The rural poor have not developed into productive forces capable of promoting their material welfare, through mobilizing internal resources available in the rural areas. The rural development programs undertaken so far in the public sector have put greater emphasis on building rural institutions from above, with very little local input from those affected. The bureaucratic-technocratic bias is so predominant in every aspect of RDPs that it cannot be ignored. It appears RDPs have been deliberately initiated under state patronage to promote and strengthen the interests of the local exploitative class, the big and middle farmers at the expense of the vast majority, marginal farmers, landless peasants, poor women etc. The members of the rural exploitative class are linked up effectively with the urban politicians, bureaucrats, and intellectuals who formulate plans and/or significantly influence policies pertaining to RDPs. Only at the implementation stage of RDPs are the rural poor and disadvantaged mobilized and put to work through propagation of lofty ideas and principles.

Participation of the rural masses in the planning and implementation of RDPs in Bangladesh will be possible only if the following take place:

1) A fundamental rethinking about rural people and existing rural institutions on the part of those who control the state apparatus is an essential prerequisite. If that occurs then obviously the restructuring of the rural power structure is bound to follow.

2) The restructuring of the rural society must include, among other things, a drastic land reform and redistribution of the surplus land among land-poor and landless peasants.

3) Rural cooperatives, which have so long been dominated by the rich farmers, must be disbanded. In their place, production cooperatives, which will allow pooling of resources, must be formed. At the same time, farmer groups must be effectively organized by the genuine small farmers. Agricultural laborers should be encouraged to form unions so that they can effectively bargain for their labor.

4) Bureaucratic management and control in any form should be eliminated. It is obvious that the bureaucrats' role as change agents in RDPs in Bangladesh has not succeeded.

5) In a highly stratified society like Bangladesh, where a microscopic minority makes all the major decisions for the vast rural majority living in abject

poverty and suffering extreme deprivation, participation for the latter is only a dream with no relation
to reality. People's participation in RDPs in Bangladesh is yet to be tried.

NOTES

1. F. Thomasson Januzzi and James T. Peach, Report on the Hierarchy of Interests in Land in Bangladesh, Washington, D.C.: Agency for International Development, September, 1977.
2. Betsy Hartman and James Boyce, "Bangladesh:
Aid to the Needy?" International Policy Report, May
1978, Vol. IV, No. 1, p. 3. Washington, D.C.: Center
for International Policy.
3. Azizur Rahman Khan, "Poverty and Inequality in
Rural Bangladesh" in Poverty and Landlessness in Rural
Asia. (Geneva: International Labor Office, 1977), 155.
Khan reaches his conclusion on the basis of information
contained in relevant issues of the monthly Economic
Indicators of Bangladesh, published by the Bangladesh
Bureau of Statistics.
4. Towards a Typology of Popular Participation,
Policy Planning and Program Review Department, The
World Bank, Washington, D.C., May 1978, 16.
5. Alastair T. White, "Why Community Partici-
pation? - A Discussion of the Arguments," Assignment
Children, 59/60, 2/1982.
6. Akthar Hamid Khan, Framework of Rural Develop-
ment in Bangladesh (Mimeo). Bogra: Rural Development
Academy, 1979, p. 1; A.M. Anisuzzaman, "Historical
Background and Current Objectives and Strategies for
Rural Development in Bangladesh," paper presented at a
National Seminar on Rural Development in Bangladesh,
March 27-31, 1979.
7. M.N. Haq, Pioneers of Rural Development in
Bangladesh: Their Programmes and Writing. Bogra:
Rural Development Academy, 1978.
8. Ibid., 15.
9. Anwarullah Chowdhury, Agrarian Social Rela-
tions and Rural Development in Bangladesh, (New Delhi:
Oxford and IBH Publishing Co., 1982), 75-76.
10. Mohammad Ayub Khan, Friends Not Masters: A
Political Autobiography, (New York: Oxford University
Press, 1967), 207.
11. Ibid., 209.
12. The Bureau of National Reconstruction and the
Pakistan Academy for Village Development, An Analysis
of the Working of Basic Democracy Institutions in East
Pakistan, (Dhaka, 1961).
13. Harry W. Blair, The Political Economy of Participation in Local Development Programmes: Short-Term

Impasse and Long-Term Change in South Asia and the United States From 1950s to the 1970s. (Ithaca: Rural Development Committee, Center for International Studies, Cornell University, 1981), 18.

14. Ibid., 18.

15. Salehuddin Ahmed, *Rural Development and Employment Expansion in Bangladesh: Experiences from Ulashi*, (Dhaka: National Foundation for Research on Human Resource Development, 1982), 1-2.

16. For criticisms of the Comilla experiment from various perspectives see the following: Princeton Lyman, "Issues in Rural Development in East Pakistan," *Journal of Comparative Administration*, Vol. 3, No. 1 (May 1971): 25-59; Swadesh R. Bose, "The Comilla Cooperative Approach and the Prospects for a Broad-Based Green Revolution in Bangladesh," *World Development*, Vol. 2, No. 8 (August 1974): 21-28.

17. Harry W. Blair, *The Elusiveness of Equity: Institutional Approaches to Rural Development in Bangladesh*. (Ithaca: Rural Development Committee, Cornell University, 1974), 1.

18. Manzur-I-Mowla; "Comilla and U-J: A Comparative Study in Rural Development Policies" in Hafiz G.A. Siddiqui, ed. *Managing Rural Development in Bangladesh: Experiences and Case Studies*. (Dhaka: Institute of Business Administration, University of Dhaka, 1983), 76.

19. For a wide-ranging criticism of all IRDP programs see Kamal Siddiqui, "Rural Development in Bangladesh - I, II", *Holiday*, June 4 and June 11, 1983; Geof Wood, "Rural Development in Bangladesh: Whose Framework?" *The Journal of Social Studies*, No. 8, April 1980, 1-31.

20. Muzaffer Ahmed, "Lessons from the Experiences of Rural Development Efforts in Bangladesh: in Hafiz G.A. Siddiqui, *Managing Rural Development in Bangladesh: Experiences and Case Studies*, (Dhaka: Institute of Business Administration, University of Dhaka, 1983), 21.

21. See, A. Mannan Majumdar, "Village Mahajanpur" in M. Ameerul Huq ed., *Exploitation of the Rural Poor*. Comilla: Bangladesh Academy for Rural Development, 1976); Anwarullah Chowdhury and Imdadul Haque, *Socio-Economic Background of KSS of Tangail District*, (Mimeo) Dhaka, 1978.

22. Harry W. Blair, *The Elusiveness of Equity*, 107-108.

23. The figures on IRDP have been taken from an article by the Director-General, IRDP. See Khandaker Asaduzzaman, "Rural Development in Bangladesh: Role of IRDP," *The Bangladesh Times*, Special Supplement on Cooperatives, November 6, 1982

24. M.A. Hamid, "Swanirvar (Self-Reliant) Rural Bangladesh: Problems and Prospects," Political Economy (Dhaka) Vol. 2, No. 1, June 1977, 200-217.

25. A.M.M. Shawkat Ali, Field Administration and Rural Development in Bangladesh. (Dhaka: Center for Social Studies, 1982), p. 177. Ali, a career civil servant served in Sylhet and Dhaka districts as deputy commissioner (district officer).

26. Mohammad Mohabbat Khan and Habib Mohammad Zafarullah, "Innovations in Village Governments in Bangladesh," Asian Profile, Vol. 9, No. 5 (October 1981): 441-453.

27. Mohammad Mohabbat Khan and Habib Mohammad Zafarullah, "Rural Development in Bangladesh: Policies, Plans and Programmes," Indian Journal of Public Administration, Vol. 27, No. 3 (July-September, 1980). 779-784.

28. "The Swanirvar Gram Sarka (Constitution and Amendment) Rules, 1980," Bangladesh Gazette Extraordinary, May 24, 1980, 110.

29. Mahbab Hossain, Raisul Awal Mahmood and Qazi Khaliquzzaman Ahmad, "Participatory" Development Efforts in Rural Bangladesh: A Case Study of Experiences in Three Areas, (Mimeo), (Dhaka: Bangladesh Institute of Development Studies, November, 1978), 29.

30. Ibid., 32.

31. Md. Manjur-ul-Alam, Md. Hazrat Ali and Bijoy Kumar Barua, Swanirvar Gram Sarkar in Bangladesh: A Preliminary Observation on Three Villages (Mimeo). (Kotbari, Comilla: Bangladesh Academy for Rural Development, November 1980),58-59.

32. Barkat-E-Khuda, Ideals and Realities in Participatory Institutions in Rural Bangladesh: The Case of the Gram Sarkar, DERAP Publications No. 123. (Bergen, Norway: The Chr. Michelsen Institute, August, 1981).

33. Muhiuddin Khan Alamgir, Development Strategy for Bangladesh. (Dhaka: Center for Social Studies, 1980), 304.

34. Ibid., 314-315; Muzaffar Ahmad, "Lessons from the Experiences of Rural Development Efforts in Bangladesh," 24; Manzur-I-Mowla, "Comilla and U-J: A Comparative Study of Rural Development Policies," 75.

35. M. Ghulam Sattar, "The Ulashi-Jadunathpur Self-Help Canal Digging Project: A Critical Analysis," The Journal of Social Studies, No. 3 (January 1979): 89.

36. Salehuddin Ahmed, Rural Development and Employment Expansion in Bangladesh: Experiences from Ulashi, 46.

37. Report of the Committee for Administrative Reorganization/Reform. June, 1982.

38. Ibid., 147-148.

202

39. Bangladesh: Country Review Paper. Second
Inter-Country Consultation for Asia and Pacific on the
Follow-up of WCARRD. Dhaka, May 1981, 43.
40. Information Collected from Proshika Brochure,
1980.
41. Mosharraf Hossain, Conscientizing Rural Disadvantaged Peasants in Bangladesh: Intervention Through
Group Action - A Case Study of Proshika. (Dhaka: Civil
Officer's Training Academy, 1981), 55.
42. Ibid.
43. B.K. Jahangir, "Local Action for Self-Reliant
Development in Bangladesh" in Mohammad Mohabbat Khan
and Habib Mohammad Zafarullah eds. Rural Development
in Bangladesh: Trends and Issues. (Dhaka: Center for
Administrative Studies, University of Dhaka, 1981),
144.

10. Self-Help and Development Planning in the Yemen Arab Republic

Sheila Carapico

Virtually all contemporary development strategies stress the importance of participation by working people in both policy formation and the benefits of economic growth. Development requires capital formation for investment in the social and economic infrastructures. Unless development investments involve mass organization, representing broad social strata, they tend to benefit only a minority of landed, administrative, or merchant capital elites. The result is an uneven pattern of development throughout the country and very often, declining standards of living for the poor majority. Moreover, numerous studies show that "top-down" programs for involving peasants in local organizations and investment projects have rarely provided a solution to the crisis of underdevelopment.[1]

Centrally dominated mobilization strategies may fail because of excessive bureaucratization, the attitudes of administrators sent to the local areas, or the inherited mistrust with which peasants view central institutions and other forms of external encroachment.[2] Research has also shown tremendous variability in the capacity of local organizations, usually imported from outside, to improve real standards of living in the Third World. Some of the most pessimistic reports come from Latin American and African case studies, whereas there is more evidence of local organizations contributing to the increase and equitable distribution of resources in Asia. Nevertheless, there is considerable variability within Asia and the Middle East.

There is also widespread agreement that local organizations in Afro-Asian and Latin countries cannot be evaluated through the prism of the civic-rational morality of the West. Many observers have argued that it is unreasonable to apply Weberian or Taylorist management models[3] to Third World institutions because the models contain certain civic and sociological presuppositions which are not merely absent from the culture but incompatible with the existing system and relations

203

of production. Case studies have contributed to criticism of the old modernization approach which assumed a priori commitment to civic values of democratic participation, rational-rules maintenance, and conflict resolution through the hierarchical institutions of the state.

A study of Middle and Far Eastern cases suggests that the importance or weakness of an institution is determined not by its legal organization or even its internal management, but by its relations to other institutions in the national system. Two kinds of relations are implied, first, linkages to other facets of the social and political structure and, second, one institution's viability relative to alternative channels. Uphoff and Esman's comparison of eighteen Asian local development organization systems offers the conclusion that horizontal and vertical linkages between and among institutions are the key to the strength of local organizations. In addition, local organizations should be evaluated in terms of their relevance to certain critical development functions: planning and goal-setting, administration and interest articulation, resource mobilization, and especially, the provision and integration of services. Relevance indicates the importance of one organizational system in performing these functions compared with the contribution of alternative institutions (e.g., the private sector or the government).

Uphoff and Esman have identified a number of structural characteristics associated with the more viable developmental organizations capable of promoting relatively equitable access to services. First, there should be more than one level of organization, preferably the lower tier functioning at the neighborhood or hamlet level. Second, multiple channels should link the community to higher levels of authority; there should be alternative channels within the system of local organizations. However, too many channels or levels may unduly complicate or clog the system. In addition, organizations with multiple functions seem to be more effective than single-purpose associations. Although again, no association can be all things to all people. Third, politics and political competition or even conflict "must be accepted as inevitable and legitimate." If resources are being mobilized and the social infrastructure altered, there is bound to be politics. Fourth, there should be sanction both from above and from below, in the form of elections, audits, public meetings, and so forth, to ensure accountability to both constituents and government. Accountability to citizens is important to assure trust in the system and equity of participation in decisions and benefits. Accountability to the state is important because in

virtually all cases the state controls essential resources for development. Finally, decentralization of
operating decisions, though not the extreme of autonomy, which implies weak linkages, enhances effectiveness in the provision of services. The deconcentration
or devolution of functions and decision-making is maxi-
mized by distribution of economic assets.[5]

Local development activities in the Yemen Arab
Republic have made a major contribution to the extension of rudimentary services to towns, villages and
hamlets during the past decade. Under particular circumstances, local and regional groups have mobilized
capital for investment in dirt roads, simple water
collection and distribution systems, primary schools,
electrical generators and other basic services. Most
observers familiar with other examples have hailed the
Yemeni development cooperatives as an unusually successful model for local participation in development.
One study of forty-one local associations in seven
least-developed countries shows the four Yemeni examples among the most viable.[6] A number of Western
researchers have concurred in the Yemeni Cooperative
Movement's claim to uniqueness, calling it "grassroots," "participatory," and a "bottom-up" development
strategy which demonstrates "the potential for indigenous organizations to achieve dramatic development
results and become important, nationally recognized
institutions."[7] Several Western and multilateral technical assistance agencies have commissioned studies of
the Yemeni development cooperatives and targeted programs to work through district development boards.

Most close observers in the late 1970s also agreed
that from the perspective of public administration, the
local development cooperatives system is very weak.
Local board members, officers of their central confederation, and foreigners hired to implement donor
strategies in conjunction with the development cooperatives, recognized difficulties in staffing, record-
keeping, project maintenance, planning and budgeting,
and interagency communication. These difficulties,
inherent in the process of institution-building, were
exacerbated by federalism, local feuds, peasant apathy,
and corruption. The government and the cooperative
confederation, as well as foreign technical assistance
projects, have repeatedly stressed the need for institution building to improve planning and management.[8]

The purpose of this paper is to explore the apparent paradox of a managerial system which remains
administratively weak and yet has been notably successful in providing very basic services. The Yemeni
associations, while adhering to few of the conventions
of public office management, have played a salient role
in the provision of services and other development

functions. The apparent paradox is partially resolved
through the application of the relevance and linkages
criteria outlined above, according to which the Yemeni
associations appear among the more organized. But
there is also tension within the system between a real
imperative for rational planning and resources allocation on the one hand and voluntary local participation on the other. While participation in fund-
raising for local services has been fairly high,
farmers' and townspeople's appreciation for planning,
budgetary, and even elections procedures is limited.
Efforts to routinize the activities of development
associations often appear as central meddling in local
affairs. Committed to local services, people have not
necessarily viewed participation in formal central
civic institutions as a means to this end. There may
exist a certain structural contradiction between political, financial, and benefit participation at the
grassroots level, and the imperatives of routinized
rational planning on a national scale.

If Yemeni self-help has achieved beyond its manifest managerial capacity, it has done so under unique
circumstances. The special conditions in Yemen in the
past two decades are not to be replicated in other
nations, nor perhaps even in the Yemeni future. The
first feature which sets north Yemen off from the
majority of Third World nations is the absence of a
Western colonial legacy. The Turks made two long but
ultimately fruitless attempts to pacify Yemen and the
British empire declared a protectorate over the southern slice of the Arabian Peninsula (now the People's
Democratic Republic of Yemen, with its capital at
Aden), but north Yemen was never truly colonized. No
Western legal or administrative forms were imported, no
cooperative or civic associations introduced. No
foreign capital entered the country. No railroads or
other modern infrastructure were built. In the mid-
twentieth century Yemen was highly traditional, a pre-
capitalist as opposed to peripheral capitalist
enclave.

The second factor which distinguishes the circumstances of local and regional development activity is
the weakness of the central state. Between 1911 and
1962 the country was ruled by autocratic Imams. The
state collected taxes, principally the zakat and
various surcharges, but returned few public services.
There was perennial resistance to the state from
tribesmen and peasants in various parts of the country
throughout the period, and a deep mistrust of central
authority among the majority. In 1962 a military coup
deposed the Imams. There followed four years of civil
war in which Egypt supported the republic against the
Saudi-backed royalists. The republic was victorious,

but there was a bloodless coup d'etat in 1968, followed
bY a military corrective movement in 1974 and presidential assassinations in 1977 and 1978. In the meantime there have been numerous border incidents (both
north and south) and local insurrections. Since 1962
and especially since 1974, the government has en-
deavored to staff service ministries with educated
Yemenis, create national highway, health, educational,
and electrification systems, secure its boundaries and
legitimize its rule in the interior. During the present
administration of Lt.-Col. 'Ali 'Abdullah Saleh, who
has outlasted most of his predecessors, true progress
has been realized on all these fronts. The state is
now perhaps stronger than it has ever been. Nonetheless, the government has only recently assumed responsibility for the welfare of its citizens.[10]

The availability and dispersion of cash due to
high rates of labor migration to the oil-rich economies
of the Arab Gulf was the most striking feature of the
Yemeni economy in the 1970s. During the peak of the
oil boom, as much as a third of the male labor force
absented itself from the farms and petty trades. Their
remitted earnings reached an estimated U.S. $1.5 bil-
lion in 1979-1980. Because migration was so widespread, most of the country's approximately seven million inhabitants benefited either directly or indirectly from this infusion of cash. According to all
reports, the lion's share of this remitted income was
spent on various forms of social prestige and direct
consumption --- bridewealth, residential construction,
home appliances, and furnishings, televisions and video
machines, yard goods and jewelry, imported foods and
tobacco products, and on the means to these luxuries,
vehicles, roads, electrical generators, and water delivery systems. The government's capacity to tax remitted income was limited to customs on legal imports.
Moreover, most of this "unrequited transfer" never
entered the banking system. Nor were private sector
institutions capable of accumulating a significant
share of aggregate remittances for investment in social
or productive infrastructure. The widespread availability of hard cash contrasted sharply with a very low
level of capitalist development.[11]

The very primitive level of services initially is
also an important point. Until after the civil war
most Yemeni women transported jugs of water for household use on their heads. Other methods were by donkey,
camel, or on foot. Most people had never seen an
electric light bulb or a motor vehicle. Some boys
studied at mosque schools; the daughters of the elite
had private tutors; ninety percent of the population
was unlettered. Limited labor migration to Aden in the
1930s, 1940s and 1950s had helped spread news of the

physical comforts available on the outside and dissent
against the Imams. During and after the revolutionary
war, awareness of and desire for commodities and
services increased. In the mid to late 1970s access to
hard currency and the economic open door made possible
the importation of bulldozers, drilling rigs, generators, pumps, pipes, and building materials.

THE HISTORICAL CONTEXT OF DEVELOPMENT ORGANIZATIONS

There have been three stages in the evolution of
what the Yemenis call their cooperative movement. The
first consisted of extra-legal, informal, and largely
uncoordinated project activity. Efforts to build small
schools, water systems, and other simple services prior
to the revolution were confined mainly to the area
which had experienced the greatest commercial influence
from the outside. After the end of the civil war,
phase two saw the foundation of formal cooperative,
welfare, and development associations by regional
elites in many parts of the country. The government
encouraged these activities in limited ways. In 1973 a
confederation of development cooperatives was founded;
the following year its president took over the government in a military corrective movement. Subsequently
the development associations were given a formal legal
identity, empowered to receive and spend tax revenues,
and accorded a role in national development planning.
Development associations were organized in nearly every
district nationwide, and each district was represented
at the provincial and national levels via the cooperative confederation. During this third stage the local
development associations made a major contribution to
the extension of road, educational, and water and electrical services to the smaller towns and rural areas.
In addition, agricultural cooperatives and a cooperative credit bank were founded to encourage capital
formation for investment in income-generating activities. It seems that 1982 marked the beginning of a
new phase in which the latter will increasingly be
emphasized, following the completion of primary infrastructure.

The seed of self-help lay deep in the traditional
society, but its germination came from the winds of
change. Much of contemporary development practice
finds precedent in Islamic tradition or local custom.
Historically, limited public services and welfare
functions were provided through religious institutions.
Mosques provided public bathing facilities. Education
and some gravity-flow water delivery systems were supported by the waqf, or religious trust. The zakat represented a pious obligation to give alms; wealthy
families were expected to give sometimes to the poor.

Both Islam and local traditions within Yemen tend to stress collective and community values. While traditional production techniques were primarily suited to a division of farm tasks within the extended family household, there were mechanisms for levying collective labor for emergency relief or other special activities. The principle of collective responsibility applied in the raising of blood money within a kin group and sometimes in tax collections within a village or tribe. Most efforts to mobilize contributions to a project have recalled these moral and primordial values. Some activities have been organized by religious dignitaries or by tribal shaykhs.

However, it is possible to overstate the role of traditional values and affiliations in development cooperation. Traditional society consists of animosity as well as affection; the extent of community cooperation should not be unduly romanticized. Preexisting institutions afforded only the barest minimum of services. Moreover, the history of the cooperative movement shows its close association with two factors which ultimately contributed to the transformation of the Imamic system [12] -- migration and the liberal movement. Both were forms of resistance to or escape from political and economic backwardness, and to increased appropriation of a dwindling agricultural surplus in the form of taxes and crop-shares. Under the Imams, many thousands of young men left the fields for Aden and points abroad. Many of them hailed from the part of north Yemen known as the southern uplands, which was closest to the bustling British port. Migrants' associations at first provided insurance and communications services, then raised funds to educate members' sons and nephews in Aden. Following this model, village associations in the southern uplands raised donations from migrants and residents for village schools and water tanks. Through migration and clandestine communications, awareness of and demand for rudimentary public services spread. This became one of the demands of the emerging anti-Imamic movement in the 1930s and 1940s.

Another issue associated with both the cooperative and the liberal movement was the release of zakat for expenditure in the region of its collection. In many regions local elites, both progressive and traditional, called for recognized bodies of regional self-governance. The republican movement also advocated rights of voluntary association and assembly, freedom of trade, liberalization of the press, secularization of education, and the creation of cooperatives to encourage agricultural modernization.

The early self-help efforts, mostly ad hoc and short-lived, often combined traditional with reformist

210

concerns. Since one-room schools, cisterns or water channels, public baths, and wayfarer shelters had generally been maintained as charitable foundations, incremental improvements to these facilities naturally recalled religious and familial values. Projects were typically simple and did not require a special ongoing organization for their execution. The first organized development board which kept records of its plans and activities was the Hodeidah city town improvement board, established just months before the September 26, 1962 revolution. Yemen's major Red Sea port was experiencing some urban growth, commercialization, and light industrialization. The town board was formed in direct response to a fire which had destroyed a large section of thatched huts. The board kept records, collected some taxes on trade, hired some workers, purchased vehicles, and drew up a plan for fire fighting brigades and drainage of unhealthful standing water after rains. Formalized in a way village welfare and projects committees were not, the Hodeidah association represented a prelude to stage two. The other major towns followed the port's example several years later.¹³

The first republican regime of Abdullah al-Sallal opened the door to political and economic liberalization and endorsed the principle of local development. Two laws in 1963 legalized the formation of voluntary associations for civic, charitable, or cultural purposes. Although vaguely worded and permissive rather than proscriptive, the laws are often cited as a landmark for local development activity. But during the next four years the government was preoccupied with the war and other pressing matters of state. Very little attention or resources were diverted to public services, especially beyond the major urban areas. There was talk of social and economic development through cooperation, but little concerted action and no vertical or horizontal coordination of efforts. The first phase of localized informal self-help activities persisted through the civil war.

During the war the perceived need for public services deepened. Unfortunately, the war coincided with several years of drought, which deprived many communities of their normal water sources and reduced agricultural output. In some areas the fighting destroyed existing cisterns or footpaths. Tanks and trucks rolled into the countryside. The Egyptian soldiers sent to fight on behalf of the republic scorned the primitive Yemeni way of life and quite possibly exaggerated the modern services available in Egypt. The Y.A.R. government, with international technical support, constructed a paved highway from the seaport of Hodeidah to the highland capital at Sana'a, and began work on roads connecting these two cities to the third urban center, the southern uplands city of Ta'iz.[14] Vehicles, water pumps, electrical generators, radios, televisions, books, and bulldozers were imported in increasing numbers, along with countless commodities and gadgets. While the war and the drought exacerbated the need for services, roads and imported innovations presented new possibilities for small-scale improvements. Local projects incorporated some new technology, but the magnitude of these projects was modest. Most organizational and project activities were undocumented.

The declaration of peace in 1968 represented a turning point in many respects. One of the last acts of the al-Sallal regime was the release of a quarter of the zakat for local development. In November, the Quadi al-Iryani quietly replaced al-Sallal. Among other things, the new government created a Department of Youth, Labor, and Social Affairs to encourage civic and cooperative institutions and local self-help initiatives. Efforts to staff and strengthen the ministries of public works, education, and health reflected a new commitment to public services. Within the next few years, a large number of international donors (both capitalist and socialist) pledged support. Still, the task of providing basic infrastructure and services to a predominantly rural population in rugged terrain was tremendous, and the capacity of the state still inchoate.

The second stage in local development activity was different from the first in that specifically organizational behavior became more salient. A number of regional, provincial, and urban associations were founded. These adopted formal names, development association, local cooperative, welfare society. They engaged in constituent activities like drawing up bylaws and budgets, holding public administrative board elections, and writing regional development plans. They organized such larger and more complex projects as regional roads and small town water systems, often combining voluntary contributions with taxes and levies, and ministerial and even international assistance.

There were several reasons for the trend toward larger organizations. First, there were limits on what could be accomplished relying on local resources alone. In many endeavors there were clear economies of scale. This was especially true in the case of roads in the hinterland; what a single clan or village could not do, many cooperating communities within a region could. There was also, of course, a political motivation for establishment of a new civic institution. For many it

represented a regionally based authority parallel to
the lower echelons of the Ministry of Local Administration, a potential instrument of local self-governance and symbol of relative autonomy from the central
state. For the politically ambitious, the cooperative
or welfare association represented a new arena defined
by the political currency of service projects. While
seeking a degree of administrative and budgetary independence from the center, many associations took pains
to register with the department of social affairs in
hopes of gaining ministerial assistance for regional
and local projects. Leaders in some areas were also
conscious of the potential for foreign aid, which they
hoped would be more generous and technically competent
than Sana'a's.

Organizational activity was something of an elite
phenomena in that most participants were literate. Two
groups were mainly involved. The progressive or per-
ceptive wing of the old landed and shaykhly clans acted
to stay the slippage in their authority under the ancient regime; and younger republican counter-elites and
military officers saw themselves as a new generation of
regional and national leadership. In founding development cooperatives, these men hoped to marshal popular
interest in improved services in order to gain concessions from government, incidentally enhancing their own
prestige both locally and nationally. Though neither
radical nor altruistic, their appeals to public welfare
and the cooperative spirit nonetheless seemed progres-
sively populistic in contrast with the old order.

In the spring of 1973 two meetings were held to
establish a confederation of self-help organizations.
The meetings were attended by representatives of the
government and of over two dozen self-help societies;
there were a few other committedly federalist groups
which declined at the time to participate in a national
union. After some debate, all member associations
agreed to a common name, which translated literally
means "local development cooperative society." This is
usually rendered "LDA" for local development association in English; in Arabic it is generally called
al-ta'awun, which implies cooperative self-help. The
purpose of the cooperative confederation, called CYDA
in English for Confederation of Yemeni Development Associations, was to encourage local development efforts,
especially by seeking government and foreign assistance
for local projects. Delegates to the second meeting
elected an articulate young military officer, Ibrahim
al-Hamdi, as president of the confederation. He
praised previous self-help efforts, noted the weakness
of the government in providing services, and called for
greater cooperation both at the local level and between

development associations and government. To demonstrate its backing for development activities, the government promised half of zakat for local projects.

A year later, al-Hamdi assumed leadership of the republic in a military coup designated the corrective movement, drawing the cooperative confederation into the national limelight. Al-Hamdi promised greater government encouragement for self-help in the provinces. In 1975, Law No. 35[15] authorized the establishment of development cooperatives whose purpose would be to foster communities' efforts to improve communications, health, education, agriculture, and general services. Development cooperatives in the towns and districts were authorized to receive municipal and customs revenues in addition to half of the zakat. In 1976, nationwide cooperative elections were culminated with much fanfare and the promulgation of a cooperative plan partially attuned to the first national five-year plan (1976-81).

Between the 1974 corrective movement and the end of the first five-year plan in 1981, the cooperative development movement expanded, diversified, and institutionalized. The expansion in project activities reflected the increased availability of cash due to heavy migration and remittances. Initially it seemed that growth in organizational and project activities rested on the leadership of President al-Hamdi. But the movement survived his assassination and the politically uncertain tenure of his successor, Ahmad al-Ghashmi, who showed his support for the LDAs by raising their share of the zakat to three-quarters. Since 1978, 'Ali' Abdullah Saleh's government has concentrated on the financial and economic aspects of local development through agricultural cooperatives and the cooperative credit bank.

During this third stage there was an exponential expansion of the numbers of development and cooperative associations and the range of their activities. The number of local development associations increased from twenty-eight in the first year to nearly 200 in 1981. The rapid increase in the numbers of associations is explained by two factors. First, many of the regional and provincial associations founded between 1968 and 1974 divided into two or several district associations after 1975. This fission was partly a response to administrative decentralization under the corrective movement, which reduced the size of basic administrative units.[16] Second, interest in roads and other projects had spread to some previously inactive regions, particularly in the north and east. The promise of regular revenues and of central assistance for district projects induced the formation of many new boards. By 1981 there were LDAs in every district, and larger towns had their own development association. In addition to the increase in numbers of LDAs, there was diversification of the kinds of associations confederated through CYDA. In particular, several agricultural cooperatives were founded. The idea of agricultural societies had been proposed even before the revolution by intellectuals. Unlike the multifunctional, services oriented development associations, whose membership was inclusive within a geographical area, the agricultural cooperatives were economically oriented, specialized associations with specific objectives. Membership was voluntary in the form of purchase of shares in the cooperative. Although a few radicals had suggested collectivization (especially of state lands), the general consensus was that north Yemeni cooperatives should encourage rather than supplant private entrepreneurship in farming. Thus the function of the agricultural coops were to make capital inputs more readily available to members and other farmers in a region, and to encourage the transition from subsistence to market-oriented production. Activities of the cooperative should both enhance the profitability of production and increase the share capital of the society through investment. For instance, farmers' cooperatives operated service and petrol stations or water drilling rigs, hoping thereby to both stimulate farm modernization and earn revenues for the society.

CYDA moved its offices from an old Sana'ani house to a modern office complex on the airport road, symbolizing its institutionalization. Gradually specialized committees and departments within the confederation (financial, foreign, technical and cultural affairs, afforestation, etc.) were staffed with administrative, clerical, and technical personnel. The cooperative press expanded from a mimeographed circular to include a newspaper, several periodicals geared towards popular audiences, a scholarly journal dealing with development issues, and the broadcast media which now reached every Yemeni home. At the provincial level, the coordinating councils, the presidents of all LDAs in the province plus the governor, a presidential appointee, established offices and acquired staff and equipment. Both CYDA and its provincial branches became visible institutions. In 1981 a separate law defined the legal status of the confederation and the coordinating councils.[17] Their prescribed function is mainly to mobilize, advise, and audit the activities of member associations.

ORGANIZATION OF THE DEVELOPMENT ASSOCIATIONS

Both the structure and the operating procedures of the development cooperatives system have evolved during a period of more than a decade, and are still being refined. The preceding historical synopsis has shown that the impetus for these activities originated neither with the grassroots nor the center, but combined bottom-up with top-down and middle-both ways initiatives. Often simultaneous, but uncoordinated, activities at several levels, local, district, regional, provincial, and national, evolved into a multitiered system. Rules and procedures have never been cogently laid out in one document, but have emerged incrementally via both legislation and praxis.

The principle of planning and implementation, as laid out in various laws, speeches, and articles, leaves considerable initiative to the localities. Project proposals originate at the village or hamlet level and are passed upward through the district's development board and the provincial coordinating council (CC) to CYDA and then to the relevant ministries for inclusion in the national plan. Once this planning exercise has been completed, the onus for initiating a particular project falls again to the beneficiaries. The actual community to be served not the development board, which represents dozens or hundreds of neighborhoods and hamlets, is expected to initiate and oversee projects.

Here is how the system is supposed to work. Each community, approximately 500 persons, elects one representative to a general assembly of the local development association. These representatives discuss the services needs of the community with their neighbors. Then the general assembly meets to elect from among their number seven or nine members of the administrative board of the development association (LDB). The board elects its own president, secretary-general, treasurer, and other officers and then meets with the general assembly to discuss their project proposals and plans. The boards should compile a district or town development plan on the basis of project proposals and estimates of its own resources, suggesting integration of individual community projects where cost-efficient. Next, the presidents of the development boards meet with the governor as the coordinating council of the province to aggregate and rationalize plans at the provincial level. Finally, three officers of each development association attend a grand national conference. The cooperative conference elects from among its membership the administrative board and officers of CYDA, and draws together the plans of the various development associations into a national cooperative plan. The

CYDA board and their staff disaggregate plans by sector
and forward them to the relevant ministries, public
works, education, health, and sometimes agriculture,
for incorporation into the national five year plan,
along with ministerial priorities such as national
roads, university and teacher training institutes, hos-
pitals, sea and airports, and so forth.

One of the multiple connotations of cooperation is
that specific projects receive funding from a diversity
of sources. Most projects should draw on at least
three kinds of resources: beneficiaries, the development board's budget, and central matching funds. The
process of collecting beneficiary shares has not been
specified by central guidelines, but left to local con-
vention. The LDA's budget derives from three-quarters
of the district's zakat, one quarter of the municipali-
ties tax in the area, a share of the 2.5 percent cooperative customs tax, and other local taxes and contributions as they are able to collect. Central
matching funds for a locally initiated project were to
be made available only upon completion of the initial
stage or stages of construction. So that development
boards could estimate their project expenditures on
primary services, a formula for the proportional division of financial responsibility among local, LDA, and
central resources was issued. Project costs should be
divided as follows:

SECTOR	CENTRAL GOVERNMENT	LDA BUDGET	PEOPLE OF LOCALITY
Education	33.3%	33.3%	33.3%
Water Projects*	25 %	25 %	50 %
Health Sector	25 %	25 %	50 %
Roads			
1-20 Kms	--	--	100 %
20-30 Kms	25 %	(cost sharing determined	
over 30 Kms	50 %	by LDA and Locality)	

* If total costs of a water project exceed YR 200,000,
the government may provide up to eighty percent.

The specification of four project areas was not
intended to limit activity, but these were the only
sectors in which the government promised material support. Subsequently, electricity projects were recognized as legitimate local development activities,[18] but
the government promised only to eventually incorporate
local systems into the national power grid. Development boards were also theoretically motivated to improve agricultural production as a means of augmenting
their zakat-based revenues. The board was also supposed to own ten percent of the share capital of local
agricultural cooperatives, if any. Other projects,

which included tree planting, youth clubs, mosque construction and repairs, and other miscellaneous activities, could be financed from local and/or development
association funds, and might receive some central assistance.

The system was rather ingenious, in that it seemed
to make the most of limited resources and local participation. There was room for variations in associations' aspirations, financial resources, and interest
and commitment. But the difficulties in routinizing
the prescribed process were manifold. Turnout for both
the 1975 and 1979 elections was uneven: in some districts men assembled in large numbers, whereas elsewhere few people voted. Likewise, plans submitted by
village and neighborhood representatives ranged from
detailed budgets for dozens of projects to a few items
hastily scribbled on a bit of brown paper. There was
too little time between election and submission of
plans for careful review. There was no formal way of
incorporating the proposals of boards formed after
promulgation of the national plan in 1976 into the
national plan. Because of this last difficulty, the
five-year cooperative plan was scrapped and a new
three-year plan (1978/79 - 1980/81) was written.

Adherence to the guidelines and regulations of
CYDA and even to boards' own plans varied considerably.
Nowhere did organizations operate purely by the book.
Records, required by CYDA prerequisite to the release
of centrally controlled funds, were haphazardly kept.
Elections results were challenged after the fact, or
members resigned. Fights and work stoppages were frequent as one locality or tribe challenged another's
appropriation of water resources, regional transport
routes, or development associations funds. The government turned out to be notoriously slow in providing
funds, so much so that beneficiaries or boards, having
already committed resources, were forced to make up the
central share. Cost estimates often proved to have
been hopelessly unrealistic. Boards found themselves
unable to keep all of their verbal commitments. Few
members serving between 1976 and 1979 understood all
the procedures or appreciated the relevance of bookkeeping guidelines. From the perspective of the char-
actered rational management model, the system was a
shambles.

Nonetheless, in the third stage the local development organizations displayed considerable strength according to the criteria used by Uphoff and Esman. This
strength, it is suggested, lies in the fragile but
salient linkages established within the system and in
the relevance of the various cooperative organizations
to economic and political change.

Most of the structural characteristics which seem
to characterize the more viable development associations in Asia are also present in the Yemeni case. A
multilevel organization evolved through simultaneous
activity at several discrete levels: within villages,
lineages, or other local communities; within towns,
especially among petty merchants and civil servants; at
the district and regional levels; at the provincial
level; and in Sana'a. These activities, which occurred
spontaneously only in a few regions of the country,
were generalized on a national scale. The result was a
two-tier organization, with each tier also consisting
of two levels. The top tier, the cooperative confederation, is divided into the central offices of CYDA and
the provincial CCs. The local development organizations likewise have two tiers: the development board
and the general assembly. There has been greater
routinization of official process in the upper tiers,
but project activity relies mainly on the less institutionalized lower tier.

The development associations are multifunctional
and have engaged in a range of interrelated developmental activities. Whereas roads, water facilities,
schools, clinics, and electrification were each handled
by separate ministries at the national level, development associations engaged in various combinations of
these activities. Roads were the main activity in mountainous districts, but more water projects were undertaken in the hot coastal plain. Again, this feature
was not a product of design but a reflection of initial, unregulated project activity. In addition to
actual project activities, the arena of the development
associations provided certain state-like functions,
including the occasional adjudication of disputes[19] and a
certain amount of verbal interest articulation. The
development associations also tax and have been responsible for a national population census. Both the flexibility and the multifunctionality of the development
associations are related to the absence of other modern
-civic institutions.

The multiple channels are also more de facto than
de jure, or at least include both sanctioned and informal or interpersonal linkages. Some of the channels
specified within the system are hypothetical or latent
rather than operative, especially at the lower echelons. Nonetheless linkages within the system approxi-
mate the criteria for multiple channels identified by
Uphoff and Esman. These suggest that "(e)very function
of rural development -- planning and goal setting, resource mobilization, provision of services, integration
of services, control of administration, and claim-
making" should be shared between local and central
organizations.[20] Linkages among levels and elements

should promote formation of a system or network of information and resources exchange. These include both channels within the local organizations' framework and linkages to national, local, and private sector institutions. Comparison of the Asian cases indicates that the linkage function is performed more effectively when a number of channels operate concurrently, since any single channel may be blocked, monopolized, dysfunctional, or otherwise unsatisfactory.

Linkages represented by the emerging cooperative framework have been very important. Historically, development of the local organizations has been an attempt to construct an alternative local or regional-to-national linkage, alternative to the only preexisting channel, an appointed, rigid, and generally unresponsive bureaucracy of local administration. In terms of local social behavior, every development organization is demonstrably tied into tribal or other traditional (but changing) power relationships. The self-help association represents a third alternative, neither of the state nor of primordial society, but a means of bridging the gap between the two. The prescribed system of project planning and implementation within the system outlined above represents a possible, but not the only available, channel for mobilizing resources, making claims, and providing services. The multiplicity of funding sources for most projects is an indicator of multiple channels. So is the fact that deviation from the prescribed procedure is more common than adherence to formal channels.

Uphoff and Esman also offer evidence that decentralization of control aids effective local organization. The optimal balance of local autonomy with central planning usually entails devolution of authority from the center to the periphery. As already noted, the Yemeni example is atypical in that resources are widely dispersed with the system, not monopolized by the center. The zakat (and related surcharges) was once the principle means of support for the state administration, but its contribution to government revenues has declined considerably.[21] Payment of the Islamic tithe was made voluntary in 1974, after which farmers could in good conscience pay to charity or local projects rather than the tax man. There were virtually no other regular taxes collected in the countryside, save those associated with local development projects. The government had very limited capacity to tax the millions of dollars which entered the country every year during the late 1970s. The government maintained only limited control beyond the administrative centers. The issue of localism vs. centralism has been salient in cooperative affairs, but it has played out differently than in most bureaucratized, heavily centralized Asian cases.

As Uphoff and Esman point out, decentralized decision-making is best suited to technologically simple, small, and relatively inexpensive projects or improvements; more complex and capital intensive operations are more likely to require scarce technical and managerial skills available only at the central level. The Yemeni experience demonstrates the same point. Ad hoc self-help groups served limited development functions where traditional solutions failed to satisfy new social needs, but more sophisticated services required more elaborate organization and linkages to the central ministries.

The three stages of development of the Yemeni development associations show an interesting pattern. The first stage was characterized by very localized, technically illegal and hence highly autonomous, activity on a small scale. In the second state there was a trend towards much larger organizations, at the supraregional and national levels. The third phase has been characterized by two countervailing tendencies, one centralizing and the other centripetal. In 1975 the government had attempted to enhance central hegemony by decentralizing local administration from the subprovince to the district level. This move made it possible, though not mandatory, for development associations covering a wide geographical area to subdivide into district associations. Fission occurred because a wealthy district wished to keep its resources to itself, or because one or more districts felt their interests were not served by the regional development association. Within districts including towns, there often developed an urban-rural split which was resolved by the formation of separate urban and district development boards. Where village associations were active, they too often sought recognized autonomy within the district association, and represented a centripetal force.

There have been numerous pressures for preservation of local or regional habits against outside incursions. The diversity of ecological and sociological niches in the country makes it possible for each area to claim unique problems, which outsiders cannot fully understand. Where self-help efforts had not emerged spontaneously, antipathy towards outside structures extended to the development associations. Where there was a history of local development activity, some participants regarded the formation of central institutions and rules as an effort to co-opt local efforts. Even where there was some local propensity to participate and trust in government to support local activities, neither working people nor elites were neces-

sarily predisposed to operate according to rules formulated at the center. In various places and at different times during the first five-year plan period, there
were incidents of armed resistance to the central
state. It is interesting to note that in several such
instances, associations calling themselves the local
cooperative have continued to function. The particular
circumstances of the 1960s and 1970s made it possible
for local or regional associations to fulfill a somewhat independent statelike role.

At the same time, there are powerful incentives to
rationalize procedures by operating within centralized
structures and guidelines. The strongest instruction
in the imperatives of rational planning and budgeting
is experience. While the initial costs of a project
may be raised in one-time-only donations, grants, and
collections, maintenance requires ongoing funds and
supervision. A few examples of water towers which
collapsed and generators which burnt out illustrated
the necessity of technical planning. Contributions and
donations were voluntary only during stages of initial
enthusiasm or in modest quantities. Larger and more
ambitious undertakings necessitated either the force of
law to ensure beneficiary financing or outside channels
of funding, or both. One or two projects could be accomplished piecemeal, with work progressing as funds
become available, but to construct several services
requires some forethought and setting of priorities.
The ambitions of cooperative leaders may also motivate
them to operate within the sanctioned rules.

The tension between localism and centralism is not
necessarily a zero sum game in which the increased
strength of the one implied a loss of authority by the
other.²² The development associations have been
strengthened by their confederation into a rule-making
body, in terms of vertical and horizontal linkages, and
as measured by the services they provide. At the same
time, the growth of the development and cooperative
associations has helped extend state authority by establishing linkages between the state and residential
communities. These include both institutional channels
and physical linkages in the form of roads and some
central-place services such as secondary schools and
health clinics.

The salience of the network of development cooperative organizations in the national civic arena is
virtually unparalleled. The 1975 cooperative elections
were the first nationwide polling experience in the
national memory, and the 1979 and 1982 cooperative
elections were each better publicized and better attended than the one before. Elections for municipal
councils and for the constituent assembly have been
patterned on the cooperative model but have not matched

it in scope. When there was discussion of a national referendum on the issue of unity between north and south Yemen, the LDAs were recognized as the most viable institution for organizing such a poll. The second national population census, in 1981, was organized through CYDA and its member associations, and later used as the basis for dividing the cooperative customs tax among districts on the basis of population density.

THE PROVISION OF SERVICES

The real relevance of the development associations has been their provision of services to the urbanizing small towns and the rural areas. They have mobilized capital for investment in regional and country roads and other infrastructure essential to capitalist development and contributed to increased rates of literacy among modern youth. Many local development projects are stop-gap or semicompleted measures. Locally initiated vehicular trails are truly extensive but never paved without special central or outside technical assistance. Many schools were built with three rooms, with additional construction after three or more years of instruction warranted fourth through sixth grade rooms. The nature of water projects varied tremendously according to environmental conditions (anything from a cistern to deepwell with piped house-to-house delivery) but were typically regarded as incomplete. The same was true of electrification schemes, which initially offered a few hour's service in the evening. Hence they do not compare in quality or durability to the government's development projects. But the numbers of small projects accomplished by self-help organizations and the extent of access to cooperatively built services makes them important. Projects initiated by communities or development boards offer rudimentary services to far more people than government services. Whereas both government and private sector investments have gravitated heavily towards the three cities and a few medium-sized towns along the paved roads, cooperative sector investments are more evenly distributed among a predominantly rural population.

Part of the managerial weakness of both the development organizations and the government lies in the absence of reliable data and records on critical development variables. All figures referring to land tenure, farm output, expenditures by government or the private or cooperative sectors, or international trade and foreign assistance are estimates. CYDA's published records reveal as much about the evolution of the budgetary system as they do about trends in expenditures. Nonetheless, records of the first three-year plan period, 1973-76, and of the 1976-81 plan, do indicate the magnitude of development investments by the cooperative sector compared with the contributions of government and private investors.

The first national three-year plan, formulated in 1973, was a very preliminary exercise in defining the parameters of development expenditures and capital formation.[23] The plan indicated general targets for growth in various sectors of the economy. Only two investment sectors were identified, the public sector and the private sector. The public sector was expected to provide somewhat more than half of all development expenditures under the plan, with the assistance of foreign donors. No mention was made of the cooperative sector.

Thanks to the infusion of remittances, actual growth (seven percent) was higher than anticipated (six percent). Growth was registered primarily by the private sector, which spent sixty percent more than planned. Although its spending increased dramatically in the last year of the plan period, the government fell short of its targets and relied increasingly on foreign assistance.

Even the broadly indicated material targets of the plan were not achieved. Investment in agriculture and industry, especially, fell short of planned objectives. The increase in private sector spending occurred mainly in commodity trade and real estate. Total public sector development spending under the plan was YR 1.37 billion (U.S. $305 million).

The CYDA records, released independently, show total development expenditures during the same period of YR 180.8 million ($40.2 million). Approximately two-thirds of this amount was raised in citizen's contributions of one form or another. The government had contributed about one percent (this was before the promise of more), and the difference came from over seven dozen reporting LDAs. By 1976, eighty boards reported having cut some 5100 kilometers of rural roads, relying on beneficiary work crews and cash donations. Seventy-four development associations reported having built 581 schools. Sixty-three associations reported having worked on nearly 700 small and medium-sized water projects. Only eleven health projects were reported by ten development associations, but twenty-two LDAs reported having contributed to eighty-five miscellaneous projects. Field observations suggest that these are reasonable counts of the numbers of projects undertaken, although the relationship between national and cooperative development spending should not be taken at face value.

In drawing up the five-year development program, the Central Planning Organization (CPO) drew on some of

the lessons of the first experience. The second plan
was more detailed and textured. Unlike the three-year
program, which identified only two investment sectors,
the five-year plan anticipated investment from the
public, the private, the cooperative, and real and projected 'mixed' sectors. A significant share of financing was expected to come from abroad, most of it in
support of public and mixed sector investments. The
public, the private, and the mixed sectors were each
expected to contribute about a third of development
financing. Projects by local development associations
were expected to represent scarcely seven percent of
total development investment. However, the local development associations were indicated to receive only a
tiny fraction of international assistance, so the cooperative sector was expected to provide twelve percent
of domestic financing.[24] A World Bank study, entitled
"Yemen Arab Republic Local Development Associations: a
New Approach to Rural Development,"[25] concluded that in
the mid-to-late 1970s the development associations were
more effective than the central government in providing
primary services to the rural areas. In the two fiscal
years 1976-77 and 1977-78, government development expenditures totaled YR 1751 million, of which YR 873
came from the state's budget. During the same period,
the development associations reported expenditures of
YR 508 million, less than the central state, to be
sure, but a respectable contribution. Clearly local
development association spending was far higher relative to state investments than supposed by the CPO.
The Bank report also points out that only a fraction of
LDA funds went towards administrative costs.
    During the 1978-1981 three-year cooperative plan
period, local projects' spending still did not conform
to submitted plans. CYDA records show the relationship
between planned and reported spending by development
associations during the period, in millions of Yemeni
riyals:[26]

	PLANNED	REPORTED	PROPORTION
Roads	YR 615	YR 811.6	123%
Education	268	245.1	91%
Water	103	151.3	146%
Health	58	21.1	36%
Other	94	70.2	74%
Miscellaneous	325	360.2	111%
	YR 1463	YR 1959.5	113%

"Other" in these figures includes electricity, youth
clubs, traffic triangles, mosques, and so forth. The
miscellaneous category groups the activities of agricultural cooperatives with foreign aid and CYDA direct
investments. Expenditures on roads and especially
water were higher than anticipated, as was foreign aid

to CYDA (negligible in the plan). Overall investment by the cooperative sector was higher than planned by the development associations, and considerably higher than planned in the national program.

The records of the cooperative confederation also show that the bulk of local development project expenses continued to be borne by citizens, both directly in the form of project financing and indirectly in the form of contributions to the LDA budget. The following table compares the contribution of local, development board, and governmental financing to projects reported to CYDA during two three-year periods.[27]

| | 1973 to 1976 | | | 1978/79 - 1980/81 | | |
	% from Citizens	% from Board	% from Gov't	% from Citizens	%from Board	% from Gov't
Roads	72	28	---	62	37	1
Schools	54	45	1	39	41	18
Water	32	68	---	52	29	10
Health	31	69	---	32	63	5
Other	17	78	5	23	79	14
Total	64	35	1	52	38	8

The government contributed more to locally initiated projects in the late 1970s than it had prior to 1976, but still failed to meet its obligations according to the CYDA formula. The total central contribution in the latter three-year span was eight percent, mostly assistance for schools, electricity and miscellaneous projects. The development associations covered a slightly higher proportion of total costs in the second period than in the first. Their proportional contribution to roads increased; they picked up the slack in government allocations to local education; and they were the primary source of financing for health and other, elective projects.

Citizen's contributions declined from two-thirds in the first period to slightly more than half in the second. Local funding for roads accounted for over half of all local development expenditures between 1973 and 1976, and remained the major items in the latter report period as well. Local resources also covered one-third to one-half of the costs of most school, water, and health projects. The category of citizens' contributions should not be understood to imply only voluntary or charitable donations but covers a wide range of local fund-raising mechanisms.[28] Variations in these are literally too numerous to examine. They have included charity drives and also taxes, levies, user fees, and various collective ownership schemes. They have varied not only regionally but from one project to the next, according to the nature and cost of

the service provided. In some cases social control and
voluntarism have served, but in others local administration authorities have enforced the obligation to
contribute. What is significant about the extent of
citizens contributions is that they represent multiple
channels for resource mobilization, not specified by
law but more or less tailored to a particular project
effort.

In addition to direct contributions to projects,
local revenues provided a major source of income to the
regular LDA budgets. The following table shows the
composition of recorded LDA incomes for two periods of
the national five-year plan:²⁹ 1976-78, the first two
years; and 1978-81, a three year span.

	1976-78	1978-81	TOTAL
Central incomes	9%	9%	9%
Local revenues from zakat	18%	34%	28%
Local revenues from citizens	73%	57%	63%

Non-zakat local revenues contributed three-quarters of
incomes in the first two years and over half in the
last three years. Proportional income from the zakat
doubled, reflecting perhaps some improvement in collections as well as the rise in the official share due
the development cooperatives from half to three-
quarters. Central revenues contributed an even nine
percent to development association revenues.

These figures demonstrate that the activities
reported by the development associations have been
financed primarily from noncentral sources. As noted
earlier, the extent of reliance on informal financial
channels is made possible by the unusual confluence of
circumstances, large amounts of cash outside the formal
banking system and practically untaxed by the central
state.

The relevance of the local development associations to capital formation and services provision
during the period of the five-year plan was substantial. Private sector spending was again higher than
targeted, but tended to concentrate in the transport
and trade of imported commodities and urban construction. The government made visible progress in the construction of national infrastructure for transport,
communications, education, and health, but its development spending was lower than planned. Most of the unanticipated growth occurred in the construction sector,
electricity and water, and public services. Agriculture was scheduled for fourteen percent of investment
under the plan, mostly from the private sector, but
reportedly attracted only eight percent.

Although a detailed account of spending during the
plan period or other reliable data comparing investment

by the development cooperatives with private, public and mixed sector investments and foreign assistance are not available, all indications are that the self-help contribution has been considerably greater than the seven percent projected in the five-year plan. While the government, with international technical assistance, has paved and culverted a basic grid of two north-south and two west-east two-lane highways, the development associations reliably report work on at least 15,000 kilometers of rural roads which now reach most inhabited sections of the country. CYDA records of expenditures in water during the final three years of the plan period represent ten percent of total national expenditures on water and electricity together over the five years. National expenditures in education and health amounted to YR 1294 million, compared with YR 266.2 million for the cooperative sector.[30] Whether or not these figures and proportions can be taken at face value, the overall relevance of spending in the cooperative sector to the development of public services has been considerable. The development associations have consistently raised and invested more resources than expected, often in the area where government has failed to meet plan targets. It is clear that the development cooperatives have been partly responsible for rapid growth in transport, water and electricity, and educational services.

The relevance of development cooperation has been in the formation of capital for investment in very basic services to smaller towns and the more densely populated rural areas. The distribution of effects and benefits from cooperative projects has been more even and equitable both geographically and socially than the effects of foreign, central, or private sector expenditures. While there is some tendency for local development spending to concentrate in administrative and commercial centers, this tendency is far more pronounced in both state and entrepreneurial investment patterns. Direct international assistance has also clustered in the urban areas and the most productive agricultural regions. Self-help activity defers to the other sectors in that LDAs and local communities tend not to pursue projects which private or state agencies seem likely to undertake. The importance of development cooperation has been in providing just those interim services which alternative channels have been unwilling or unable to foster. If there had been no local development activity the alternative channels may have behaved a bit differently, but there would probably be greater inequities in access to services than existed at the beginning of the second national five-year plan in 1982.

In contemplating a new development program for the 1980s, both the nation and the CYDA organizations faced new circumstances and challenges. On the one hand, there was a clear national imperative for rational planning and management of resources. With the end of the oil boom, remittances from the Arab Gulf into the Y.A.R. leveled off. But imports continued to rise. Faced with growing budget deficits and its first balance of payments deficit, the government called for "less consumerism and more investment," particularly in agriculture and agro-industry.[31] A certain level of services had been attained, but it would be necessary to further extend, integrate, and maintain utilities, roads and schools. The government sought to bring all primary schools under a unified public curriculum and to produce a new generation of literate men and women. Roads require repair after rain or heavy use, at least until drainage and embankments are provided. Work was in progress to bring the whole country into an integrated twenty-four-hour-a-day electricity system. Urban health services had improved, but access to medical facilities in the countryside remained poor. While many communities still lacked adequate water resources, high rates of drilling and pumping in certain regions raised fears of depleted aquafers. Overall, the improvement in services, especially in the truly rural areas, was relative only to the very low starting point.

The cooperative associations had provided very basic services and made a leading contribution to expansion of the national road network. They provided for some integration of services at the regional and local level. Agricultural cooperatives, still in their infancy during the first five-year plan, nonetheless represented a possible solution to the dilemma of private sector underinvestment in agriculture. In view of the government's incapacity to tax rural incomes, the mobilization of resources through informal and semiformal channels was impressive. The development associations provided necessary and sufficient organization for investment in basic services. Cooperative investments in roads and utilities facilitated the penetration of capitalism into the periphery and the emergence of a rural and semiurban bourgeoisie. Roads, schools, and other projects and the cooperative associations themselves constituted important material and institutional linkages within the Y.A.R., thus contributing also to the augmentation of state power.

The end of the first five-year plan period seemed to signify the beginning of a new stage for the development cooperatives associations. First, in many regions what could be accomplished relying primarily on local resources had been accomplished. Rural roads had

been the most important development activity in the
mountainous interior of the country, but new road construction leveled off in most regions between 1978 and
1981. With international assistance, the Ministry of
Education was building more rural schools and assuming
responsibility for administration and curriculum in
locally constructed schools. Local development of
water resources was seriously constrained by geophysi-
cal factors in some areas. One very rudimentary level
of services had been achieved, but to improve this
basic infrastructure required higher financial, technical, and managerial inputs. Heretofore the strength
of local development associations had been in activat-
ing informal channels for technically simple projects.
To raise the level of services now required greater
degrees of coordination and planning.

There was an effort to both rationalize and
centralize local development channels. For the 1982
cooperative elections guidelines were pursued for voter
and candidate registration. The CYDA law of 1981
formalized the identity and role of the cooperative
confederation and the coordinating councils, and the
participation of deputy ministers of public works,
health, education, planning, and other government
agencies on the administrative board of CYDA. The
exact channeling of zakat from taxpayer to development
board account had always been left vague, but was now
to be collected centrally and dispersed to the LDAs
through CYDA upon review of their accounts. Poor and
sparsely populated districts which had been unable or
unwilling to undertake self-help were granted an additional share of the cooperative customs tax as an
inducement. Village associations, which had been
active mostly in the southern uplands, were discredited
for their failure to respect plans and formal procedures; having formalized the central cooperative
institutions, the government pointed out that the
village associations lacked any legal basis. Steps
were taken to encourage the more even and regular participation of the district and town associations in cooperative affairs. All of these represented efforts to
institutionalize the system and to encourage new allocations of resources consistent with national goals.[32]

At the 1983 cooperative conference, emphasis was
on investments in income-generating and productive
activities. Development associations would continue to
help provide public services, especially in the heretofore neglected health sector. However, the new direction in the 1980s would be toward projects which
either generated revenue or stimulated capital investment in the private sector. It was therefore hoped
that the cooperative associations would supply institutional support for productive investments. While

diversifying away from very primary services, the development cooperative organizations would continue to support investments in projects relatively neglected by the government and the private sector. Credits for projects which promised a return on the initial investment would be offered by the cooperative credit bank to qualifying associations. Both local development associations and shareholder cooperatives should participate in investment credits. In the case of LDAs, income from equipment or facility rental or other revenue-bearing activities would be used to support truly public services, from clinic to welfare to cultural events. Shareholder cooperatives were expected both to provide services to a specialized group, farmers, fishermen, craftspeople, and to pursue corporate goals of capital accumulation for shareholder dividends as well as reinvestment. As with previous developments within the cooperative movement, this new direction called for widespread adoption of policies already practiced by some vanguard associations.

Administration of a credit system and management of more sophisticated services will, of course, require tighter supervision than in the past. Centralization and routinization of process are further warranted by several considerations. Central initiatives are probably necessary to offset the increased peripheralization of districts and regions which haven't participated in self-help. From a national perspective it is crucial to raise farm and industrial output if a widening balance of payments deficit is to be avoided. More complex services, projects, and events will necessitate the maintenance of a system of files and more efficient auditing. This is especially true if investment capital is borrowed. Operation of any of the known investment projects, tractors, bulldozers, drilling rigs, service stations, agricultural experiment and extension stations, utilities companies, refrigeration of fresh fish, light manufacturers, and new irrigation schemes, requires both technical skill and office back-up.

Although some Yemenis fear overregulation of self-help, the Y.A.R. development associations and cooperatives are considerably less controlled than comparable organizations elsewhere in the Third World. The question now seems to be whether more management and routinization of process will make local development more efficient and equitable, or merely stifle the element of spontaneity and success realized in the past two decades. If the development cooperative associations are to have the same relevance in the 1980s as they have shown in the first development decade, major adaptations of financial and political practice will be necessary. If self-help cannot evolve to accommodate more complex issues, then it will be necessary to conclude that the relative success of local development associations was a unique and fleeting result of extraordinary circumstances at a particular stage of development.

NOTES

1. For a discussion of the problems associated with this approach, see Norman T. Uphoff and Milton J. Esman, Local Organization for Rural Development: Analysis of Asian Experience. (Ithaca: Cornell University Rural Development Committee, 1974). Rene Dumont, in Socialism and Development. (New York:; Praeger, 1973) argues a similar point from a more radical perspective.

2. Goran Hyden, Beyond Ujamaa in Tanzania: Underdevelopment and an Uncaptured Peasantry. (Berkeley: University of California, 1980) argues that the public sphere often fails to foster a civic morality.

3. See James B. Mayfield's discussion of the application of Western management in "The Egyptian Basic Village Service Program," in this volume.

4. Uphoff and Esman, Local Organization, xi - xii, summarize their major findings and conclusions.

5. They place greater emphasis on the distribution of economic assets, particularly land tenure, than I indicate here. Discussion of land tenure and equity issues, though important, are beyond the scope of this paper. See pp. 99-102 for a discussion of the criteria listed.

6. The study by David D. Gow et al. Local Development Organizations and Rural Development: A Comparative Reappraisal, 2 Vols. (Washington, D.C.: Development Alternatives, Inc., 1979). The other countries studied were Upper Volta, Cameroon, Guatemala, Peru, the Philippines, and Jamaica.

7. John M. Cohen, et. al. "Development from Below: Local Development Associations in the Yemen Arab Republic." (World Development, Vol. 9, No. 11/12: 1981), p. 1039. This article reviews the "fugitive" literature on development associations in the Y.A.R.

8. This point is noted in the World Bank, Yemen Arab Republic Local Development Associations: A New Approach to Rural Development. (Country Programs Department 1, Report No. 2963a - Y.A.R.: March 2, 1981). For more ethnographic detail, see Jon C. Swanson and Mary Hebert, Rural Society and Participatory Development: Case Studies of Two Villages in the Yemen Arab Republic. (Ithaca: Cornell University Rural Development Committee, Yemen Research Program, September, 1981).

9. I have argued this point at greater length in a paper presented to the Middle East Studies Association Conference in Philadelphia, November, 1982: "The Transition to Peripheral Capitalism in the Y.A.R." See also Samir Amin, The Arab Nation. (London: Zed Press, 1978), 20,29.

10. The best recent political history of the Y.A.R. is J.E. Peterson. Yemen: The Search for a Modern State. (Baltimore: Johns Hopkins University Press, 1982).

11. The effects of migration and remittances is one of the most interesting research questions in Yemen. For a review of literature on the subject, see John M. Cohen and David B. Lewis, "Capital Surplus, Labor-Short Economies: Yemen as a Challenge to Rural Development Strategies" (American Journal of Agricultural Economics, Vol. LXI, Nov. 8, 1979).

12. Leigh Douglas has recently completed his study of the liberal movement, including its relationship to early migration and the formation of village associations. "The Free Yemeni Movement, 1935-1962," Ph.D dissertation for the Department of Political Science, School of Oriental and African Studies, University of London, 1983.

13. I have chronicled the history and the details of many points raised herein in my dissertation, "The Political Economy of Self-Help: Development Cooperatives in the Yemen Arab Republic," for the Department of Political Science, SUNY-Binghamton, September, 1983.

14. For a list of national roads and international sources of construction financing see the World Bank, Yemen Arab Republic: Development of a Traditional Economy. (Washington, D.C.: World Bank Report No. 2057a - Y.A.R., 1978), 277.

15. This law has been published several times. One source is Ta'awan Book No. 3, Majmua'ah al-Qanawin wa al-Lawah al-Ta'awuniyyah fi J.A.Y. (Sana's: CYDA, n.d.), 29-41.

16. Under the Imams and the first years of the republic, the basic administrative unit was the sub-province or quda. Each quda was divided into several districts. The 1975-1976 decentralization made the district, or nahiyah, the lowest unit of national administration.

17. The CYDA law, the 1975 Cooperative Law, the Cooperative Credit Bank Law, and other documents pertaining to cooperative organization have been published by CYDA, al-Ta'awum: al-tashriya'at al-Ta'awantyyah (no place or date).

18. Inclusion of electricity within the priorities for local development was decided at the Fourth Cooperative Conference, 1979. The formula for project cost-sharing comes from CYDA records.

19. For a discussion of the socio-political role of
one development board, see Richard Tutwiler, "Ta'awun
Mahwit: The Social History of a Local Development
Association in Highland Yemen" (paper presented to the
Conference on Strategies of Local Development in the
Middle East, University of Maryland, September 1978).
20. Uphoff and Esman, Local Organization, 70. Sharing of responsibility maximizes both local benefits and
central management and technical inputs.
21. Mohammad al-Azazi, translated by Barbara Croken
under the title "The Financial Resources of the LDAs
and Some Possibilities for Their Development" (in al-
Ghad, No. 4 Year 3: Oct./Nov. 1977).
22. Uphoff and Esman, Local Organization, 79, point
out that it is possible for each to draw strength from
their cooperation.
23. The first section of the five-year plan issued
in 1976 is an evaluation of the three-year plan. Central Planning Organization. Yemen Arab Republic First
Five-Year Plan, 1976-1977 - 1980-1981. (Sana'a The
Prime Minister's Office, 1977), English version, 11-55.
24. For allotments by investment sector, see pp.
221-224 of the plan. CYDA and development association
plans (pp. 341-342) include roads, schools, water,
health, electricity, mosque, and environmental projects. Road building equipment for CYDA and fifty
agricultural cooperatives were also indicated.
25. The World Bank, 1981. Summary and conclusions,
i - xiii.
26. A detailed account of cooperative activities
between 1978 and 1981 is Abdu 'Ali' Othman and Hamoud
al-Awdi, "The Yemeni Cooperative Movement and Development: Participation of Local Development Cooperative
Associations in the Projects of the First Five-Year
Development Plan" (in Arabic: paper presented to the
CPO, Sana'a, January 1982). Their study also includes
a cross-sectional survey of development and cooperative
associations.
27. These data are compiled from CYDA records. I
have analyzed variations and trends in greater depth in
my dissertation. For evidence of variations among
rural districts, see also S. Tjip Walker, Sheila
Carapico, and John Cohen, Emerging Rural Patterns in
the Yemen Arab Republic: Results of a 21 - Community
Cross-Sectional Study. (Ithaca: Cornell University
Rural Development Committee, Yemen Research Program,
1983).
28. Hyden's comment on comparable resource mobilization schemes in East Africa is applicable: "Although
it is wrong to expect that ... benefits are equally
shared within communities, people do make a contribution, whether in the form of money or labor. This is
a form of local taxation, which is usually far more

acceptable than government taxation, because it is
usually more progressive -- the big men in the communities make the largest contributions -- and above
all, because it is locally approved and administered."
(p. 28).

29. Othman and la-Awdi Yemeni Cooperative 75-76,
citing CYDA records.

30. CYDA data are compared with Nigel Harvey's reports of spending under the plan, in Middle East Economic Digest, February 10, 1981.

31. Nigel Harvey, in the Middle East Economic Digest, January 8, 1981, reports a projected 1982 deficit
of YR 3200 mil ($700 million) in a budget of YR 8470
million ($1850 million). This would be three times
greater than the 1980 deficit. For the prime minister's views, see the interview with A.R. Haideri, MEED,
April 3, 1981.

32. These changes were reported in two issues of
al-Ta'awun magazine: No. 173, April, 1982, especially
13-14; and No. 174/175, May-June, 1982, especially
8-10, 19, 28-29, and the report of an international
development conference, 33-43. For analysis of the
activities of the village associations, see Othman and
al-Awdi, "Yemeni Cooperative."

Introduction to Part IV

Jean-Claude Garcia-Zamor

The first chapter of this part, entitled "Can Participative Planning and Management be Institutionalized in Developing Countries?" reviews the experiences of five industrialized countries with some form of PPM and contrasts the suitability of these countries versus developing countries for a PPM approach. In answering the question asked in the title, the author argues that PPM cannot be institutionalized in developing countries in its present conceptual framework. He suggests a less radical approach, such as the concept of "guidance," which is defined in the chapter. In such a context, participation would be seen as merely the coordination of roles of the outside advisers, the national decision-makers, and the local beneficiaries, to achieve effective guidance of the development process.

This chapter is followed by a selected bibliography on participative planning and management. The wide range of literature included in it is divided into two sections. The first contains not only books but other documents published in book form by consulting firms, universities, and some international organizations. The second section covers articles published in professional journals in the United States and abroad.

11. Can Participative Planning and Management Be Institutionalized in Developing Countries?

Jean-Claude Garcia-Zamor

Most of the developing countries are a composite world of two contrasting realities. There is on the one hand, the so-called urban elite, civil servants, politicians, military officers, and teachers, and on the other, the rural poor who have no participation whatsoever in the planning or managing of development strategies that supposedly would help them. Most of these countries do not have the administrative framework to handle the requirements imposed by the donors of foreign aid. In some cases, the national leaders do not have the wisdom to plan and work for long-term development activities in the rural areas where their accomplishment will be less visible. They opt instead for high status projects. They seem to be unaware of the fact that all of the highly industrialized nations first became highly successful agricultural nations. The political systems that prevail in the former countries make PPM quite difficult.

The Argentines sometimes refer to people from similar systems as <u>verticalista</u> who believe in <u>dedocracia</u>, meaning that the finger of the leader points and his will moves vertically down through the structures.[1] Furthermore, in developing countries, the bulk of the population does not understand the process of public administration and economic development. At the local level, people may be in a better situation to perceive the needs of their village or province than the planning specialist who is operating in the capital, because the latter's global plan encompasses many variables that are not manageable at the local level. But despite their knowledge of the right variables, people at the local level need the guidance of technocrats to develop large-scale projects that could have a significant impact on development. Experience has shown that beneficiaries' participation is not easily achieved when specific actions are required not only from the designers of the project but also from a centralized bureaucracy located several hundred, sometimes thousands of miles away.

Another impediment to successful participation at the grassroots level is what Albert O. Hirschman refers to as fracasomania in the Latin American context, but is also found in some of the countries of Africa and Asia: a highly damaging tendency to categorize most of the experiences in social and political reform and in economic development as utter failures. Hirschman argues that this failure complex, or fracasomania, may itself lead to real failures.

If a serious attempt has to be made to institutionalize PPM in developing countries in order to contribute to efficient and effective orientation of the development process, some new approaches, possibly different from the ones advocated in many of the chapters of this book, might be necessary. A good example of such approaches could be the one suggested at a seminar sponsored by the Inter-American Institute of Agricultural Sciences regarding participation in the programs of the institute. PPM was viewed more as a "guidance" mechanism. This guidance concept assumes different dimensions at different levels. It could be visualized as societywide, as agricultural or rural, as a reference in the guidance of the development process in general or the agricultural or rural development process specifically. Also, it could be seen in terms of an institution, program, project, etc. In this case it would mean the guidance of the planning-implementation process at each of these levels. Guidance is conceived as the ensemble of decisions adopted and taken into action with the purpose of transforming the socioeconomic and political situation in a defined way. In this sense it is an integrated whole which occurs, with different components, at all the administrative levels indicated, ranging from the national, sectorial, and subsectoral levels to the regional, local, and enterprise levels. Through strategic and focused decisions, guidance defines a general framework for assigning society's resources as a means of transforming reality. Guidance makes operational decisions that should produce an effective allocation of these resources, mobilizing them and truly transforming them. It also mobilizes individual and group efforts to achieve the results previously mentioned. Priority is given to the concept of operating groups, an approach which describes the person as a social subject, emphasizing his or her primacy in labor relations. This stands in contrast to approaches that appear to be concerned for people, when in reality, the concern is for institutions, projects, etc., to which people are subordinated. For example, rural development projects that maintain an apparent humanism emphasize that the beneficiaries must participate in decision-making. This appears to be more functional than humanistic.[4]

PPM IN INDUSTRIALIZED NATIONS

An examination of some cases of participatory planning and/or management in a few industrialized societies will contrast the suitability of these countries for a PPM approach to that of the developing countries. This examination, however brief and selective, reveals that PPM can best take place in developed countries where the local communities possess more experienced and skilled people to deal with outside agencies. These countries also have a tradition of broad-based participation as an essential part of their political process and therefore apply PPM as part of an integrated approach to development. The PPM strategy can then be very effective. The following cases, concisely reviewed, involve five highly industrialized countries, The Netherlands, Sweden, France, Canada and Great Britain.

The Netherlands and Sweden. In a recent study of The Netherlands and Sweden, archetypical welfare states, Estelle James of the State University of New York at Stonybrook notes that churches, unions and similar community groups can assume wide responsibility for the delivery of specific social services with little threat to the progressive goals of these societies. In fact, the broad objectives of political democracy, widespread participation in economic decision-making and cultural pluralism, may be best served by a welfare system that centralizes the financing of social services but which decentralizes responsibility for actually delivering services.[5]

France. For over fifteen years, alternative approaches to development plans have been tried in France, with a view toward proposing other perspectives and modes of development. In this respect a French scholar, Bernard Eme, makes a distinction between small groups of individual initiatives which attempt to master new lifestyles in an often limited spatial framework, and local and microregional initiatives attempting to promote global strategies of endogenous development within the context of their own territory, with the participation of the local populations. In the first case, the system remains, according to Eme, elitist and sector based and constitutes a peripheral field of innovation which cannot change the dominant system of development. But in the second case, the study of these local and microregional global development initiatives gives reason to believe that real alternatives to industrial development have asserted themselves.[6]

Canada. In Canada, community economic development projects use public money for government programs as "seed money" or for research and training purposes. However, projects organize themselves around the social, economic and cultural problems of their respective communities. Local development workers want outsiders to be involved in terms of giving advice and assistance, but they recognize that the lasting benefits of a community venture will be much greater if the final decisions about a project are made within the community by its own members. Two students of the community economic development organizations in Canada state that these organizations begin with the idea that people have the intelligence and ability to control their own lives. This does not mean that people at the local level always have the necessary skills and knowledge to make good decisions. It does mean, however, that given the opportunity, there are very few people who cannot make good decisions about what is best for them, including decisions about when expert advice is needed.[7]

Great Britain. Stan Windass makes the same point in the book, Local Initiatives in Great Britain, which he edited in 1981. He believes that releasing local energy and initiative is a bit like splitting the atom. It is hard to do; but once it is done, the results in terms of energy release are incalculable. His survey of local initiatives in Great Britain convinced him that there is no point in talking about decentralized society unless there are local groups with resources and competence which can exercise a leadership role.[8]

In the cases mentioned above, the countries involved have skilled labor and good technocrats even at the local level, and the governments of these countries in no way view participation at the local level as a possible threat to their survival or to the political stability of their systems. Therefore, a large degree of decentralization permits there a greater participation without so much guidance from central authority.

However, even in industrialized societies where the participative approach to the management of human resources has been a beneficial tool, there is a growing trend towards limiting its use. Some of the reasons frequently mentioned for this lack of enthusiasm for participative management include the lack of timely or effective follow-up with regard to the ideas submitted, resulting in disenchantment with the program and the increasingly automated environment of some industrialized societies which exclude human participation. This last factor is a significant one because it may be a warning that the popularity of the participatory approach to management may have peaked. Since there has been a correlation between the increased use of the participatory approach and the advent of the modern worker, conversely it may be appropriate to hypothesize that there will be a correlation between the increasing automated environment of industrialized societies with the diminishing use of the participatory approach there. Despite the growth of the scholarly literature on participation, no scholar has systematically addressed this hypothesis yet. Attention to this question may be appropriate at this time.[9]

PPM IN DEVELOPING COUNTRIES

In developing countries, most government officials see themselves and are seen by the citizens as instruments of regulation and control. Any attempt at PPM would involve changes which may affect strong vested interests. Government officials usually play the role of planners of programs which the people are told about and exhorted to carry out. However, continuous pressures from outside donors and lenders have led many developing countries, even those with authoritarian regimes, to accept incremental changes to establish and increase participation at the local level. As expressed earlier, PPM can best be detected where there are more skilled people at the local level and where the political risk for government leaders is the least. The administrative structures of these countries are not suited to the task of national economic development. Most of the following constraints usually can be found in developing countries and severely restrict a genuine experiment with PPM:

1. A centralized political system which views local initiatives with some suspicions.
2. A tightly controlled national planning mechanism closely related to the allocation of scarce resources, where political priorities play an important role.
3. The national bureaucracy tends to rule out participatory methods as an obstacle to the economies of scale that is sought.
4. The untested effectiveness of PPM as a facilitator of development. The bureaucracy has serious doubts that an activity that works well in a small village can be equally effective as part of a nationwide program.
5. Lack of coordination at the national level where the government is not presently capable of formulating coherent development strategies.
6. Lack of coordination at the local level where no formal mechanism exists for development agents to discuss among themselves the technical and physical inputs required by their programs, the implications their

programs have for each other's activities, or any sequencing of activities that could make everyone's tasks
easier.

7. And finally, the gap between the national and
local governments. In the developing countries, most
governmental resources are concentrated in the capital.
There is usually a total dearth of administrative manpower, even poorly trained manpower, in other areas of
these countries. This gap between the national and
local governments in developing countries is constantly
widening because a lack of a modern communications
network.

Attempts to institutionalize PPM have only led to
some donors making ineffectual gestures to the beneficiaries, such as having them debate already decided
issues without the power either to change or amend
them. This follows the "human relations" approach, in
which the goal of such participation is to create
favorable relations with the subordinates without the
risk of sharing any real power with them. Therefore a
less radical approach, such as the concept of "guidance" may be more suitable in developing countries.
Since most projects depend on some form of participation in order to attain their objectives, guidance
could be subtly enforced through the use of incentives.
In such a context, participation would be seen as
merely the coordination of roles of the outside ad-
viser, the national decision-makers and the local beneficiaries to achieve effective guidance of the development process.

NOTES

1. Although not typical of democratic societies,
this phenomenon can also be found there. In U.S. terms
for example, the late Mayor Richard Daley of Chicago
was a verticalist and a dedocrat.
2. Albert O. Hirschman, "The Principle of Conser-
vation and Mutation of Social Energy" in Grassroots
Development - Journal of the Inter-American Foundation
- 1983, Volume 7, No. 2, 8-9.
3. Inter-American Institute for Cooperation on
Agriculture, Planning and Project Management Division.
Improving Rural Development Planning and Management:
Proceedings of IICA-PROPLAN/USDA-DPMC Seminar. (San
Jose, Costa Rica: IICA, December 1981).
4. Ibid., and correspondence with P. Lizardo de
las Casas, Director of Planning and Management Program
at IICA.
5. Bruce Stokes, "Self-Reliance in the Welfare
State" in Development, 1982: 3, 33.

6. Bernard Ewe, "The French Search for Alternatives: Decentralization and Local Self-Reliance" in Development, 1982: 3, 36-37.

7. David Pell and Susan Wismer, Community Profit: Community-Based Economic Development in Canada, (Toronto: Is Five Press, 1981) excerpted in Development, 1982: 3, 40-43.

8. Stan Windass, "Grass Roots Initiatives in Britain," in Development, 1982: 3, 56-57.

9. Douglas McGregor raised this question concerning the applicability of Scanlon philosophy in situations which are highly automated, and where the technology is of a kind that leaves little room for improvement and change originating anywhere but in engineering or research. In The Human Side of Enterprise: (Highstown, NJ: McGraw-Hill, 1960), 119.

Selected Bibliography on Participative Planning and Management

Jean-Claude Garcia-Zamor

A. Books*

Abrahamson, Bengt. Bureaucracy of Participation.
Beverly Hills: Sage Publications, 1977.

Abramson, Robert. An Integrated Approach to Organization Development and Performance Improvement Planning: Experiences from America, Asia, and Africa. West Hartford, CT: Kumarian Press, 1978.

Amin, Samir. Unequal Development. New York: Monthly Review Press, 1976.

Anthony, William P. Participative Management.
Reading, MA: Addison-Wesley Publishing Co., 1978.

Apthrope, Raymond (ed.) People Planning and Development Studies, London: Frank Cass, 1970.

Beach, Dale S. Personnel: The Management of People At Work. New York: Macmillan Co., 1965.

Bennis, Warren G. et al. The Planning of Change. New York: Holt, Rinehart and Winston, 3d. 1976.

Berger, Peter L. and Richard J. Neuhaus. To Employ People: The Role of Mediating Structures in Public Policy. Washington, D.C.: American Enterprise Institute for Public Policy Research, 1977.

Bienen, Henry. Kenya: The Politics of Participation and Control. Princeton: Princeton University Press, 1974.

_____. Tanzania: Party Transformation and Economic Development. Princeton: Princeton University Press, 1970.

Binder, Leonard, James Coleman, et al. Crises and Sequence in Political Development. Princeton: Princeton University Press, 1971.

Black, Joseph E., et al (eds.) Education and Training for Public Sector Management in the Developing Countries. New York: Rockefeller Foundation, 1977.

---

* Studies published in book format by consulting firms, universities, and international agencies are also included in this section.

245

Blair, Harry, W. The Elusiveness of Equity: Institutional Approaches to Rural Development in Bangladesh. Ithaca, NY: Rural Development Committee, Cornell University, 1974.

_____. The Political Economy of Participation in Local Development Programmes: Short-Term Impasse and Long-Term Change in South Asia and the United States From the 1950s to the 1970s. Ithaca, NY: Rural Development Committee. Center for International Studies, Cornell University, 1981.

Blanchard, Kenneth H., and Paul Hersey. Management of Organizational Behavior, Utilizing Human Resources. Englewood Cliffs, NJ: Prentice-Hall, 1969.

Bobbit, Randolph H. Jr., et al. Organizational Behavior-Understanding and Prediction. Englewood Cliffs, NJ: Prentice Hall, 1978.

The Brandt Report. North-South: A Programme for Survival. London: Pan Books Ltd., 1980.

Bryant, Coralie and Louise White. Managing Development in the Third World. Bolder CO: Westview Press, 1982.

Burack, Elmer H. Organizational Analysis: Theory and Application. Hinsdale, IL: The Dryden Press, 1975.

Caiden, Naomi and Aaron Wildavsky. Planning and Budgeting in Poor Countries. New York: John Wiley and Sons, 1974.

Carner, George and David C. Korten. "People-Centered Planning: The USAID/Philippines Experience." Working Paper No. 2, Washington, D.C.: NASPAA, 1982.

Carroll, Stephen J. and Henry L. Tosi. Organizational Behavior. Chicago: St. Clair Press, 1977.

Chambers, R. Managing Rural Development: Ideas and Experiences From East Africa. Appsala: Scandinavian Institute of African Studies, 1974.

Chowdhury, Anwarullah. Agrarian Social Relations and Rural Development in Bangladesh, New Delhi: Oxford and IBH Publishing Co., 1982.

Chung, Kae A. and Leon C. Megginson. Organizational Behavior Developing Managerial Skills. Philadelphia: Harper and Row Publishers, 1981.

Cohen, John M. and Norman Uphoff. Rural Development Participation: Concepts and Measures for Project Design, Implementation and Evaluation. Ithaca, NY: Rural Development Committee, Cornell University, 1977.

Coombs, Philip. Meeting the Basic Needs of the Rural Poor. London: Pergamon Press, 1980.

Davis, Keith. Human Relations at Work: The Dynamics of Organizational Behavior. New York: McGraw-Hill, 1957.

_____ and John W. Bewstrom. Organizational Behavior. New York: McGraw-Hill, 1981.

Donnelly, James H. et al. Fundamentals of Management. Dallas: Business Publications, 1975.

Dunn, Edgar S. Jr. Economic and Social Development: A Process of Social Learning. Baltimore: Johns Hopkins University Press, 1971.

Esman, Milton J. and John D. Montgomery. "The Administration of Human Development," in Implementing Programs of Human Development, Staff Working Paper No. 403, Washington, DC: The World Bank, 1980.

_____ and Norman Uphoff. Local Organizations: Intermediaries in Rural Development. Ithaca, NY: Cornell University Press, 1984.

Faber, M. and D. Seers (eds.) The Crisis in Planning. London: Chatto and Windus, 1972.

Fadil, Muhamond A. Development, Income Distribution and Social Change in Rural Egypt, 1952-1970. New York: Cambridge University Press, 1975.

Filley, A.C. and R.J. House. Managerial Process and Organizational Behavior, Glenview, IL: Scott, Foresman and Co., 1969.

Gable, Richard W. Development Administration: Background Terms, Concepts, Theories and a New Approach. Washington, DC: SICA-American Society for Public Administration, 1976.

Gadalla, Saad M. Land Reform in Relation to Social Development in Egypt. Columbia, MO: University of Missouri Press, 1967.

Garcia-Zamor, Jean-Claude and Steward E. Sutin. Financing Development in Latin America. New York: Praeger Publishers, 1980.

Ghai, Dharam and Anisur Rahman. Rural Poverty and the Small Farmers' Development Program in Nepal. Geneva: Rural Employment Policies Branch, International Labor Organization, 1979.

Glajart, Benno and Dieke Buijs (eds.) Participation of the Poor in Development: Contributions to a Seminar. Leiden, The Netherlands: Institute of Cultural and Social Studies, 1980.

Gould, David. Law and the Administrative Process: Analytic Framework for Understanding Public Policy-Making. Washington, DC: University Press of America, 1979.

_____. Bureaucratic Corruption and Underdevelopment in the Third World: The Case of Zaire. Elmsford, NY: Pergamon, 1980.

Gow, David D. et al. Local Development Organizations and Rural Development: A Comparative Reappraisal, Vol. 2, Washington, DC: Development Alternatives, Inc. 1979.

Graham, Gerald H. Management: The Individual, The
     Organization, The Process. Belmont, CA: Wadsworth
     Publishing Company, 1975.
Groom, Victor H. and Philip W. Yetton. Leadership and
     Decision Making. Pittsburgh, PA: University of
     Pittsburgh Press, 1973.
Harik, Iliya. The Political Mobilization of Peasants:
     A Study of an Egyptian Community. Bloomington,
     IN: Indiana University Press, 1974.
Hilgert, Raymond L. Supervision: Concepts and
     Practices of Management. Chicago: Southwestern
     Publishing Company, 1972.
Hirschman, Albert O. Development Projects Observed.
     Washington, DC: Brookings Institution, 1967.
Hodge, B.J. and William P. Anthony. Organization
     Theory: An Environmental Approach. Boston:
     Allyn and Bacon, 1975.
Holdcroft, Lane E. The Rise and Fall of Community
     Development in Developing Countries, 1950-65: A
     Critical Analysis and an Annotated Bibliography.
     MSU Rural Development Papers, East Lansing,
     Department of Agricultural Economics, Michigan
     State University, 1977.
Honadle, George. "Fishing for Sustainability: The
     Role of Capacity Building in Development Admini-
     stration." IRD Working Paper #8. Washington,
     DC: Development Alternatives, Inc., 1981.
Hoole, Francis W. Evaluation Research and Development
     Activities. Beverly Hills: Sage Publications,
     1978.
Hunter, G. and A. Bottrall, eds. Serving the Small
     Farmer: Policy Choices in Indian Agricultural
     Development. London: Croom Helm, 1974.
Huntington, Samuel. Political Order in Changing
     Societies. New Haven: Yale University Press,
     1968.
Ingle, Marcus. Procalfer Management and Imple-
     mentation Manual. Washington, DC: Development
     Project Management Center, U.S. Department of
     Agriculture, 1981.
_____ and Thyra Riley. Managing Benefits for
     the Poor: Approaches, Experience, and Strategies
     for Improvement. Washington, DC: Practical
     Concepts Incorporated, 1981.
Januzzi, Thomasson F. and James T. Peach. Report on
     the Hierarchy of Interests in Land in Bangladesh.
     Washington, DC: Agency for International Develop-
     ment, September, 1977.
Khan, Mohammad A. Friends Not Masters: A Political
     Autobiography. New York: Oxford University
     Press, 1967.

Kramer, D. Participatory Democracy: Developing Ideals of the Political Left. Cambridge, MA: Scheinkman Publishing Company, 1972.

Kranz, H. The Participatory Bureaucracy. New York: Lexington Books, 1976.

Koehler, Jerry, W.E. Anatoe and Ronald Applebaum. Organizational Communication. New York: Holt, Rinehart and Winston, 1976.

Korten, David C. The Working Group as a Mechanism for Managing Bureaucratic Reorientation: Experience from the Philippines, Working Paper No. 4. Washington, DC: NASPAA, 1982.

_____ and Felipe Alfonso, ed. Bureaucracy and the Poor: Closing the Gap. West Hartford, CT: Kumarian, 1983.

_____ and Norman Uphoff, Bureaucratic Reorientation and Participatory Rural Development, Working Paper No. 1, Washington, DC: NASPAA, 1981.

Korten, Frances F. 1981. Building National Capacity to Develop Water Users Associations: Experience from the Philippines. World Bank Staff Working Paper #528. Washington, DC: The World Bank, 1982.

Lassen, Cheryl A. Reaching the Assetless Poor: Projects and Strategies for Self-Reliant Development. Ithaca, NY: Rural Development Committee, Cornell University, 1980.

Lawler III, Edward. Motivations in Work Organizations, Monterey: Brooks/Cole Publishing Co., 1973.

Leonard, David K. Reaching the Small Farmers: Organization Theory and Practice in Kenya. Chicago: University of Chicago Press, 1977.

Lele, Uma. The Design of Rural Development: Lessons from Africa, Baltimore: Johns Hopkins University Press, 1975.

Leys, Colin (ed.). Politics and Change in Developing Countries, New York: Cambridge University Press, 1969.

Macy, Joanna. Dharma and Development: Religion as a Resource in the Sarvodaya Self-Help Movement. West Hartford, CT: Kumarian Press, 1983.

Mahbub-ul-Haq. The Poverty Curtain: Choices for the Third World. New York: Columbia University Press, 1976.

March, James G. and Herbert A. Simon. Organizations. New York: John Wiley and Sons, 1958.

Marini, Frank (ed.) Toward a New Public Administration - The Minnowbrook Perspective. Scranton: Chandler Publishing, 1971.

Mayfield, James B. Rural Politics of Nasser's Egypt. Austin: University of Texas Press, 1970.

McGregor, Douglas. The Human Side of Enterprise. Hightstown, NJ: McGraw-Hill, 1960.

Meehan, Eugene J. In Partnership with People: An
    Alternative Development Strategy. Washington,
    DC: Inter-American Foundation, 1978.
Mehmet, Ozay. Economic Planning and Social Justice in
    Developing Countries. New York: St. Martin's
    Press, 1978.
Michael, Donald N. On Learning to Plan -- and Planning
    to Learn. San Francisco: Jossey-Bass Publishers,
    1973.
Millett, J.D. Government and Public Administration.
    The Quest for Responsible Performance. Hightstown,
    NJ: McGraw-Hill, 1954.
Mohr, Lawrence B. Explaining Organizational Behavior.
    San Francisco: Jossey-Bass Publishers, 1982.
Mondy, R. Wayne, Robert E. Holmes, and Edwin Flippo.
    Management: Concepts and Practices. Boston:
    Allyn and Bacon, 1980.
Moore, Franklin G. The Management of Organization.
    New York: Wiley and Sons, 1982.
Moris, Jon R. Managing Induced Rural Development.
    Bloomington, IN, International Development
    Institute, Indiana University, 1981.
Newman, William and E. Kirby Warren. The Process of
    Management: Concepts, Behavior and Practice.
    Englewood Cliffs, NJ: Prentice-Hall, 1977.
O'Donnelly, Guillermo. Modernization and Bureau-
    Authoritarianism. Berkeley: University of
    California, Institute of International Studies,
    1973.
Olson, Maneour. The Logic of Collective Action.
    Cambridge, MA: Harvard University Press, 1977.
O'Shaughnessy, John. Patterns of Business Organization.
    New York: John Wiley and Sons, 1976.
Patchen, Martin. Participation, Achievement and In-
    volvement on the Job. Englewood Cliffs, NJ:
    Prentice-Hall, 1970.
Patten, Thomas H., Jr. Organizational Development
    Through Teambuilding. New York: John Wiley and
    Sons, 1981.
Patton, Michael Quinn. Utilization-Focused Evaluation.
    Beverly Hills: Sage Publications, 1981.
Porter, Lyman W., Edward E. Lawler, and J. Richard
    Hackman. Behavior in Organizations. New York:
    McGraw-Hill, 1975.
Redfield, Charles E. Communication in Management.
    Chicago: The University of Chicago Press, 1958.
Robbins, Stephen P. Managing Organizational Conflict.
    Englewood Cliffs, NJ: Prentice-Hall, 1974.
Roberts, Hayden. Community Development: Learning and
    Action. Toronto: University of Toronto Press,
    1982.
Saab, Gabriel S. The Egyptian Agrarian Reform,
    1952-1962. London: Oxford University Press, 1967.

Samoff, Joel. Tanzania: Local Politics and the Structure of Power. Madison, WI: University of Wisconsin Press, 1974.

Shivji, Issa. Class Struggles in Tanzania. London: Heinemann, 1976.

Steers, Richard M. and Lyman W. Porter, Motivational and Work Behavior. New York: McGraw-Hill, 1979.

Steers, Richard M. Introduction to Organizational Behavior. Glenview, IL: Scott, Foreman and Co., 1981.

Stern, David. Managing Human Resources: The Art of Full Employment. Boston: Auburn House Publishing Co., 1982.

Sutermeister, Robert A. People and Productivity. 3d ed. New York: McGraw Hill, 1976.

Swanson, Jon C. and Mary Herbert. Rural Society and Participatory Development: Case Studies of Two Villages in the Yemen Arab Republic. Ithaca, NY: Cornell University Rural Development Committee, Yemen Research Program, September, 1981.

Tabb, J. and A. Goldfarb. Workers' Participation in Management. Oxford: Pergamon Press, 1970.

Tannenbaum, Robert. Leadership and Organization. New York: McGraw-Hill, 1981.

Tendler, Judith. Inside Foreign Aid. Baltimore, MD: Johns Hopkins University Press, 1975.

Thomas, Theodore H. and Derick Brinkerhoff. "Revolutionary Strategies for Development Administration." SICA Occasional Papers." American Society for Public Administration, Washington, DC, 1978.

Tosi, Henry L. and Stephen J. Carroll. Management. New York: John Wiley and Sons, 1982.

Tushman, Michael L. and William L. Moore, eds. Readings in the Management of Innovation. Boston: Pitman Publishing, 1982.

Uphoff, Norman and Milton J. Esman. Local Organization for Rural Development: Analysis of Asian Experience. Ithaca, NY: Cornell University Rural Development Committee, 1974.

Verba, S. and N. Nie. Participation in American Political Democracy and Social Equality. New York: Harper and Row, 1972.

Walker, S. Tjip, Sheila Carapico, and John Cohen. Emerging Rural Patterns in the Yemen Arab Republic: Results of a 21-Community Cross-Sectional Study. Ithaca, NY: Cornell University Rural Development Committee. Yemen Research Program, 1983.

Ward, Barbara, Lenore d'Anjou and J.D. Runnalls (eds.) The Widening Gap: Development in the 1970's. New York: Columbia University Press, 1971.

252

Waterburg, John. Hydropolitics of the Nile Valley.
    Syracuse, NY: Syracuse University Press, 1979.
Waterston, Albert. Development Planning: Lessons of
    Experience. Baltimore, MD: Johns Hopkins
    University Press, 1965.
Williams, Ervin (ed.) Participative Management:
    Concepts, Theory and Implementation. Atlanta:
    School of Business Administration, Georgia State
    University, 1976.
The World Bank. Toward a Typology of Popular Partici-
    pation. Policy Planning and Program Review
    Department. Washington, DC: The World Bank, May,
    1978.
Zahedami, Abdolhossain et al. The Basic Village
    Service Program, Egypt: Technical and Financial
    Assessment. Washington, DC: Development
    Alternatives, Inc., 1980.

B. Articles

Aaron, Lowin. "Participative Decision-Making: A Model
    Literature Critique, and Prescriptions for
    Research." Organizational Behavior and Human
    Performance 3 (February, 1968).
Alutto, Joseph A. "Participative Management."
    Administrative Science Quarterly 17, (March 1972).
    _____ and James A. Belasco. "A Typology for
    Participation in Organizational Decision-Making."
    Administrative Science Quarterly. 17, (1) (March
    1972).
Bartolke, Klaus, Walter Eschweiler, Dieter
    Flechsenberger and Arnold S. Tannenbaum.
    "Workers' Participation and the Distribution of
    Control as Perceived by Members of Ten German
    Companies." Administrative Science Quarterly, 27,
    (3) (September 1982).
Bass, Bernard M. and V.T. Schackleton. "Industrial
    Democracy and Participative Management: A Case
    for a Synthesis." The Academy of Management
    Review 4, (3) (July 1979).
Bate, P.S. and Murphy, J.A. "Can Joint Consultation
    Become Employee Participation?" Journal of
    Management Studies 18, (4) (October 1981).
Beckman, M. "Participative Management Urged as Best
    Option." Library Journal 102 (February 1, 1977).
Bejovich, S. "Codetermination: Labor Participation in
    Management." Modern Age 22 (Winter 1978).
Bernstein, Paul. "Modeling the Internal Dynamics of
    Workplace Democratization: First Necessary
    Component-Participation in Decision-Making."
    Organization and Administrative Sciences, 7, (3)
    (Fall 1976).

Blan, Judith R. and Richard D. Alba. "Empowering Nets
    of Participation." Administrative Science
    Quarterly 27 (3) (September 1982).
Brinkerhoff, Derick W. "Inside Public Bureaucracy:
    Empowering Managers to Empower Clients." Rural
    Development Participation Review 1 (1) (Summer
    1979).
Bryant, Coralie. "Organizational Impediments to Making
    Participation a Reality: 'Swimming Upstream' in
    AID." Rural Development Participation Review 1,
    (3) (Spring 1980).
Chacko, Thomas I., Thomas H. Stone, and Arthur P.
    Brief. Participation in Goal-Setting Programs:
    An Attributional Analysis." Academy of Manage-
    ment Review 4, (3) (July 1979).
Chambers, Robert. "Project Selection for Poverty-
    Focuses Rural Development: Simple is Optimal."
    World Development 6 (1978).
Chelimsky, Eleanor. "Program Evaluation and Appropri-
    ate Governmental Change." The Annals 466, (March
    1983).
Cochran, Nancy. "Society as Emergent and More Than
    Rational: An Essay on the Inappropriateness of
    Program Evaluation." Policy Sciences, 12, (1980).
Cohen, John M. and Norman T. Uphoff. "Participation's
    Place in Rural Development: Seeking Clarity
    Through Specificity." World Development 8 (1980).
    _____, et al. "Development from Below: Local
    Development Associations in the Yemen Arab
    Republic." World Development 9, (1981).
Coward, Jr., Walter E. "Principles of Social Organi-
    zation in an Indigenous Irrigation System." Human
    Organization 38, (1).
Dachler, H. Peter and Bernhard Wilpert. "Conceptual
    Dimensions and Boundaries of Participation in
    Organizations: A Critical Evaluation." Adminis-
    trative Science Quarterly 23, (1) (March 1978).
Dickson, John W. "Participation as Means of Organi-
    zational Control." Journal of Management Studies
    18, (2) (April 1981).
Driscull, James W. "Trust and Participation in Organi-
    zational Decision-Making as Predictors of Satis-
    faction." Academy of Management Journal 21 (1).
Dyson, R.G. and M.J. Foster. "The Relationship of
    Participation and Effectiveness in Strategic
    Planning." Strategic Management Journal 3 (1982).
Fanon, K.C. "Disembodied Technical Progress: Does
    Employee Participation in Decision-making Con-
    tribute to Change and Growth?" American Economic
    Review 68 (May 1978).

Feuerstein, Marie Therese. "Evaluation as Education --
An Appropriate Technology for a Rural Health
Program." Community Development Journal 13 (2)
(1978).

Fleishman, Edwin A. "Attitude Versus Skill Factors in
Work Group Productivity." Personnel Psychology 18
(1965).

Fortmann, Louise. "Taking the Data Back to the
Village." Rural Development Participation Review
3 (2) (Winter 1982).

_____. "Pitfalls in Implementing Partici-
pation: An African Example." Rural Development
Participation Review 1 (1) (Summer 1979).

"Gallup Survey". Fortune 163, (12) (June 15, 1981):
72.

Garcia-Zamor, Jean-Claude. "Micro-Bureaucracies and
Development Administration" in International
Review of Administrative Sciences 39 (4), 1973.

Gowler, Dan and Karen Legge. "Participation in Context:
Towards a Synthesis of the Theory and Practice of
Organizational Change, Part I." Journal of
Management Studies 15 (2) (May 1978).

Grant, James P. "Development: The End of Trickle Down?"
Foreign Policy 12 (Fall 1973).

Hartman, Betsy and James Boyce. "Bangladesh: Aid to
the Needy?" International Policy Report (1): 3.
Washington, DC: Center for International Policy
(May 1978).

Hawley, Karen E. and Mary Lippitt Nichols. "A Con-
textual Approach to Modeling the Decision to
Participate in a 'Political' Issue." Administrative Science Quarterly 27 (1), (March 1982).

Heron, A.R. "Why Men Work." Personnel Journal (July-
August 1948).

Hollensteiner, Mary. "Mobilizing the Rural Poor Through
Community Organization." Philippines Studies 27
(1979).

Honadle, George. "Development Administration in the
Eighties: New Agenda or Old Perspectives?" Public
Administration Review 42 (2) (March-April 1982).

House, Robert J. and Terence R. Mitchell. "Path-Goal
Theory of Leadership," Journal of Contemporary
Business (Autumn 1974).

Isenman, Paul. "Basic Needs: The Case of Sri Lanka."
World Development 8 (3) (March 1980).

Islam, Nasir and George M. Herrault. "From GNP to Basic
Needs: A Critical Review of Development and
Development Administration." International Review
of Administrative Science 45 (3) (1979).

Isles, Carlos D. and Manuel L. Collado. "Farmers
Participation in Communal Irrigation Development:
Lessons from Laur." Philippine Agricultural
Engineering Journal 10 (1979).

Jenkins, Jr., G. Douglas. "Impact of Employee Partici-
     pation in Pay Plan Development." Organizational
     Behavior and Human Performance 28 (1) (August
     1981).
Johnson, Rossale J. "Problem Resolution and Imposition
     of Change Through a Participative Group Effort."
     The Journal of Management Studies 11 (2) (May
     1974).
Kahn, Melvin L. "Occupational Experience and Psycho-
     logical Functioning." American Sociological
     Review (February 1973).
Korten, David C. "Community Organization and Rural
     Development: A Learning Process Approach."
     Public Administration Review 40 (5) (September-
     October 1980).
_____. "The Management of Social Transfor-
     mation." Public Administration Review 41 (6)
     (November-December 1981).
Lammers, J.C. "Power and Participation in Decision-
     Making in Formal Organization." The American
     Journal of Sociology 73 (2) (September 1967).
Lawrence, L.C. and P.C. Smith. "Group Decision and
     Employee Participation." Journal of Applied
     Psychology 39 (1955).
Lyman, Princeton. "Issues in Rural Development in East
     Pakistan." Journal of Comparative Administration
     3 (1) (May 1971).
McGregor, Douglas. "Working Smarter." Fortune 163
     (12) (June 15, 1981).
McMahon, Timothy. "A Study of Control in a Manufactur-
     ing Organization." Administrative Science
     Quarterly 21 (March 1976).
McMurray, Robert. "The Case for Benevolent Autocracy."
     Harvard Business Review 36 (January-February
     1958).
Montgomery, John D. "The Populist Front in Rural
     Development: Or, Shall We Eliminate the Bureau-
     crats and Get on with the Job?" Public Adminis-
     tration Review 39 (1) (January-February 1958).
Moris, Jon R. "Administrative Authority and the
     Problem of Effective Agricultural Administration
     in East Africa. African Review, 2 (1) (June
     1972).
Mulder, Mark and Henk Wilke. "Participation and Power
     Equalization." Organizational Behavior and Human
     Performance 1 (5)(September 1970).
Naylor, Thomas H. "How to Integrate Strategic Planning
     Into Your Management Process." Long Range
     Planning 14 (5) (1981).
Nellis, John R. "Socialist Management in Algeria."
     Journal of Modern African Studies 15 (4) (December
     1977).

Penniys, Johannes M. "Dimensions of Organizational
    Influence and Their Effectiveness Correlates."
    Administrative Science Quarterly 21 (December
    1976).
Perlman, Janice. "Grass-Roots Empowerment and Govern-
    ment Responses." Social Policy (September/October
    2979).
Porket, J.L. "Participation in Management in Communist
    Systems in 1970s." British Journal of Industrial
    Relations 13 (3) (November 1975).
Rosenfield, M. Joel and Smith J. Mathew. "Participative
    Management: An Overview." Personnel Journal 46
    (2) (February 1967).
Satter, M. Ghulam. "The Ulashi-Jadunathpur Self-Help
    Canal Digging Project: A Critical Analysis." The
    Journal of Social Studies (3) (January 1979).
Schuler, Randall S. "A Role and Expectancy Perception
    Model of Participation in Decision-Making."
    Academy of Management Journal 23 (2) (June 1980).
Schultz, George P. and Robert B. McKersie. "Partici-
    pation-Achievement-Reward Systems." The Journal
    of Management Studies 10 (2) (May 1973).
Strachan, Harry W. "Side-Effects of Planning in the
    Aid Control System." World Development 6 (4)
    (April 1978).
Tannenbaum, Arnold S. and Robert A. Cooke. "Control
    and Participation." Journal of Contemporary
    Business 3 (4) (Autumn 1974).
Thomas, Theodore H. "People Strategies for Inter-
    national Development: Administrative Alternatives
    of National, Political, and Economic Ideologies."
    Journal of Comparative Administration 5 (1) (May
    1973).
Vroom, Victor H. "Some Personality Determinants of the
    Effects of Participation." The Journal of Abnormal
    and Social Psychology 59 (3) (November 1959).
Wall, T.D. and J.A. Lischerson. "Worker Participation:
    A Critique of the Literature and Some Fresh
    Evidence." Administrative Science Quarterly 23
    (1) (March 1978).

Index

About the Editor and Contributors

JEAN-CLAUDE GARCIA-ZAMOR is a professor of public policy and administration in the Department of Political Science at Howard University. Previously, he taught at the Brazilian School of Public Administration (EBAP) of the Getulio Vargas Foundation in Rio de Janeiro (1967-69), and at the University of Texas at Austin (1969-71). He has also lectured at the Venezuelan National School of Public Administration, Caracas, Venezuela; the U.S. Air Force Academy, Colorado Springs; the Catholic University of Argentina, Mendoza, Argentina; University of Pittsburgh; the American University; the Foreign Service Institute of the U.S. Department of State; the University of Idaho, Moscow, Idaho; and the National School of Public Administration, Montreal, Canada. He has also visited the Caribbean and Europe under the sponsorship of the United States Information Agency and the National Institute of Public Management to lecture on U.S. public administration theory and practice.

From 1971 to 1975, Dr. Garcia-Zamor was a senior specialist in public administration at the Organization of American States, and from 1975 to 1977 he was president of the International Development Group, Inc. a Washington-based consulting firm with twenty-five associates. In 1977, he was elected to a two-year term as Controller of the Inter-American Development Bank (IDB) by the Board of Executive Directors of IDB. In recent years, he has done extensive consulting work in the United States and abroad for the World Bank, the United States Agency for International Development, the Research Triangle Institute in North Carolina, the Pan American Development Foundation, and the National Association of Schools of Public Affairs and Administration (NASPAA).

Dr. Garcia-Zamor is the author of La Administracion Publica en Haiti (1966); Public Administration and Social Changes in Argentina: 1943-1955 (1968); The Ecology of Development Administration in Trinidad and Tobago, Jamaica, and Barbados (1977); and is the editor of Politics and Administration in Brazil (1978). He also co-edited a book: The Financing of Development in Latin America (1980). His seventh book, Politics, Projects, and Peasants: Institutional Development in Haiti, will be published in the fall of 1985. He is

261

the author of numerous articles which have appeared in professional journals in the United States, Puerto Rico, Brazil, Belgium, Great Britain, The Netherlands, and India.

Dr. Garcia-Zamor holds a Ph.D. from the Graduate School of Public Administration of New York University. He is a life member of the American Society for Public Administration.

Contributors

DERICK W. BRINKERHOFF is on the staff of the International Development Management Center at the University of Maryland, College Park. He is currently resident advisor on monitoring and evaluation to the Ministry of Planning in Port-au-Prince, Haiti through an arrangement with the U.S. Department of Agriculture's Development Project Management Center and the Haiti field mission of the U.S. Agency for International Development. He holds a doctorate in planning and management from Harvard University.

SHEILA CARAPICO is at the World Issues Program, School for International Training, Brattleboro, Vermont. She previously taught at Wilkes College. She worked in Yemen for several years and did research and data analysis for the Center for International Studies at Cornell University. She holds a doctorate in political science from the State University of New York at Binghamton.

DAVID J. GOULD is an associate professor at the Graduate School of Public and International Affairs, University of Pittsburgh, where he is director of the Francophone Development Management Seminar. Formerly a professor in Zaire and Venezuela, he has served as a consultant to USAID, IBRD, NASPAA and CAFRAD, and directed several development management seminars in Africa. The author of five books, he holds J.D. and Ph.D. (public administration) degrees from New York University.

MOHAMMAD MOHABBAT KHAN is a professor and chairman of the Department of Public Administration at the University of Dhaka, Bangladesh. He is also the director of the Center for Administrative Studies and The Center for Development Research at the university. He has been a visiting associate professor of public administration at the University of Benin in Nigeria. He is the author or editor of numerous books and articles in public administration. He holds a doctorate in public

administration from the University of Southern
California.

FRANCES F. KORTEN received her Ph.D. in social
psychology from Stanford University in 1968. She has
spent most of her professional life in Third World
countries, concentrating on issues of the management of
government programs, community organization, and the
interface between the two. She taught at the Haile
Sellassie I University in Ethiopia; researched family
planning program management while at INCAE in Nica-
ragua; and worked on irrigation programs in the Philippines and Indonesia. Since 1978 she has been a program
officer with the Ford Foundation in Manila and Jakarta.

JAMES B. MAYFIELD is a professor of political
science at the University of Utah. He has published
extensively on the Middle East in general and on Egypt
in particular. He holds a doctorate in political
science from the University of Texas.

RICHARD W. RYAN is an associate professor of
public administration at San Diego State's Imperial
Valley Campus adjacent to the Mexican border. From
1978 to 1980 he worked in Upper Volta and Togo as program manager for a U.S. private voluntary organization.
For the following two years, he was the assistant
director of the International Development Institute at
Indiana University.

THEODORE THOMAS is a Consultant to the Public
Administration Training Center, Savar, Bangladesh, and
a senior staff member at the Institute of Public
Administration, New York. Formerly with the University
of Southern California, he has also been a development
management consultant in Pakistan, Bahrain and Somalia
and an organizing member of the Social Development
Management Network. He holds AB and MA degrees from
Duke University and a Ph.D. in political science from
UCLA.

NORMAN UPHOFF is an associate professor in the
Department of Government, and chairman of the Rural
Development Committee in the Center for International
Studies at Cornell University. Before coming to Cor-
nell in 1970, Professor Uphoff did research in Nigeria
on manpower development and in Ghana on the use of
foreign aid. He worked with the Center for Economic
Development and Administration in Nepal for the Ford
Foundation in 1972 and 1973, and from 1972-1974, he was
chairman of the Development Administration panel of the
Southeast Asia Development Advisory Group (SEADAG). He
was a consultant for the African Centre for Training

and Research on Development Administration (CAFRAD) in
Morocco and Ghana in 1975.   Professor Uphoff has
published numerous books and articles.